					Speed (knots)						
2.5	3.0	3.5	4.0	4.5	5.0	5.5	6.0	6.5	7.0	7.5	8.0
- -	- -	- -	0.1	0.1	0.1	0.1	0.1	0.1	0.1	0.1	0.1
0.1	0.1	0.1	0.1	0.1	0.2	0.2	0.2	0.2	0.2	0.2	0.3
0.1	0.1	0.2	0.2	0.2	0.2	0.3	0.3	0.3	0.3	0.4	0.4
0.1	0.2	0.2	0.3	0.3	0.3	0.4	0.4	0.4	0.5	0.5	0.5
0.2	0.2	0.3	0.3	0.4	0.4	0.5	0.5	0.5	0.6	0.6	0.7
0.2	0.3	0.3	0.4	0.4	0.5	0.5	0.6	0.6	0.7	0.7	0.8
0.3	0.4	0.4	0.5	0.5	0.6	0.6	0.7	0.8	0.8	0.9	0.9
0.3	0.4	0.5	0.5	0.6	0.7	0.7	0.8	0.9	0.9	1.0	1.1
0.4	0.4	0.5	0.6	0.7	0.7	0.8	0.9	1.0	1.0	1.1	1.2
0.4	0.5	0.6	0.7	0.8	0.8	0.9	1.0	1.1	1.2	1.3	1.3
0.5	0.5	0.6	0.7	0.8	0.9	1.0	1.1	1.2	1.3	1.4	1.5
0.5	0.6	0.7	0.8	0.9	1.0	1.1	1.2	1.3	1.4	1.5	1.6
0.5	0.6	0.8	0.9	1.0	1.1	1.2	1.3	1.4	1.5	1.6	1.7
0.6	0.7	0.8	0.9	1.0	1.2	1.3	1.4	1.5	1.6	1.7	1.9
0.6	0.7	0.9	1.0	1.1	1.2	1.4	1.5	1.6	1.8	1.9	2.0
0.7	0.8	0.9	1.1	1.2	1.3	1.5	1.6	1.7	1.9	2.0	2.1
0.7	0.8	1.0	1.1	1.3	1.4	1.6	1.7	1.8	2.0	2.1	2.3
0.7	0.9	1.0	1.2	1.3	1.5	1.6	1.8	1.9	2.1	2.2	2.4
0.8	1.0	1.1	1.3	1.4	1.6	1.7	1.9	2.1	2.2	2.4	2.5
0.8	1.0	1.2	1.3	1.5	1.7	1.8	2.0	2.2	2.3	2.5	2.7
0.9	1.0	1.2	1.4	1.6	1.7	1.9	2.1	2.3	2.4	2.6	2.8
0.9	1.1	1.3	1.5	1.7	1.8	2.1	2.2	2.4	2.6	2.8	2.9
1.0	1.1	1.3	1.5	1.7	1.9	2.1	2.3	2.5	2.7	2.9	3.1
1.0	1.2	1.4	1.6	1.8	2.0	2.2	2.4	2.6	2.8	3.0	3.2
1.0	1.3	1.5	1.7	1.9	2.1	2.3	2.5	2.7	2.9	3.1	3.3
1.1	1.3	1.5	1.7	1.9	2.2	2.4	2.6	2.8	3.0	3.2	3.5
1.1	1.3	1.6	1.8	2.0	2.2	2.5	2.7	2.9	3.1	3.4	3.6
1.2	1.4	1.6	1.9	2.1	2.3	2.6	2.8	3.0	3.3	3.5	3.7
1.2	1.5	1.7	1.9	2.2	2.4	2.7	2.9	3.1	3.4	3.6	3.9
1.2	1.5	1.7	2.0	2.2	2.5	2.7	3.0	3.2	3.5	3.7	4.0
1.3	1.6	1.8	2.1	2.3	2.6	2.8	3.1	3.4	3.6	3.9	4.1
1.3	1.6	1.9	2.1	2.4	2.7	2.9	3.2	3.5	3.7	4.0	4.3
1.4	1.6	1.9	2.2	2.5	2.7	3.0	3.3	3.6	3.8	4.1	4.4
1.4	1.7	2.0	2.3	2.6	2.8	3.1	3.4	3.7	4.0	4.3	4.5
1.5	1.7	2.0	2.3	2.6	2.9	3.2	3.5	3.8	4.1	4.4	4.7
1.5	1.8	2.1	2.4	2.7	3.0	3.3	3.6	3.9	4.2	4.5	4.8
1.6	1.8	2.1	2.4	2.8	3.1	3.4	3.7	4.0	4.3	4.6	4.9
1.6	1.9	2.2	2.5	2.8	3.2	3.5	3.8	4.1	4.4	4.7	5.1
1.6	1.9	2.3	2.6	2.9	3.2	3.6	3.9	4.2	4.5	4.9	5.2
1.7	2.0	2.3	2.7	3.0	3.3	3.7	4.0	4.3	4.7	5.0	5.3
1.7	2.0	2.4	2.7	3.1	3.4	3.8	4.1	4.4	4.8	5.1	5.5
1.7	2.1	2.4	2.8	3.1	3.5	3.8	4.2	4.5	4.9	5.2	5.6
1.8	2.2	2.5	2.9	3.2	3.6	3.9	4.3	4.7	5.0	5.4	5.7
1.8	2.2	2.6	2.9	3.3	3.7	4.0	4.4	4.8	5.1	5.5	5.9
1.9	2.2	2.6	3.0	3.4	3.7	4.1	4.5	4.9	5.2	5.6	6.0
1.9	2.3	2.7	3.1	3.5	3.8	4.2	4.6	5.0	5.4	5.8	6.1
2.0	2.3	2.7	3.1	3.5	3.9	4.3	4.7	5.1	5.5	5.9	6.3
2.0	2.4	2.8	3.2	3.6	4.0	4.4	4.8	5.2	5.6	6.0	6.4
2.0	2.5	2.9	3.3	3.7	4.1	4.5	4.9	5.3	5.7	6.1	6.5
2.1	2.5	2.9	3.3	3.7	4.2	4.6	5.0	5.4	5.8	6.2	6.7
2.1	2.5	3.0	3.4	3.8	4.2	4.7	5.1	5.5	5.9	6.4	6.8
2.2	2.6	3.0	3.5	3.9	4.3	4.8	5.2	5.6	6.1	6.5	6.9
2.2	2.6	3.1	3.5	4.0	4.4	4.9	5.3	5.7	6.2	6.6	7.1
2.2	2.7	3.1	3.6	4.0	4.5	4.9	5.4	5.8	6.3	6.7	7.2
2.3	2.8	3.2	3.7	4.1	4.6	5.0	5.5	6.0	6.4	6.9	7.3
2.3	2.8	3.3	3.7	4.2	4.7	5.1	5.6	6.1	6.5	7.0	7.5
2.4	2.8	3.3	3.8	4.3	4.7	5.2	5.7	6.2	6.6	7.1	7.6
2.4	2.9	3.4	3.9	4.4	4.8	5.3	5.8	6.3	6.8	7.3	7.7
2.5	2.9	3.4	3.9	4.4	4.9	5.4	5.9	6.4	6.9	7.4	7.9
2.5	3.0	3.5	4.0	4.5	5.0	5.5	6.0	6.5	7.0	7.5	8.0

HARBOUR SEAMANSHIP

HARBOUR SEAMANSHIP

by

BERNARD HAYMAN

PERGAMON PRESS

OXFORD · NEW YORK · TORONTO · SYDNEY · FRANKFURT

U.K.	Pergamon Press Ltd., Headington Hill Hall, Oxford OX3 0BW, England
U.S.A.	Pergamon Press Inc., Maxwell House, Fairview Park, Elmsford, New York 10523, U.S.A.
CANADA	Pergamon Press Canada Ltd., Suite 104, 150 Consumers Road, Willowdale, Ontario M2J 1P9, Canada
AUSTRALIA	Pergamon Press (Aust.) Pty. Ltd., P.O. Box 544, Potts Point, N.S.W. 2011, Australia
FEDERAL REPUBLIC OF GERMANY	Pergamon Press GmbH, Hammerweg 6, D-6242 Kronberg-Taunus, Federal Republic of Germany
JAPAN	Pergamon Press Ltd., 8th Floor, Matsuoka Central Building, 1–7–1 Nishishinjuku, Shinjuku-ku, Tokyo 160, Japan
BRAZIL	Pergamon Editora Ltda., Rua Eca de Queiros, 346, CEP 04011, São Paulo, Brazil
PEOPLE'S REPUBLIC OF CHINA	Pergamon Press, Qianmen Hotel, Beijing, People's Republic of China

First edition 1986

Library of Congress Cataloguing in Publication Data
Hayman, Bernard.
Harbour seamanship.
1. Harbors.   2. Yachts and yachting.
3. Navigation.   I. Title.
VK321.H38 1985   623.89′29   85–12232

British Library Cataloguing in Publication Data
Hayman, Bernard.
Harbour seamanship.
1. Yachts and yachting.   2. Seamanship.
3. Harbors.   I. Title.
623.88′223   GV813

ISBN 0–08–033389–3 (Hardcover)
ISBN 0–08–032652–8 (Flexicover)

Printed in Great Britain by A. Wheaton & Co. Ltd. Exeter

Contents

List of Illustrations   ix

Introduction   xi

1. Harbour Entry   1
New International Port Entry Signals   2
Other National Port Entry Signals   5
Tidal Signals   8
Way-point Reporting   9

2. VHF Radiotelephony   12
The Principles   13
Simplex, Semi-duplex and Duplex   14
Harbour Radio   18
Development of VTS   19
Model Calls and Acknowledgements   23
Selective Calling   31

3. Vessel Traffic Services   33
General Principles   33
"Seaspeak"   36
Where Do Small Craft Fit In?   40

4. Collision Regulations   43
Rules 9 and 10   44
Close Quarters   48
A Planned Approach   48
Hampered Vessels   53
Small Craft Lights and Shapes   57

5. The Navigator's Trade   65
Charts   65
Tides   67
Publications   74
Electronic Aids   75
Navigational Warnings   79
Weather Messages   81

6. Restricted Visibility 83

Sailing at Night 83
How much light? 83
Fog 88
Signals 90
Radar 93

7. Seamanship at Close Quarters 96

Crossing Narrow Channels 97
Slowing and Stopping 98
Heaving-to 100
Picking Up a Buoy 102
Drogues at Harbour Mouths 104
Coming Alongside 108
Wind and Tide 110
Within a Marina 111
Slip Ropes 112

8. Mooring, Anchoring and Making Fast 115

Anchoring 116
Fast Alongside 124
Alongside Others 131
Making Fast in Locks 133
Leaving a Berth 135

9. Harbour Authorities and the Law 138

Special Signals 139
Moorings 141
Insurance 141
Salvage 142
Club Custom and Behaviour 144

10. Other Rules and Regulations 145

Ensigns 145
Customs and Excise 147
Immigration 151
Registration 151
Certificate of Competence 153
Ship Licence 154
Light Dues 155

11. Distress and Urgency 156

Radio 156
Distress Other Than Radio 163
Other Visual Distress and Urgency Signals 164
Club Rescue Boats and the Use of Ch "M" 166
Citizen's Band (CB) 168
Safety Boats 168

APPENDICES

A. VHF Procedural Words and Their Meanings   170

B. Standard Marine Navigational Vocabulary   172

C. Ten Golden Rules for the Use of VHF Radiotelephones   174

D. Metric Units and Their Symbols and Other Useful Measurements   175

E. Useful Abbreviations   177

Index   179

List of Illustrations

1.1. French and Belgian port entry signals (Lisbon agreement)   2
1.2. International port traffic signals   4
1.3. Federal Republic of Germany port entry signals   6
1.4. Netherlands bridge and lock signals   8
1.5. French and Belgian tidal height signals   9
1.6. Way-point reporting   10

2.1. The capture effect   13
2.2. VHF frequency table   15
2.3. Summary calling and working procedures   22
2.4. Dangers of bridge-to-bridge communication   25

4.1. Crossing a channel: heading not course-made-good   50
4.2. Mounting shapes   52
4.3. Lack of visibility from the bridge   59
4.4. Positions of small craft lights   59
4.5. Shielding against glare   61
4.6. Shielding against scatter   62
4.7. Danger of anchor lights on centreline   63

5.1. Charts 2182a, 1406, 1610, 2052, 2693, 1492   68/69
5.2. Tidal height curves: (a) Devonport; (b) Southampton and
     Vlissingen   72
5.3. BH tidal height graph   73
5.4. BH tidal stream atlas time   74

6.1. Deceptive speed of large vessels   86/87
6.2. Vessels restricted in their ability to manoeuvre, constrained by
     their draught and night confusions   89
6.3. Dredger signals   91

7.1. The concept of a waiting area   99
7.2. Drogues: (a) in wave; (b) anti-tangle cone   107
7.3. Use of slip ropes   113

8.1. Anchoring scope   118

8.2.	Rope and chain	118
8.3.	Pawl	123
8.4.	Alongside: (a) basic geometry; (b) lay-out of fairleads and cleats; (c) warps and fenders	126
8.5.	Fenders and slack breast ropes	127
8.6.	Fairleads	129
8.7.	Effect of tidal range	130
8.8.	Warps for a tier of yachts	132
8.9.	Warps in locks	134
11.1.	Distress frequencies	159

Illustrations on pages 25, 86, 87, 89 and 134 by Colin Mudie

Introduction

DURING the past 15–20 years there has been a transformation in both the types of ships as well as in the number of ships that use our commercial ports. Today, in most parts of the world, yachts far outnumber all commercial craft. Furthermore, the size, the character and the manner in which the remaining commercial craft are operated is completely different.

Until a few decades ago, a commercial ship would spend days, and sometimes weeks, in port unloading and then reloading. Today most ships, although they are very much larger than their older sisters, will be turned around in a matter of hours. Thus we have far larger ships working to very much tighter schedules and because of the development of infinitely more sophisticated equipment all the ships now have very much smaller crews.

Several factors have led to the change. Two important ones are the use of containers for mixed cargo, and the use of roll-on roll-off ships where lorries drive straight on and off the ship. However, the greatest port operational change is in the use of the radiotelephone. Today a ship can keep in constant touch with her owners, she can communicate with the pilot boat, she can speak to other ships and, most important of all (from the organizational point of view), she can talk to the port and the port can talk to her.

That last point—the ability of a port to inform approaching ships whether a berth is ready, whether there are any hazards to safe navigation and whether there is any other shipping movements in the area—has been the key to the whole transformation of the movement of shipping in the commercial ports of the world.

From the yachtsman's point of view, there are still hundreds of creeks and anchorages which, apart from the number of yachtsmen using them, have remained basically unchanged for centuries. And long may that state of affairs remain. The River Blackwater, in Essex—one of my favourite anchorages—is unchanged, in many parts, since the Vikings invaded nearly 1000 years ago. In contrast, the ports of Harwich, Felixstowe and Ipswich, which are only a few miles north-east of the Blackwater, have more shipping tonnage moving in one tide than they might have had in a month only a few years ago.

That is the key to the purpose of this book. Yachtsmen use commercial ports, and will continue to do so, but the days when a yacht merely bumbled along—approximately in the centre of any buoyed channel—and then asked questions afterwards have gone for good. With a few, highly specialized, exceptions, yachts can still come and go without having to seek prior permission. However, increasingly, there is a need to monitor what is happening in the port.

The manner in which a yacht can minimize her effect on the commercial operation of the port is a new art. It is one that needs to be developed. Without such development, our freedom to continue to come and go is at risk.

Most sports attract a healthy number of *How to* . . . books, and yachting is no exception. There are books galore helping yachtsmen to navigate, to repair, to maintain and to improve the efficiency of their boats. Here, in addition to the chapters introducing the subject of the use of ports—a subject called "Port Operations" in the world of commerce—I hope to cover everything connected with the business of handling small craft in confined waters.

To try to achieve the main objective, the use of VHF radio is described in so far as it affects a port operation, and Vessel Traffic Services (VTS)—as they are called—are both given chapters of their own. Further, the regulations affecting ports—both the International Regulations for Preventing Collisions at Sea (The Collision Regulations) and various port authority rules—are outlined.

For the secondary objective, all close-quarters operations, like berthing, anchoring and manoeuvring in confined places, are described, as is inshore navigation and chartwork.

The word "seaman" is unambiguous: it means a man who goes to sea. Thus the word "seamanship" is similarly clear and stands for all the operations connected with handling ships at sea. If there was such a word, "harbourmanship" would cover the subject of this book.

Most of the surface of the world is covered with water, and there should be plenty for everyone. However, as with traffic flow on our roads, or even for the movement of pedestrians, it is when moving objects are concentrated into small areas—ports and harbours in this context—that difficulties can arise.

Most things in life are more satisfying when they can be done efficiently, and that philosophy certainly applies to the handling of small boats. However, the new dimension—introduced by the development of radiotelephony—is the ability to be well informed about the intentions of others in a harbour area.

The man who can remain well informed is all the more likely to behave in a responsible manner. Thus, the more the yachtsman can do that, the longer will those who go to sea for pleasure continue to enjoy the freedom to use the commercial ports of the world.

Harbour Entry

SINCE the earliest attempts to introduce any form of entry signals for the world's ports, flags or shapes have been used by day and lights by night. However, although flags and shapes are still used in a great many places—including many major commercial ports—the *need* to use flags and shapes has gone. Nowadays lights can be used by day as well as night, in a manner that makes it possible for the seaman to identify the purpose of the signal even when the older types of day shapes would still have been indistinguishable because of their distance off.

One of the most impressive modern-day signals is the pair of leading lights at the Hoek van Holland. The Nieuwe Waterweg, as the canal is called, is not often used by small craft because it gives access to the highly commercial parts of industrial Holland rather than to the many delightful holiday areas—and the leading lights, at the centre of the deep water channel, are most certainly not the line of approach for a yacht. Nevertheless, even when passing The Hoek many miles off, these lights seem almost unbelievably bright. They have a range of 12 miles even in daylight; a range at which the coast itself and even large buildings are hardly visible.

In contrast, at Zeebrugge, on the Belgian coast only a few miles away, day shapes are still used. A combination of shapes has the advantage that it can be read from all angles. On the other hand, even shapes 1 metre in diameter can be identified at only about 1 mile off.

The precise distance depends on the background, but as a generalization a shape has to be between 1:500 and 1:1000 times the distance off to be certain to be seen for what it is.

In further contrast to the Hoek leading lights—and they are bright enough to be seen through a degree of fog when shapes of whatever size would be useless—smaller ports, like Ramsgate in Kent, still use the traditional one black flag as an entry signal and two black balls to signal: "No Entry" but that vessels may leave.

New International Port Entry Signals

Thus, with a range extending from nothing—for a great many small ports—to highly sophisticated lights such as at the entrance to Dover, it is not surprising that the lighthouse authorities of the world realized that new standards were needed.

An attempt had been made by the League of Nations in 1930 to reach an agreed system and, considering the limitations of the available equipment, a reasonable system was developed. The main problem was that hardly anyone adopted it. The 1930 system, agreed at Lisbon, is still (1985) in use in the Belgian ports of Zeebrugge and Oostende and in many of the French Channel ports. It is based on all-round lights at night and balls or cones by day, and although an attempt was made to make the meaning easily distinguished from afar, by having all cones to signal "Entry permitted" and combinations of cones and balls to signal otherwise (Fig. 1.1) the system has obvious limitations, especially in restricted visibility.

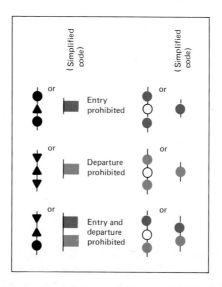

Fig. 1.1. *French and Belgian port entry signals (Lisbon agreement)*

Once the decision to rethink the old Lisbon agreement had been made, two vital changes were possible. First, the use of day shapes was abandoned, and secondly, following the first decision, it was realized that a signal showing to seaward did not necessarily have to be repeated in the same form when shown to landward. Obviously an arrangement that suits one port may not suit another, but a new system—agreed internationally towards the end of 1982—has great flexibility. Furthermore, and as a result of that flexibility, it was possible to introduce special signals for small craft.

The new system (Fig. 1.2) is based on the use of three vertical lights for the principal messages, with additional lights (mounted to the right or the left of the main group) to signal additional information. A few ports may need additional signals to warn of special local conditions, or of a dredger working in the channel, and in those circumstances the additional white or yellow lights will be placed to the right of the main column of lights. However, it is the additional **yellow** lights—placed to the **left** of the main column—which are of particular interest to small craft.

These are exemption signals for vessels which can navigate outside the main channel. They do not apply to a port like Dover—the first port in the United Kingdom to adopt the new international signals—because the entrances are narrow openings between pierheads, but it is obvious that ports where there are deep water main channels, but ample shallow water to the sides, might use them.

The meanings are unambiguous and they represent regulation at its best, because their use will help the port as well as the small craft. The latter are not kept waiting unnecessarily and the port does not have small craft hanging about outside the entrance, causing a potential hazard by their presence, when there is plenty of water for them inshore.

Local Anomalies

Although the world now has an internationally agreed set of port entry signals, as has just been described, it is unlikely that many ports will change to the new system straight away. The wording of the announcement of their adoption read:

> "The signals . . . may be introduced, from 1983, at any port throughout the world, as circumstances permit. . . . They may be recognized as traffic signals because the main lights are always three lights in a vertical line. These signals may also be used to control movements at locks and bridges."

In practice, harbour authorities in most north-west European ports had already introduced signals, of one type or another, by the time the international agreement was reached. Thus there will be many local differences, but one of the difficulties for the yachtsman without local knowledge is that in some ports—Zeebrugge and Oostende, for example—the old Lisbon agreement lights are strictly enforced for **all** vessels, but only a few miles down the coast the port of Calais uses similar signals, but they apply to the ferries only. Small craft do not have signals exhibited for them. When there is no ferry due, there is no signal shown and small craft can come and go, with caution, as they please.

A type of local anomaly that is even more confusing is where a local harbour authority does not even expect small craft to take any notice of its signals. At the lock into Grimsby, some years ago (before the port adopted

MAIN SIGNALS	MAIN MESSAGES	REMARKS
1 (FLASHING)	SERIOUS EMERGENCY— ALL VESSELS TO STOP OR DIVERT ACCORDING TO INSTRUCTIONS	
2	VESSELS SHALL NOT PROCEED	Some ports may use an Exemption Signal with Signal 2: see 2a.
3	VESSELS MAY PROCEED. ONE-WAY TRAFFIC	Some ports may not use the full range of main signals, e.g. they may use only Signals 2 and 4, or only Signal 1.
4	VESSELS MAY PROCEED. TWO-WAY TRAFFIC	The uncoloured circle in Signals 4, 5 and 5a represents a **white** light.
5	A VESSEL MAY PROCEED ONLY WHEN IT HAS RECEIVED SPECIFIC ORDERS TO DO SO	Used when a vessel or special group of vessels must receive specific instructions in order to proceed. All other vessels must not proceed. Specific instructions may be given by Auxiliary Signal or by other means such as radio, signal lamp or patrol boat. Some ports may use an Exemption Signal with Signal 5: see 5a.

(Signals 2 and 3: OCCULTING. Signals 4 and 5: FIXED OR SLOW-OCCULTING)

EXEMPTION SIGNALS	EXEMPTION MESSAGES	REMARKS
2a	Vessels shall not proceed, except that vessels which navigate outside the main channel need not comply with the main message.	Some ports may use the additional yellow light (always displayed to the **left** of the top main light) to allow smaller vessels to disregard Messages 2 and 5.
5a	A vessel may proceed only when it has received specific orders to do so; except that vessels which navigate outside the main channel need not comply with the main message.	

(2a: OCCULTING. 5a: FIXED OR SLOW-OCCULTING)

AUXILIARY SIGNALS	AUXILIARY MESSAGES	REMARKS
Normally white and/or yellow lights, displayed to the **right** of the main lights.	Local meanings: e.g. added to Signal 5 to instruct a vessel to proceed; to give information about the situation of traffic in the opposite direction; or to warn of a dredger operating in the channel.	Special messages may apply at some ports with a complex layout, or complicated traffic situation. Nautical documents should be consulted for the details.

FIG. 1.2. *International port traffic signals*

the international signals) I stood off, well clear of the entrance, because the "No Entry" signal, one black ball, was flying. After about half an hour I realized I was being "waved in" by a uniformed figure on the pierhead. As soon as I was in the lock he asked: "What were you hanging about out there for? You nearly missed the tide?" When I pointed to the "No Entry" black ball, still flying, he replied: "Oh, but we don't expect yachts to take any notice of that."

That type of anomaly is unacceptable, because it breeds confusion elsewhere. Thus the small craft exemption signals in the new international port traffic signals are all the more welcome. The idea was sown, over lunch, during an informal discussion with the Secretary of the International Association of Lighthouse Authorities (IALA)—himself a yachtsman. The precedent was an occasional signal used at a lock entrance in Southampton, and it is highly satisfactory to me that the idea should have been accepted internationally.

To some it might appear strange that the IALA—an international lighthouse authority—should be involved in port entry signals which are the responsibility of the local port authority. However, although in the United Kingdom the principal lighthouse authorities—Trinity House, the Northern Lighthouse Board and the Commissioners of Irish Lights—are unconnected with port administration, in most parts of the world—especially France, Belgium, Holland and Germany and the Scandinavian countries—the ports and the seamarks are both controlled by state run organizations. Thus the IALA is deeply involved with port operation guidelines and will figure prominently in later parts of this book.

Other National Port Entry Signals

Apart from the group of French and Belgian ports still using the Lisbon agreement signals—even if the interpretations of their meaning is not always the same—there are also other national signals that are likely to be in use for some time to come.

Once again the actual signals used do not always apply to small craft. As a generalization a "No Entry" signal almost certainly does apply to all, but a "You may Proceed" signal does not necessarily apply. In many continental ports and waterways priority is given to commercial traffic and, especially in Holland, the lock keepers may make their wishes clear to small craft by the use of a loud-hailer or by a bold sweep of an arm to beckon or warn off.

Increasingly, however, the harbour authority is using radiotelephony to give advice or instruction to particular vessels both as main port entry signals as well as at docks or locks.

Radiotelephony, and the way in which small craft can best benefit from its use, is the major part of the next two chapters. Here it is visual signals that apply, because, despite the introduction of harbour radio, visual signals will continue to be employed.

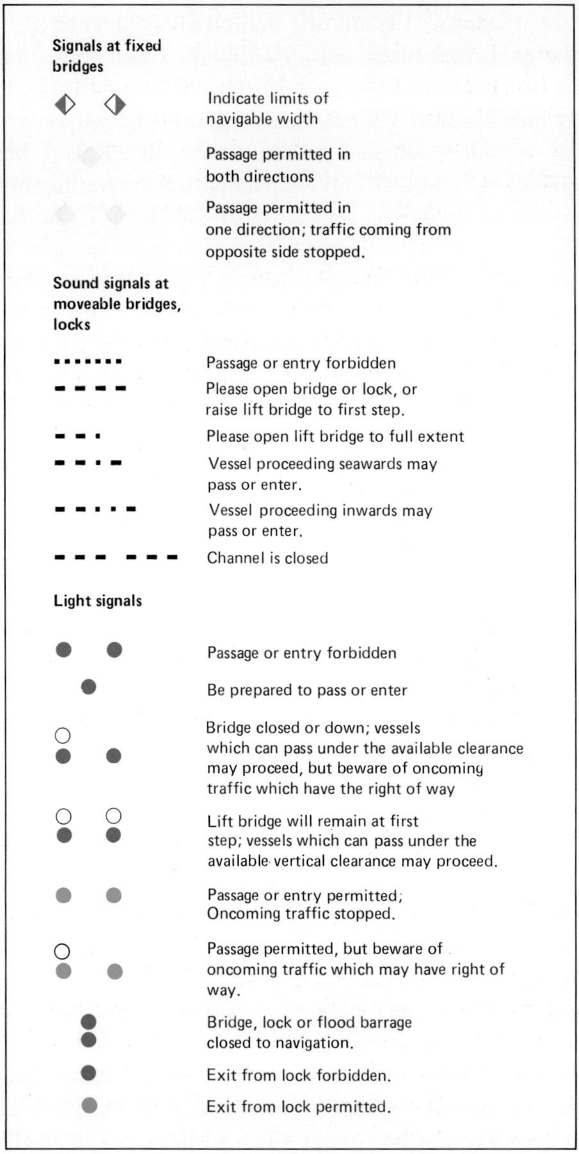

Signals at fixed bridges

◆ ◇ Indicate limits of navigable width

Passage permitted in both directions

Passage permitted in one direction; traffic coming from opposite side stopped.

Sound signals at moveable bridges, locks

▪ ▪ ▪ ▪ ▪ ▪ ▪ Passage or entry forbidden

▬ ▬ ▬ ▬ Please open bridge or lock, or raise lift bridge to first step.

▬ ▬ ▪ Please open lift bridge to full extent

▬ ▬ ▪ ▬ Vessel proceeding seawards may pass or enter.

▬ ▬ ▪ ▪ ▬ Vessel proceeding inwards may pass or enter.

▬ ▬ ▬ ▬ ▬ Channel is closed

Light signals

● ● Passage or entry forbidden

● Be prepared to pass or enter

○
● ● Bridge closed or down; vessels which can pass under the available clearance may proceed, but beware of oncoming traffic which have the right of way

○ ○
● ● Lift bridge will remain at first step; vessels which can pass under the available vertical clearance may proceed.

● ● Passage or entry permitted; Oncoming traffic stopped.

○
● ● Passage permitted, but beware of oncoming traffic which may have right of way.

● Bridge, lock or flood barrage closed to navigation.
●

● Exit from lock forbidden.

● Exit from lock permitted.

FIG. 1.3. *Federal Republic of Germany port entry signals*

A radio signal means something to the station to which it is transmitted and/or to any station which heard what was said. The visual signal, on the other hand, goes on giving its message so long as it is displayed. Thus visual signals will continue to be used, even when radiotelephony is in use as well, and the relevant reference books will have to be consulted as necessary.

For U.K. yachtsmen the Admiralty Sailing Directions—so-called "Pilots"—are nowadays very much more informative than they were only a few years ago. Possibly because of a more enlightened policy and possibly because of the sheer weight of numbers of small craft—probably both—the Hydrographic Office takes considerably more notice of the needs of small craft than it did. However, the Admiralty "Pilot" concentrates on the access ports, and they have little of detailed value, for instance, for the Dutch inland waterways.

As a generalization, both German and Dutch coastal ports tend to have individual signals to suit local conditions—although it is to be hoped that the new international system will be adopted progressively—but both German (Fig. 1.3) and The Netherlands (Fig. 1.4) are reasonably consistent with their inland waterway signalling. The main problem, however, is that they do not use the same system.

Not a great many U.K. yachtsmen cruise in German waters, but those that do can get the detailed information from the Deutscher Segler Verbund publications. For The Netherlands, on the other hand, British yachtsmen join the nationals of many other countries in enjoying the seemingly limitless water available for recreation. Tourism in Holland is very big business and the Dutch *Hydrografische Kaarten*, (booklets of charts for small craft), both for the Dutch and Belgian coast as well as for the Dutch main inland waters, are outstandingly good.

From the port entry point of view, not only do they include chartlets at a large scale of most major ports, but the *Scheepvaartekens* (traffic signs) are summarized in English as well as Dutch.

For the rivers and smaller inland waters—which are generally outside the scope of this book—the waters and facilities are again covered in an excellent manner by charts of the Koninklijke Nederlandse Toeristenbond (ANWB), but the ANWB also publishes two volumes giving details of the various regulations on the major waterways (Volume 1) and details of the hundreds of small ports and overnight stopping places (Volume 2).

The second volume of this book—the *Almanak voor watertoerisme*—is so useful that it becomes almost obligatory to have it. It is hardly necessary to add that it is all in Dutch, but the times of bridge openings, the costs of marina berths and suchlike information is usually understandable. It does not take much imagination to decipher the fact that *ma. t/m vr* means Mon.–Fri. or that *Gesloten* means closed.

In addition to the specialized sources of information, the well-known almanacs—Reeds or Macmillans—contain a great deal of information, but neither are able to devote much space to port entry information, and the recent improvements in the Hydrographic Department "Pilots" makes the traditional almanac by no means the "Bible" that it used to be. Furthermore, those who take Admiralty Notices to Mariners—and the more complex the business of taking a small boat to sea becomes, the greater the need to keep

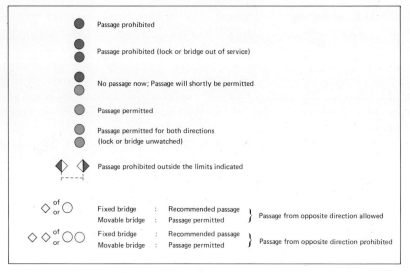

Fig. 1.4. *Netherlands bridge and lock signals*

the sources of information corrected—will find it a simple matter to keep the "Pilots" corrected so that they are up to date.

Tidal Signals

Nowadays, with dredging becoming so quick and efficient, the precise depth of water at a harbour entrance is less likely to be of concern to small craft than it might have been in the past. Nevertheless, many ports still exhibit tidal height signals at their entrances and it is as well to recognize them, even if only to realize that they are what they are.

Generalizing once again, the Belgian and French ports which still use the Lisbon agreement port entry signals also use the same tidal height signals (Fig. 1.5).

The Dutch, on the other hand, use different tidal height signals with IJmuiden, for example, having a complex system of lights giving the channel depths to the nearest 0.2 metre.

In the United Kingdom visual tidal signals are not normally used, but for the many shallow channels in the Thames Estuary the actual tidal heights at any particular moment in relation to those that were predicted, are broadcast from Gravesend Radio at regular intervals (see also Chapter 10). Normally a yacht is highly unlikely to have to depend on a broadcast of an "actual" tidal height, before deciding whether to use a particular approach channel or not. On the other hand, to know that a particular tide was a metre or more, more or less, than the predicted height—a condition that is by no means unusual—might be of interest even if it was unlikely to be significant.

Way-point Reporting

Yet another type of harbour entry signal—but one which the ship transmits to the port rather than the other way round—is summarized by the expression "Way Points". Many commercial ports like to monitor the approach of the ships that are about to enter by asking—and sometimes requiring—radiotelephone reports from a number of places in the approach channels.

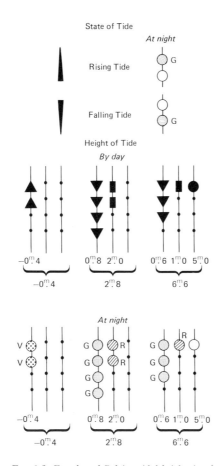

Fig. 1.5. *French and Belgian tidal height signals*

The German River Elbe has one of the more complex (Fig. 1.6), and it serves as a good example of what has been happening during the past few years. Until only a few years ago the service did not exist: within the next few years it is likely that many more concentrations of shipping will have similar facilities. For the Rivers Jade, Weser and Elbe, the system is mandatory for all

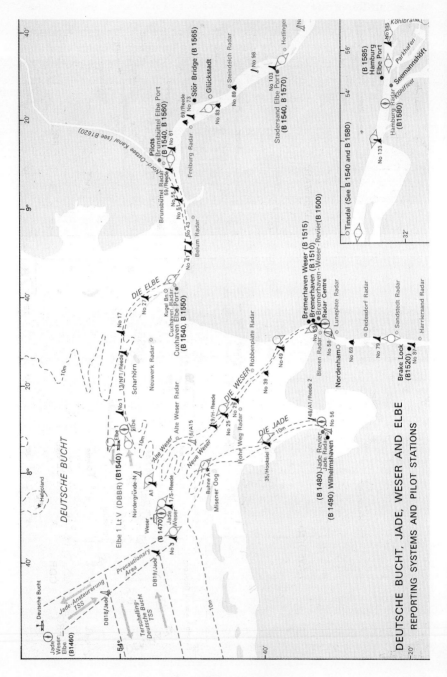

Fig. 1.6. Way-point reporting

vessels (including tows) that are over 50 metres in length, and also to all vessels carrying dangerous cargoes.

In practice, the reports themselves are extremely brief. Once the approaching vessel has "reported in" at the designated outer approach reporting point, the subsequent reports are merely her name and the name of the way point—usually a buoy. Also, in many of the more complex way-point reporting systems the ship changes the VHF channel as she progresses up the river.

For a system such as for the Elbe, her progress will be monitored by a series of radar stations, and regular information broadcasts are often made to give a brief "running commentary" of the movements of shipping in special areas.

Chapter 3 and 9 have a good deal more to say regarding way-point reports. Very rarely will it be necessary for small craft to report more than once—if at all—but increasingly a port authority likes to identify a radar "blip", as a small craft first enters the area.

Chapter 3 explains how, and in what circumstances, a small craft can be involved in Vessel Traffic Services (VTS) as they are called, and her obligations towards the harbour authority.

On our roads a crossing was first unmanned, then manned by police, then controlled by traffic lights, and now, increasingly, by bigger and more complex roundabouts and slip roads; sometimes with lights as well. Similarly, our ports used to have no signals at all. Later many adopted day shapes and lights for night-time. Now many are finding a need for monitoring the approach of shipping, as well as monitoring the movement of ships when within the port area. That is what a Port Operation is all about, and it is to explain how small craft fit into this complex scene that this book came into being.

Similarly, the supplement to this book—*Coast and Port Radio*—was developed to give a quick and easy way to look up the radio facilities and regulations in any particular port and, possibly more important still, to keep that information up to date. The supplement is self-explanatory and is described in greater detail in Chapter 3.

2

VHF Radiotelephony

RADIO, as a means of communication between ships and the shore, first began to have an affect on shipping in the late 1920s. At that time, and for several decades to come, the traffic was by means of wireless telegraphy (WT). All the traffic was by use of the Morse Code: thus only skilled, professional operators could use it. In certain circumstances immense distances could be covered, but WT was not used as a means of communication for port traffic at all.

Radiotelephony (RT), the use of speech on the air, followed on the medium frequency (MF) bands, but for many years the sets themselves were both bulky and expensive. It was not until the 1970s that Very High Frequency (VHF) radio began to be generally available on ships.

Early in the 1970s, when I first installed a VHF radiotelephone in a 10-metre sailing yacht, it was considered very odd indeed. Apart from a small handful of major ports like London and Southampton, there was no VHF port radio at all, and there were less than 1500 "VHF only" licenses issued in the whole of the United Kingdom.

Today—little more than a decade later—it would be the small craft that did **not** have VHF radio available that would be the oddity. Today there is almost continuous coastal coverage on VHF from Coast Radio Stations—the stations that handle ship-to-shore telephone traffic. There is almost continuous coverage as well, in the United Kingdom to HM Coastguard for VHF distress traffic and for direct contact with Coastguard for advice for small craft. Furthermore, and far more important as far as this book is concerned, virtually all commercial ports, and many yacht harbours as well, now have Port Operations VHF radio. (See Chapter 3 and the loose Supplement.)

Port Operations is a blanket phrase that covers all types of harbour radio. It can range from the highly sophisticated monitoring system, that includes continuous reporting and continuous radar cover, to the small port where the radio may be manned merely an hour or two either side of High Water or even only when a vessel is expected. Both are "Port Operations", and there are many grades of service in between.

In addition, the phrase Port Operations covers both the type of operation

12

when local by-laws give the port authority the power to control the movement of shipping, as well as the type of service that is purely advisory and informative. The subject is huge, but for any of the systems to operate successfully there has to be discipline, and discipline implies a knowledge of the way maritime radio works.

The Principles

For the longer range methods of communication—both telegraphy and telephony—the signals are normally bounced off layers of the upper atmosphere. The resultant ranges can be hundreds of miles for MF transmissions and thousands of miles for HF sets. For VHF radiotelephony, on the other hand, the range is normally, approximately line-of-sight.

At first, that might be thought to be a disadvantage, but for port operation radio, the range of VHF is just about right. The one overriding problem connected with the tool—because VHF radiotelephony is really a communications tool of the mariner—is summarized by what is called the "Capture Effect". That phenomenon has to be properly understood or everyone suffers.

In one sense it is a pity that VHF radiotelephony was ever connected with the word "telephone", for it is really a giant "party line". On shore, if there is a shortage of telephone lines in a particular area, it is sometimes necessary for two subscribers to share the same, so-called, "party line". In those circumstances, if one of the subscribers picks up his handset and starts speaking, without first listening to see if the line if free, he merely superimposes his voice on the conversation that is already in progress. On VHF, on the other hand, the strongest signal dominates the air. It "captures" the frequency and blots out all of the other signals (Fig. 2.1), even if the station that was originally transmitting continues to transmit.

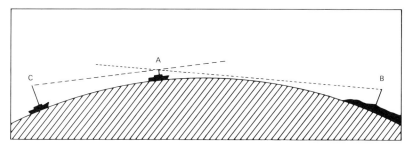

FIG. 2.1. *The capture effect. If C transmits while A is listening to a transmission from B, C "captures" the frequency. Her transmission blots out B and A therefore has to waste time for everyone while she asks C to wait and then asks B to repeat her message*

On the land-line "party line"—and on ordinary conversation for that matter—if two speak at once a third person within earshot would hear both conversations, even if they were somewhat jumbled. With VHF radiotelephony it is one **or** the other that captures the air waves.

It is not the intention here to write about the general technical aspects of radiotelephony, but it is necessary to summarize the subject if full advantage can be taken of the port radio facilities. [The author has written a book, *Yacht Signalling* (published by Macmillan in 1983), which devotes most of its pages to all aspects of small craft communication by VHF radio.]

Nowadays there are fifty-five channels available on a modern, synthesized VHF set and they are allocated, by international agreement, to one of four broad types: *Ship-to-Ship, Port Operations, Ship Movement* and *Public Correspondence* (Fig. 2.2). However, before understanding what that means it is necessary to explain the difference between what is called Simplex working and Duplex working, because there are three different types of transmission and reception.

Simplex, Semi-duplex and Duplex

To understand what follows, remember that there are two separate circuits within any VHF radiotelephone set. One is used for transmission and the other for reception, and *in most of the equipment used on small craft* the two circuits are never live together.

On commercial ships, however, and in the equipment used by Coast Radio Stations, both circuits can be in operation at the same time; a man can speak and listen simultaneously, as on a land-line telephone. The difference is fundamental. To listen and to speak simultaneously it is necessary to use what is called **Duplex** equipment and not only are Duplex sets themselves considerably more expensive, it is necessary to have two separate aerials, or highly sophisticated Duplex filters.

For **Simplex** only—the other extreme—the set can be used only on the channels which use the same frequency both for transmission and reception. In practice, that is highly restrictive and Simplex circuitry is used mainly on portables: because "Simplex only" sets can never be used for traffic to Coast Radio Stations.

Thus the compromise—used on almost all small craft—is equipment called **Semi-duplex.** The sets can be used on all channels—both Simplex and Duplex—but speech can travel in only one direction at any one time.

All **Ship-to-ship** channels are Simplex; they use one frequency only. Thus all the three types of equipment can be used for ship-to-ship traffic. **Port Operation** traffic is partly on Simplex channels and partly on Duplex channels that use two different frequencies. **Ship Movement** traffic is so similar to Port Operation traffic that the difference does not matter at this stage.

At first glance the table (Fig. 2.2) may look confusing, but it is an essential part of the smooth running of the VHF communications service that only channels allocated to a particular type of traffic should be used for that traffic. Some channels are allocated to more than one type of service; others, like many of the public correspondence channels, are unique.

Channel designators	Notes	Ship-to-ship	Port Operations		Ship Movement		Public Correspondence
			Single Frequency	Two Frequency	Single Frequency	Two Frequency	
60	(c)			17		9	25
01				10		15	8
61				23		3	19
02				8		17	10
62				20		6	22
03				9		16	9
63				18		8	24
04				11		14	7
64				22		4	20
05				6		19	12
65				21		5	21
06	(b)	1					
66				19		7	23
07				7		18	11
67	(e)	9	10		9		
08		2					
68	(g)		6		2		
09	(f)	5	5		12		
69	(g)	8	11		4		
10	(e)	3	9		10		
70	(i)	Digital selective calling for distress and safety					
11	(g)		3		1		
71	(g)		7		6		
12	(g)		1		3		
72	(f)	6					
13	(g)	4	4		5		
73	(e)	7	12		11		
14	(g)		2		7		
74	(g)		8		8		
15	(d)	11	14				
75		Guardband					
16		DISTRESS SAFETY AND CALLING					
76		Direct-printing for distress and safety purposes					
17	(d)	12	13				
77		10					
18	(a)			3		22	
78				12		13	27
19	(a)			4		21	
79	(a) (g)			14		1	
20	(a)			1		23	
80	(a) (g)			16		2	
21	(a)			5		20	
81				15		10	28
22	(a)			2		24	
82				13		11	26
23							5
83							16
24							4
84				24		12	13
25							3
85							17
26							1
86							15
27							2
87							14
28							6
88	(c)						18

FIG. 2.2. *VHF frequency table*

NOTES TO TABLE

(a)   The two frequency channels for port operations may also be used for public correspondence by special arrangement.
(b)   Ch 06 may also be used for ship-to-aircraft traffic during co-ordinated search and rescue operations.
(c)   Used only with special arrangements by interested administrations.
(d)   Ch 15 and 17 may also be used for on-board communication at 1 W.
(e)   In Europe and Canada Ch 10, 67 and 73 may also be used in co-ordinated search and rescue or anti-pollution operations.
(f)   The preferred first three frequencies for ship to air traffic in co-ordinated search and rescue operations. Ch 09, 72 and 73.
(g)   These ship movement channels may be used for port operations if required for a specific area.
        Ch 13 is also used world-wide for intership navigational safety traffic.
(h)   Ch 70 is to be used exclusively for digital selective calling for distress and safety purposes as from 1 January 1986.

These notes are considerably abbreviated from the official version which appears in *Admiralty List of Radio Signals*, Vol. 6.

With hindsight, it is obvious that the whole frequency allocation is over-congested, but that merely underlines the need for discipline. One of the commoner abuses is the use of port operation channels for ship-to-ship working.

The fact that a particular port operation channel was not being used at any particular time does not imply that the channel is available for *any* use. Furthermore, the essence of the change to the system of calling on working channels—to be discussed later—is based on the assumption that those channels will not be overloaded with spurious traffic and thus be unavailable for calls.

Calling and Being Called

With fifty-five channels available on most sets, it might be thought that there were therefore fifty-five ways of calling. In fact that is far from the truth. With the exception of specialized scanning receivers, which are well outside the scope of this chapter, a ship station or a shore station can be called only on the channel or channels on which she is listening; to try to call on any other channel is like kicking a dead jelly-fish: nothing happens.

What is even worse, the calls on the channel on which the other station is *not* listening are blocking the airwaves on that particular frequency so that no one else in that particular locality can use it even if it was perfectly legitimate for him to try to do so.

Thus it is of the utmost importance to understand how to call and what channels should be used for the purpose.

Ch 16 is designated the **Distress, Safety** and **Calling** frequency, and when VHF first came on the maritime scene Ch 16 was used for all calling. The regulations state that a call must not last more than a maximum of 60 seconds, and after making the call and the exchange of identities the two stations involved then change to a working channel.

Today that simplistic principle no longer applies in practice: the volume of traffic on VHF radio channels has made it impossible. As has just been explained, the prime requirement of a call is that it should be on a channel on which the station called will be listening. Thus although Ch 16 is still, and will remain, the correct calling channel for Distress and Safety traffic, and although it is also still the usual channel to use for a ship-to-ship call, Ch 16 is used less and less for calls to Coast Radio Stations and practically never for calls to Port Operations. Both Coast Radio Stations (CRS) and ports worldwide are changing to the system where ships call direct on the working channels. (See later for "model" calls.)

The reason for the change is two-fold. First, Ch 16 was becoming so congested that it was difficult to get a call through without interruption. Second, the amount of traffic on Ch 16 was making it less and less available for distress working.

Dual Watch

As has just been explained, a call to a port radio operator is now likely to be on the port's primary working channel. Similarly, a port operator will expect—and sometimes require—a ship to be monitoring that channel so that the port too can use the working channels for its calls.

From the safety point of view the port will also be monitoring Ch 16—for Safety, Urgency and Distress traffic—and thus the need for a ship to be monitoring Ch 16 as well is not quite so obvious as it is when a ship is on passage. However, most ships will also be monitoring Ch 16 either by the use of another radiotelephone or, more often, by the use of a facility called "dual-watch".

In theory dual-watch—the ability of one receiver to listen to two channels at the same time—is excellent: in practice it has severe disadvantages. For dual-watch the receive circuit of the radiotelephone is switched, automatically, between Ch 16 and one other selected channel. However, because Ch 16 is the Distress, Safety and Calling channel, Ch 16 always takes precedence. In other words, even if the set was receiving traffic on the chosen working channel, that traffic would be switched off and the set would change to receive the Ch 16 traffic.

In practice that means that an important message from a Port Operations Centre might be switched off in the middle of a sentence by some other vessel using Ch 16 for a routine ship-to-ship call. The fact that the Port Operations traffic might have been really important and the ship-to-ship call of low priority does not alter the outcome.

In other words, although dual-watch can be useful for keeping a check on what is happening on a particular channel, while still keeping Ch 16 "open" in case the vessel herself is called, it is certainly not a reliable "tool" on the occasions when it is important that the working channel is carefully monitored.

For that circumstance the installation of two separate VHF sets is the only satisfactory answer.

Dual Installation

Considering the importance of VHF to those responsible for the safety of ships in confined waters, it is surprising that the idea of dual installation has not become the norm, even on large vessels. The advantages are obvious, but although two sets require two aerials, it is not necessary that both aerials should be high. In small craft it is best to place the primary VHF aerial at the masthead in order to achieve the best range for long-distance communication. The aerial for a back-up set, on the other hand, can well be sited on a house top or similar position so long as it is well away from rigging. The range is basically line-of-sight, and bearing in mind that the back-up set will be used for close-quarters communication, such as port operation traffic, a comparatively low position for the aerial might be an advantage: the possibility of interference is actually lessened.

Harbour Radio

All commercial aircraft—and in many places all private aircraft as well —are *controlled*. An Air Traffic Controller organizes the sequence of arriving aircraft into an orderly stream and by means of radiotelephony the pilot is issued with instructions regarding how he is to proceed. The Air Traffic Controller—himself a highly qualified man—is in charge of what happens.

At sea, on the other hand, there are similarities with the air but also great differences. The similarities are fairly obvious, but the numerous differences may not be so clear.

In the first place, everything happens so very much more slowly at sea that there is not—or at least has not been up until now—the need to **control** traffic. Traditionally it has always been the Master who is the ultimate man in charge of his ship and, with a few specialized exceptions, that is still true today. The port radio operator is advising. He is informing the master of an approaching vessel of any known hazards; he keeps account of the movement of others in the vicinity and he advises on the availability of tugs or the state of readiness of the berth towards which the ship is bound.

Again there are exceptions, because the expression Port Operations traffic covers everything from the enormously comprehensive radio and radar cover for commercial ports like Rotterdam, Göteborg or London to a harbour radio, manned for a few hours a day by a harassed harbour official who has no radar cover and who cannot even see some parts of his "patch". The local bylaws will cover a Harbour Master's powers, but those powers will never be akin to the control exercised in the air.

Yet another difference, and one that, for the purposes of this book, is even more important, is that in the air the Controller is speaking on a dedicated frequency. The exchange between the two is an exchange between only those two, even though others will be listening. At sea, on the other hand, although a harbour radio will have an allocated channel or channels, the primary channel will be listened to by almost everyone. The Harbour operator will speak to "A" and to "B", but "C", "D" and "E" will be listening and **may adjust their actions as a result of what they hear.**

That is the fundamental difference between the sea and the air. Many ships may be monitoring the traffic of a few, and it is that type of participation, participation only by listening, that applies most frequently to the small craft.

Development of VTS

The expression Vessel Traffic Services (VTS) for all harbour radio has now been used for long enough for those involved with the subject to take it for granted, but in fact it grew from the less easily accepted (although more easily understood) term Vessel Traffic Management (VTM). For understandable reasons the idea of a harbour authority acting as "Manager" for a ship was resented by many ship masters, and thus the earlier expression VTM has only rarely been adopted.

By emphasizing the "Service" element in the operation, the "pill" was less "bitter" and at the same time shipowners could not escape from the fact that a well-managed harbour was better for them too.

The demurrage charge—the amount payable for the failure to load within an agreed time—runs into thousands of pounds sterling a day for a large vessel, and the more the Harbour Authority, the Pilots, the Shipping Agents and the numerous other organizations involved with a ship can work to a schedule the better for everyone.

Once upon a time a ship would sail into and drop anchor in, say, Falmouth Roads "for orders". Her arrival time might vary by days or even weeks from that when she had been expected. Today a ship might be "singling-up" (taking in all but one of her mooring ropes) as the next occupant of her berth is actually approaching the same berth.

Without an efficient VTS and without a dependence on VHF radiotelephony, that would be unthinkable: only a decade ago it would have been impossible.

The idea of having—and in many instances requiring—ships to report in has snowballed. At first, and for many major ports, the need to report—at positions marked as Way-points on the chart—was restricted only to the largest vessels. However, the advantages of having an orderly flow into, or out of, any restricted area such as a port soon showed such benefits both to the ports as well as to the shipping companies that the early objections and suspicions are vanishing fast.

At first the requirement was connected with the risks of pollution as much as anything else. Nations such as Britain and France, that had vast tonnages of oil and other hazardous cargoes passing close to their shores every day, were increasingly concerned about the affects on the environment by collisions or stranding. Dover Strait is one of the more obvious concentrations of shipping, and all vessels above a certain size started, during the 1970s, to come under the control of the shore.

From that basic ship movement reporting spread the organization we see today. All major ports, as well as a great many minor ones, have continuous VHF "cover" of their waters.

As was explained in the Introduction, small craft are generally exempted from any requirement to report to a VTS, although there are specialized areas where all vessels, regardless of size, do have to report or otherwise obtain prior permission. The barrier across the River Thames at Woolwich is one of the more obvious examples in Home waters. There are also areas on the French Coast—off Oeussant (Ushant) for example—where all vessels are required to report their presence on Ch 16 and off the River Seine and off Saint Malo where the regulations say that all vessels should do so.

Off the Rotterdam Waterweg approaches the regulations also state that all vessels should report, but it is an interesting sign of the times that, in the short interval between writing the Introduction to this book, and writing Chapter 2, the Dutch authorities have introduced a special monitoring service for coastal small craft off the Hoek, and allocated a specific VHF channel for what they refer to as "coastal recreational traffic", with the recommendation that all report name, position and course.

The implications of this trend are discussed more fully in the next chapter. In 1984 the idea of yachts having to report in merely because they were sailing along a particular stretch of coast might have seemed strange, at the very least, and an infringement on personal freedom to come and go at the worst. Nevertheless, within a very few years the discipline of reporting is likely to be the norm in many congested areas.

The Dutch have done what they have done for the waters just off the Hoek van Holland: it would be difficult to argue that that was not an area that needs particular attention. Thus, if we have reached the point in the development of small craft radiotelephony when small craft are—or may be—asked and/or required to report, how is the equipment to be arranged?

Installation

From what has been said already, it should be obvious that if any small vessel is to monitor any channel at least one loudspeaker must be installed within easy earshot of the man on watch. For monitoring a port operations channel, while entering or manoeuvring in a port, it is not too onerous to suggest that the VHF set volume is merely turned up enough for the loudspeaker to be heard from on deck. While entering port, the crew is likely to be active and on deck, and thus the inconvenience of having a radio "blasting away" in the cabin could be acceptable.

However, nobody would suggest that that is the best answer. For an entry to London River, for example, there might be a need to listen to Gravesend Radio and then to Woolwich Radio for a period of many hours, possibly all day. Thus the idea of relying on a cabin-mounted louspeaker alone is something that ought to be dismissed from the outset. It may be the commonest type of installation, but it is not satisfactory.

There are two objectives. First, a loudspeaker needs to be installed within easy earshot of the man on watch. In a motor yacht, with the steering position within a wheelhouse, there is little or no problem. However, for all sailing yachts and motor-sailers, and for all motor yachts likely to be steered from an open steering position, a separate, cockpit-mounted loudspeaker becomes essential.

Separate loudspeakers—waterproof of course—are readily available, and they are not difficult to install. The key technical point is to ensure that the impedance of the speaker suits the circuitry of the set.

Specialist firms, advertising exterior VHF speakers, can offer what is necessary—usually a speaker with an impedance of 4 ohms—but the switching, too, needs a little thought.

At its most crude, a cabin speaker can be merely unplugged and the cockpit speaker plugged in, the jack-plug of the cockpit speaker isolating the cabin speaker. However, plugs are not really the answer. A switch by the companionway is my choice; mounted at a point where it is simple to use when going on deck or when coming below.

On the other hand, some might call for switching offering either or both. But in any event, the problem is not great and once a sensible mounting can be arranged it is difficult to understand how the crew ever managed without it.

The cockpit speaker allows the man at the helm to monitor whatever needs monitoring. He can monitor Ch 16 when on passage. And he can do all that without any need to disturb the watch below.

The second requirement concerns the use of the transmitter. For the best solution, waterproof handsets are available, and there arc also sets with more than one handset mounting so that not only can the radiotelephone be used, but channels can be changed, and volume and squelch adjusted as well, from the cockpit mounting.

For a large vessel that has obvious advantages, but for small family yachts a compromise is probably adequate. A modern VHF set is little larger than a book, and many are designed so that they can be mounted on the deckhead. The deckhead has the advantage, over all other places, in that it is likely to remain dry and is unlikely to be used for anything else. Thus the choice might be a deckhead mounted set that can **just** be reached from the companion, with a cabin louspeaker mounted wherever thought best, with a cockpit mounted speaker well away from the companion, and with a change-over switch alongside the companion itself.

Almost always the set, when needed, would be used from below, but if short-handed there might be an occasion when there was a need to transmit from on deck—even if the transmitted message consisted of "THIS IS BARBICAN—WAIT—OUT".

Obviously, in a book of this sort, it is the use of radio in harbour that is most important, but radio in distress is also of importance in all circumstances. If assisting, in any manner, in a search and rescue operation, a cockpit mounted speaker might well make all the difference between success and failure.

Distress and Urgency Traffic

Radio, in distress, is obviously an important subject, and it has been given a chapter of its own, Chapter 11. The key point, is that all distress traffic has a particular procedure laid down internationally.

Figure 2.3 shows how complex the intermingling can be. Normally any distress call in inshore waters would be picked up by a CRS or in U.K. waters by HM Coastguard and it would then be HM Coastguard's responsibility to co-ordinate all subsequent efforts.

Within a harbour VTS, on the other hand, an incident might first be reported on the VTS primary channel, and subsequent involvement of pilot

CALL	WORK
Distress Ch 16	Ch 16
Urgency Ch 16	Ch16
Safety Ch 16	Normally some other working channel
HM Coastguard Ch 16	Ch 67
Ship-to-shore Normally the appropriate working channel	Normally the working channel used for the call but otherwise a working channel designated by the Coast Radio Station.
Port Operation Normally the port's primary working channel. Otherwise Ch 16	Normally the working channel used for the call. Otherwise another working channel designated by the port.
Ship-to-ship Ch 16, unless other prior arrangements had been made.	Any ship-to-ship working channel found to be free but preferably avoiding ship-to-ship channels that are port operational working channels as well.

FIG. 2.3. *Summary calling and working procedures*

vessels or tugs—within the area—might be co-ordinated from the VTS centre, at least in the initial stages.

Obviously there is the possibility of a conflict of interests, but most harbour offices already have an agreed plan to involve HMCG as soon as possible.

The implications of this situation are explained in Chapter 11, but whether the traffic is for Distress, Urgency, Safety or merely the normal business of the vessel, a degree of discipline is essential.

Throughout the exchange, that discipline is important, but nowhere is it more important than in the method of calling and acknowledging a call.

Model Calls and Acknowledgements

There is no, one, correct way to call, or to answer a call, on VHF radiotelephony. The best method depends on the type of station being called, the nature of the call and on the conditions prevailing.

Ship-to-Ship Traffic in Harbour: Calling on Ch 16

The use of radio in harbour is restricted to certain specific purposes. The regulations state that: "A ship station in harbour may not communicate with other ship stations, but only with coast stations....Except in case of emergency involving safety...".

In practice, that regulation is not observed nearly as well as it deserves to be. However, ship-to-ship traffic concerned with the business of the port can probably come under the heading of "...involving safety..." if the procedure is sensible. Thus, subject to that proviso, a ship-to-ship call in harbour would be as any other ship-to-ship call (except when prior arrangement had been made) on Ch 16.

The call would be the name of the station called, once (twice if thought necessary), followed by the pro-words "This is", followed by the name of the calling station, twice (or once if the name is likely to be recognized), followed by the invitation to reply:

    "FANFARE—THIS IS BARBICAN, BARBICAN—OVER".

In addition, although the International Telecommunications Union (ITU) recommendations state that it is the station called that should name the channel to be used for the exchange of messages—the procedure that applies for all ship-to-shore exchanges—there is logic in the idea that, for a ship-to-ship call, the calling station should switch among the available ship-to-ship channels (prior to making her initial call) to find a suitable one that is free of other traffic.

If she did that, the initial call might be:

    "FANFARE—THIS IS BARBICAN,
    BARBICAN—CHANNEL SEVEN TWO—OVER".

In that circumstance the acknowledgement might be:

"BARBICAN—THIS IS FANFARE—
CHANNEL SEVEN TWO—OVER".

Both stations then change to Ch 72 and the whole call and acknowledgement has occupied only two, short sentences on Ch 16.

Alternatively, if the calling station had not recommended a channel to be used for the exchange, it is the duty of the station called to so so. The calling station then acknowledges and they both change channel.

The disadvantage of that (official) sequence is first that the exchange occupies three sentences on Ch 16 instead of two; also the station called might well recommend a channel that was occupied, because she would not have had the opportunity to listen to those available before acknowledging the call.

All that applies to ship-to-ship traffic in general, but it needs to be stressed that "normal" ship-to-ship traffic in harbour is not allowed.

Calling on a Working Channel

An alternative type of ship-to-ship call, that is more likely to be heard within a port area, is a call to another ship on the port's primary working channel. First, the station called is likely to be monitoring the port's channel and, on the assumption that the traffic affects the business of the safety of the port, the port operator will also be aware that ship "a" has called ship "b" and that they will therefore not be monitoring the port's primary channel for a few moments.

At all times it is the shore that controls, and it hardly needs to be stressed that traffic on the port's primary channel should have priority. Nevertheless, even if not precisely "according to the book", a brief call on the port's working channel might well be the correct way to start an exchange with another ship.

What then happens, after the opening exchange, would depend on the circumstances. For a very brief exchange the two pilots—or the two masters—might remain on the port operation working channel for the exchange, rather than change. However, in general, bridge-to-bridge traffic is to be discouraged. First, because it is the Collision Regulations, rather than any verbal understanding between two ships, which should control the movements of those ships. Secondly, as is described later in Chapter 4, it is so easy for one ship to think she is speaking to one particular ship whereas she is actually speaking to another (Fig. 2.4).

Recently Ch 13 has been designated as the appropriate working channel for bridge-to-bridge navigational safety traffic. Thus, is any traffic between masters of vessels under way was to be more than a brief exchange, that would be the correct channel for the exchange.

Finally, under this heading, it should be made clear that any question of

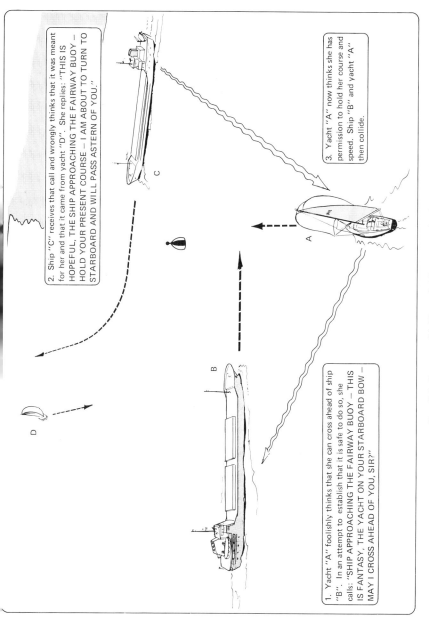

2. Ship "C" receives that call and wrongly thinks that it was meant for her and that it came from yacht "D". She replies: "THIS IS HOPEFUL, THE SHIP APPROACHING THE FAIRWAY BUOY – HOLD YOUR PRESENT COURSE – I AM ABOUT TO TURN TO STARBOARD AND WILL PASS ASTERN OF YOU."

3. Yacht "A" now thinks she has permission to hold her course and speed. Ship "B" and yacht "A" then collide.

1. Yacht "A" foolishly thinks that she can cross ahead of ship "B". In an attempt to establish that it is safe to do so, she calls: "SHIP APPROACHING THE FAIRWAY BUOY – THIS IS FANTASY, THE YACHT ON YOUR STARBOARD BOW – MAY I CROSS AHEAD OF YOU, SIR?"

FIG. 2.4. *Dangers of bridge-to-bridge communication*

small craft using port operation primary channels for calling should be reserved for exceptional circumstances. There might be occasions when small craft needed to call the port operation itself on the port operation channel, but, as has been explained, that is **not** merely an alternative calling frequency: it is a calling frequency for use in certain specific circumstances.

Calling Port Operations

Many small ports and virtually all large ports have recently changed from the traditional procedure of calling on Ch 16 to one where ships are asked (and sometimes required) to call on the port's primary working channel. A small port might have only one working channel, and it might use that both for calling and for the traffic. However, increasingly the large commercial ports are introducing a system where they have one primary working channel—usually printed in bold type in any list of radio signals—and other working channels allocated for specific purposes. To use Harwich as an example, there are two harbour operations channels listed, Ch 14 and **71**; the latter printed in bold type to indicate it is the primary calling channel. Ch 16 is still monitored as the Distress and Calling channel, but the fact that the port will be monitoring Ch 16 as well as at least one other working channel shows the need to state the number of the channel in use in the initial call.

In a major port there will always be more than one operator on duty, and calls on different channels will be automatically switched to different men. However, the object of stating the channel in use is that there are many occasions when one operator will be monitoring more than one frequency. A call

"HARWICH HARBOUR—THIS IS BARBICAN—OVER"

alerts the Harwich operator that a vessel called *Barbican* is calling, but unless the operator was actually looking at his instruments at the time of the call, he would not know which of the two channels that he was monitoring was being used.

Thus a call to a harbour radio—where more than one frequency is likely to be watched—should always follow the recommendation in the "M" Notice, *Proper Use of VHF Channels at Sea,* and include the channel in use in the initial call.

"HARWICH HARBOUR CONTROL—THIS IS BARBICAN,
BARBICAN, ON CHANNEL SEVEN ONE—OVER."

That is the complete call. The name of the station called once and the name of the calling station twice. Only rarely is it necessary to repeat more than that.

However, for a small port, where the harbour authority does not list itself as monitoring a working channel, the call is then on Ch 16 and the procedure is as for an intership call.

Note that, in contrast to ship-to-shore traffic via CRS, there is no charge either for ship-to-ship or port operation radiotelephone use.

Calling Coast Radio Stations

The term Coast Radio Station (CRS) is reserved for the numerous radio stations which handle commercial ship-to-shore traffic. They all include the word radio in their names.

North Foreland Radio, Niton Radio and Scheveningen Radio are three of the better known examples, but unfortunately some port operation radio stations also include radio as a suffix to their names and that can cause confusion.

In the useful guidelines that have recently been produced by an International Association of Lighthouse Authorities (IALA) Working Party, it is recommended that that anomaly should be phased out.

A port might call itself, for example, Harwich Harbour Control or Dover Port Control—to avoid confusion with a ship-to-shore radio station—but the IALA recommendation is for "Landfall VTS" (such as Ouessant) or "Through Traffic VTS" (such as Dover) to use the word "Traffic" as the suffix: *Ouessant Traffic* and *Dover Traffic*.

Pilot stations such as Rotterdam would then use "Pilot Traffic" as their suffix: *Rotterdam Pilot Traffic,* and the port would use "Port Traffic": *Rotterdam Port Traffic.*

In that manner—and the recommendation is eminently sensible—the possibility of confusion is minimized. The use of the word "Radio" identifies the station as a coast radio station and the use of the word "Traffic" (in one of its forms) identifies the station as a port operational station.

Thus here, and throughout this book, the phrase Coast Radio Station (CRS) refers to stations handling ship-to-shore telephone calls.

All U.K. CRS and most Continental CRS prefer calls on one of the station's working channels, but unlike harbour VTS radio stations there is no primary channel for calls; the choice of the particular channel depends on the location of the vessel.

The procedure for calling is the same whether a vessel is in port or at sea.

If the CRS to be called is one that still accepts calls on Ch 16 (see the Supplement to this book), the procedure is similar to a call to another ship with the exception that the identity of the ship should be given, in the initial call, as the ship's call sign, not her name.

By the summer of 1985 all the CRS around our coastline, except Jersey in the Channel Islands and Malin Head in Northern Ireland, had changed to the system where calls are made on the appropriate working channel. This is similar to the system used in Holland and Belgium. Calls will still be accepted if made on Ch 16, but the CRS much prefer the call on the appropriate working channel and, in busy periods, calls made in that manner are far more likely to be acknowledged. The exception is in France, when calls on Ch 16 are not acknowledged; that channel is reserved for distress only.

To call on a working channel, look up the channel or channels that are appropriate to the station and/or to the geographical position of the vessel and then listen, in turn, until one of the appropriate working channels is found to be free. An engaged channel is indicated by speech or by an engaged tone. Silence indicates a channel is free.

In the United Kingdom the engaged tone is a series of pips, similar to those used on land, and after a call has been made (on a channel that is silent) the fact that the call has been accepted is indicated by similar pips. In Holland the acceptance signal is a jingle, which lasts for 90 seconds, after which, if the call has not been acknowledged, the calling station should call again. In France the acceptance signal is a series of "buzzes" and the CRS will then ask for the call sign of the station calling.

A call on a working channel should last at least 5 seconds in order to trigger the automatic switching equipment.

The call varies somewhat from country to country. In the United Kingdom the call is always the name of the station followed by the word "Radio"— Niton Radio or North Foreland Radio, for example—and the choice of channel depends on which is found to be free. In Belgium the call is to a station named in a similar manner—Oostende Radio or Antwerpen Radio— but the working channel on which the call is made will vary according to the location of the vessel.

In Holland the system is slightly different again. The Dutch system, which is extremely efficient, uses "Scheveningen Radio" as the call for the whole country, but there are about twelve different channels to choose from, again the choice depending on the location of the calling station. In Holland, too, some localities have more than one frequency allocation.

After checking on the frequency to be used for the call and listening to ensure that it is free, the call is:

—name of station called once (twice if thought necessary);
—call sign of calling station twice (three times if conditions are poor) spoken phonetically, slowly.

Thus a complete call might be:

> NORTH FORELAND RADIO—THIS IS MIKE ALPHA BRAVO
> ALPHA, MIKE ALPHA BRAVO ALPHA—OVER."

The acknowledgement might be:

> "MIKE ALPHA BRAVO ALPHA—THIS IS NORTH FORELAND
> RADIO"

possibly followed by a courtesty comment such as "Good afternoon".
That is followed by:

> "THIS IS MIKE ALPHA BRAVO ALPHA—SHIP'S NAME
> BARBICAN—I SPELL BRAVO ALPHA ROMEO BRAVO INDIA
> CHARLIE ALPHA NOVEMBER—BARBICAN—ONE LINK CALL,
> PLEASE TO . . .".

The operator will want the ship's name (spelt phonetically, unless the spelling is obvious and the conditions good); the area code (if known) or the name of the exchange required; the number required; and the accounting authority indicator code.

Paying for the Calls

The accounting authority is the organization to which the cost of the ship-to-shore call will be sent. Large organizations have special arrangements for their accounting, but small craft will use one of two methods.

The simplest for yachtsmen, from the authorities' point of view, is to use a new system called Yacht Telephone Debit (YTD). It applies only to calls from U.K. yachts, to U.K. telephone numbers and via U.K. CRS, but as that covers the majority of all U.K. calls it will soon become the norm. With a VTD call the calling station adds the abbreviation "YTD" after transmitting the number of the subscriber required, and that is followed by the telephone number to which the call should be charged.

That is all. As far as the yacht is concerned, the cost is the same, but the use of YTD means that the cost of the call, or calls, is added to the existing subscribers' telephone account as an itemized addition each quarter.

The alternative, which applies to all other calls, is to use the accounting authority indicator code which was allocated when the licence was issued. Unless special arrangements have been made, all small craft use British Telecom International, for which the indicator code is **"GB 14"**.

The disadvantage of failing to use YTD, for a call for which it would have been appropriate, is that British Telecom have to initiate a special account for the purpose. If the ship uses the radiotelephone a lot, that is no problem, but for the very occasional use that many yachts make of the service it costs BTI more to send in the bill than the profit margin on the call.

The procedure for making ship-to-shore calls has been described in some detail, because there is a good deal of confusion, but there is yet another problem that can arise, and it is appropriate to explain it here.

In Chapter 10 the procedures for reporting to HM Customs and Excise are summarized. In certain circumstances there is a requirement to make a notification of arrival by telephone, and as an obvious alternative to having to go ashore to find a call box many yachtsmen, returning from abroad, use the yacht's radiotelephone. The problem arises because many of the smaller Customs and Excise offices rely on telephone answering machines.

The regulations, outlined in Chapter 11, make it clear that certain details have to be given concerning the name of the vessel, where she is lying, and so on, but if speaking to an answering machine and if the facts had been assembled properly beforehand, the complete transmission need not take more than 1 minute at the most. The problem arises because an answering machine does not switch itself off after you have stopped speaking to it: it is switched off only by a disconnection of the line.

In theory, the CRS operator listens to the beginning of the exchange, so that he would know that the ship was connected to an answering machine, and he would therefore listen, at intervals, to find out if the calling station had finished the call. In practice, if the CRS is busy, the operator may carry on dealing with another call as soon as he has made the connection and before the answering machine has "answered". So long as the answering machine is running, his switchboard tells him that a "conversation" is still taking place because the "subscriber" ashore—the answering machine—has not replaced his receiver.

Once a subscriber on shore replaces his receiver, the line is broken, a light comes up on the CRS switchboard and the CRS operator then calls the ship and informs her of the length of the call. With an answering machine that does not happen.

The only way to avoid waiting a long period after the end of the call (and risking being charged for that period of waiting) is to notify the CRS operator **when the call is first made** that the station called is likely to be "manned" by an answering machine.

I learnt that lesson, for which there is no official answer, the hard way. After a 45-second call I waited about 8 or 9 minutes until a CRS operator came back and asked if I was finished. The fact that he accepted my statement regarding the length of my wait and thus charged me the minimum 3 minutes for my call did not alter the fact that I was frustrated and that the channel had been occupied unnecessarily for all that time.

Distress and Urgency traffic is given a chapter of its own, but for all normal use the most important point of all is to keep off Ch 16 as much as possible. It is still, and will remain, the International Distress, Safety and Calling frequency, but today the emphasis is to use it for calling as little as possible.

Chapter 3 outlines the principle of the radiotelephony discipline "Seaspeak", but, even without learning any particular discipline, it should be obvious by now that a degree of personal discipline is essential.

Over or Out

In the examples given here the need to end every sentence with "OVER", the invitation to reply, has been included. The theory is that with Simplex and Semi-duplex equipment the recipient of any call cannot know whether the man speaking has finished what he intends to say or not until he hears that invitation to reply. On hearing "OVER" he can press his transmit button and, on doing so, will no longer hear anything.

With Duplex equipment that restriction does not apply. Thus the professional communicator, working from the switchboard in the CRS, hears the small craft whether the CRS operator is speaking himself or not. In practice, that means that the CRS rarely uses the expression "OVER", but that does mean that it is superfluous and, for the initial exchange at any rate, it should always be used. Later, if conditions are good, the tone of voice can often indicate whether a man has merely paused or whether he is inviting a reply.

If in any doubt, follow "the book". Use "OVER" at the end of every message when a reply is invited and use "OUT" at the end of the traffic. Never both, they mean totally different things.

Some of the other "Pro" words (pro standing for "procedural" not, as often described, for "professional") are listed with their meanings in Appendix A, but just as some communicators seem to find difficulty regarding the use of "OVER", there is also confusion regarding "OUT".

"OUT", in radiotelephony, means "As far as I am concerned this is the end of my working to you." It does not mean the end of the station's transmissions, nor does it mean that the station is closing down or ceasing to keep watch. Ideally, and according to the regulations, **both** stations say "OUT" at the end of an exchange. In practice, in good conditions, only one station uses out and the other does not bother to reply. (See also Appendix A.)

Selective Calling

In a chapter dealing with the various methods of calling on VHF radiotelephone, it would be wrong not to mention what is called Selcall, a system of selective calling that is not nearly as widely used as it ought to be.

Any vessels can obtain a Selcall number (at present the system uses a five-digit number), there is no charge for the service, and as far as ship-to-shore traffic and emergency traffic is concerned Selcall becomes a private "paging" system.

When a CRS gets a request for a link call to a ship it normally waits until the next Traffic List broadcast. However, if the ship is fitted with Selcall, and if the caller knows the ship's Selcall number, the CRS merely puts the number into its encoder, presses a transmit switch, and the signal—transmitted on Ch 16 in milliseconds—triggers a corresponding switch on board the vessel.

With most small craft Selcall sets there are two red lights and a buzzer. The buzzer is triggered by the signal and lasts for 15 seconds or so. One or other of the lights is also switched on and remains on until the signal is cancelled. One light is for a normal ship-to-shore call, labelled "Call"; the other for what is usually called a CQ call. CQ stands for "All ships" in the wireless operators Q Code.

The "All ships" call is used by the CRS to alert everyone within range if there was a distress message to relay. Normally, however, the "Call" light and buzzer saves time for everyone. The CRS does not have to wait to broadcast the fact that it has a call, and the ship gets her call without having to listen to the next Traffic List.

Finally, and in one sense the most interesting point of all from the small craft's point of view, there might well be occasions when a call was received when there was nobody near the set to handle it or even nobody on board! On a return from shopping a man might find his "call" light on (and, of course, the system works only when the radio itself is switched on) and all he has to do is call the nearest CRS and say:

"THIS IS MIKE ALPHA BRAVO ALPHA—YOU HAVE TRAFFIC FOR ME."

Why the system has not caught the attention of the public is not clear. Most of the better quality sets either have the facility built-in or it can be added comparatively cheaply. All CRS have the facility, and it works—at home or abroad.

Cost

Inevitably radiotelephone calls cost a little more than calls made from a man's home or office. However, the extra is only a small proportion of the cost of a land-line call and the service, generally, is extremely efficient.

To give but one example, during a 12-week cruise in 1977, when I visited eight different countries in north-west Europe, I kept in touch with my office at about 5-day intervals throughout the period and on only one occasion—when I was outside the theoretical range of a Finnish CRS—did I not get through within less than 2 minutes of first picking up the handset.

3

Vessel Traffic Services

MUCH of the basic idea of a Vessel Traffic Service arose from the need to report the movement of unusually large ships and/or dangerous cargoes. During the 1970s and the early years of the 1980s there were many different arguments and committee discussions regarding the best way to achieve the objectives, but a large part of the problem arose because of the different interpretations regarding what was the objective.

Broadly the authority—the government, the port or the international organization—favoured "control" in the sense that it was they who decided what happened, and the shipmaster and the shipping company favoured the maximum possible freedom for the individual ship. Both wanted to avoid the devastating affects of marine pollution, but the mariner—understandably—was concerned about the idea of some faceless voice on a radio telling him how to navigate his ship.

Gradually the advantages of VTS, as far as ports were concerned, became more and more obvious commercially—as well as from the point of view of the necessary protection of the marine environment—and the two sides came closer together.

Yachtsmen will never be involved in the type of detailed, coded reports that a 100 000 tonne tanker is likely to have to submit to, but it does help to understand the principle of Ship Movement Reporting if the method is outlined.

General Principles

Ship reporting systems are used to gather information by radio reports to provide data for many purposes, including search and rescue, traffic management, weather forecasting and the prevention of marine pollution.

Ideally a reporting system should contain only essential information. It should be in a standard format and the times when, and the geographical positions where, to submit reports should be clearly specified.

Bearing in mind that the report will be transmitted by radio and that the man transmitting and the man receiving will not necessarily have English as their mother tongue, the need for the report to be in a standard format is probably the prime requirement. **If a man receiving a message is told beforehand what type of traffic he is about to hear, he is far less likely to be confused.**

Later in this chapter the speech discipline "Seaspeak" will be outlined, because it is a direct development of the same philosophy, but chronologically the idea of a predetermined format for a report came first.

For commercial shipping there are several different types of reporting system, with MAREP one of the better known. The information is given in an alphabetical list with "A" standing for the name of the ship, "B" the date and time, "C" the position as a latitude and longitude, "D" the position as a bearing and distance (as an alternative), "E" the true course, "F" the speed and so on.

Any section which is inappropriate is omitted, but the point of the whole report is that if the receiving operator hears any letter, he knows what to expect: "delta" will be a bearing and distance.

If MAREP is an example of the more sophisticated end of the reporting ladder, the other extreme is found merely as a name and a position or way-point. A ship, having once checked in to a VTS, may make occasional reports as brief as:

> "GRAVESEND RADIO—THIS IS BARBICAN—NO. 5 SEA
> REACH—OVER."

Or even briefer:

> "GRAVESEND—BARBICAN—NO. 5."

If conditions are good, and if the Gravesend VTS operator knows the name "Barbican" and knows (or does not need to know) what type of ship she is, then even that four-word message is satisfactory. However, even then, in a four-word message, the order of those words follows the recommended format for any VHF call: "Name of station called"—"Name of calling station"—"message".

Next in this outline of the reporting guidelines is the question of how to present the facts. Once again yachts are unlikely to have to use the reports in anything like the manner that commercial ships use them, but the manner in which a message is sent has a great deal to do with the effect it has on the recipient. The point becomes almost one of basic courtesy; to "um" and "er" and stumble over a simple message not only takes up the time of a man who may be very busy, but it causes needless possibilities of confusion.

Time is an excellent example. Time—"Bravo" in the IMO recommended format—is the word used for a "Time group" or a Date-time group. In person-to-person speech or during a ship-to-ship call it might be perfectly reasonable to say that you expect to arrive by half-past four, and normally it would be perfectly obvious that you were referring to local time and to either the morning or afternoon. In a report, on the other hand, the receiving station is logging the facts of the message and it might be thoroughly confusing if one man says: "Half-past four", another "Half four" and a third "Four thirty".

A time group is either four or six digits; four for time alone and six for date and time. In a date-time group the first two digits are the day of the month, the second two the hour, and the third two the minutes. Thus half-past four in the afternoon on the sixth day of the month is 061630 followed by a time zone letter if the time is not Universal Time.

At first the idea of stating time in that manner might appear top-heavy, but it very soon becomes second nature and it is far, far easier to record a message when time is given in that manner than to have to translate "Half four" into "1630".

A course should be transmitted as a three-digit group: true unless stated otherwise.

A speed is also best given as a three-digit group in knots and tenths of a knot. From the VTS operator's point of view few ships will be doing less than 10 knots and none more than 99. Thus the occasional speed sent as "Zero six decimal five", for the occasions when a small vessel might be asked her speed, is easier to log than "About six and a half knots".

From a small craft's point of view, especially in the proximity of a harbour, position is most likely to be given as a bearing and a distance in relation to a well-known mark. The expression "bearing and distance" is a common one, and at first it might be assumed that the meaning was obvious. In fact that is far from the case.

At sea, bearings of headlands, or other features being used for navigation, are taken from seaward, as are all bearings of the sectors of lights. Thus the mariner tends to think of a bearing as something taken from seaward. For a position, on the other hand, the bearing is *always* given **FROM** the mark that has been chosen as the data base. A ship is 180 degrees from St Catherine's Point; the position is not that St Catherine's Point bears 000 degrees. Furthermore, bearings are given as true bearings, not magnetic.

In official publications, including the original edition of the *International Marine Navigational Vocabulary*, the example of a position was given as "POSITION 137 DEGREES SIX MILES FROM ST CATHERINE'S LIGHT"; in some other publications the word "from" is printed in bold type. However, even that is not completely clear: the word "from" needs to be associated in the mind of the mariner with the bearing, not the distance. It is obvious that the distance is so much "from" the prominent mark; it is the bearing, too, that has to be **from** the mark.

Following representation to the U.K. Department of Transport Search and Rescue Committee, from the Royal Yachting Association representatives, the point was picked up by the appropriate IMO Safety of Navigation Committee and an amendment to the *International Marine Navigational Vocabulary* was issued in 1985. By no means were amateurs the only people to cause confusion by misunderstanding this point. The first helicopter to arrive on the scene for what turned out to be the largest helicopter rescue ever performed—when 140 passengers and crew were lifted off the ferry *Antrim Princess*—went to the wrong position. A reciprocal bearing had been given in the distress message!

Offshore, on the other hand, the increasing use of hyperbolic radio position-fixing devices, such as Decca, means that a position is far more likely to be given as a latitude and longitude rather than as a bearing and a distance.

If giving a position in latitude and longitude, the latitude is a four- (plus decimals) digit group and longitude a five- (plus decimals) digit group; each suffixed with N or S and E or W. Nowadays positions are usually given in degrees and minutes, with decimals of a minute added if accuracy is needed. The digitized machines used today use that method (not degrees, minutes and seconds), and when extreme accuracy is needed decimals allow a greater flexibility as well as eliminating a unit. Thus modern charts are increasingly being subdivided into degrees, minutes and decimals of minutes.

All that may seem a long way from the traditional "North by East, a quarter East" type of direction, but the 360 degree compass itself was treated with considerable suspicion when it first began to be adopted in the early 1930s.

I submit that the digital presentation of course, speed and position and the digitalized description of time will be universal and second nature to all within a decade at the outside: it is already in constant use in the commercial world today.

The change has been slow because individuals cling to the style and to the symbols that they were taught when young. However, we, in the United Kingdom, should remember that even if we have resisted the change to metrication, most of the rest of the world has had to undergo the change to the use of the English language. We have struggled to dismiss the yard and the degree Fahrenheit; many have had to relearn their whole seagoing language.

"Seaspeak"

In the IMO Guidelines for the development of VTS is the paragraph:

> "In international waters communication in a VTS should take place primarily in the English language. When in addition to the English language a local language is used to communicate with a specific vessel, navigational information relevant to other vessels should be repeated in English."

The reasons are purely practical. The world has not developed multilingual ship's officers, as are found in Holland and much of Scandinavia, and even in

Holland the ability to exchange messages in English and German—and sometimes French—in addition to the mother tongue, would be the limit. Thus, if the world has decided to speak English, it must be agreed what type of English is to be used.

The initial "standardization" was in the *International Marine Navigational Vocabulary*. It was first produced in the late 1970s, and was a useful and basically sensible start, but—probably because the British are somewhat insular, by nature—it never received the publicity it deserved in the United Kingdom; nor was it used outside some nautical schools and colleges. (See Appendix "B" for a summary and 1985 amendments.)

During 1981 and 1982 a completely separate research was undertaken by a small group into the structure of the English language and the manner in which it was used at sea. The prime movers were a linguist from Cambridge University, Peter Strevens, who had spent most of his life connected with teaching English, and Captain Fred Weeks from the Faculty of Maritime Studies at the Plymouth Polytechnic. The research was originally financed in part by Pergamon Press Limited (the publishers of this book) and by the Ship and Marine Technology Requirements Board, of the U.K. Department of Industry. By early 1983 the main research was complete and the *Seaspeak Reference Manual* was available for use in nautical colleges and other teaching establishments throughout the world.

At about the same time as this research was being completed, the VTS Guidelines were already being discussed by several different bodies. The International Chamber of Shipping (representing shipowners), the Nautical Institute (representing those professionally involved with the sea) and the International Association of Ports and Harbours were all involved, among others, but the VTS Guidelines that were eventually submitted to the International Maritime Organization, and which became the guidelines in use today, were finally brought together by the International Association of Lighthouse Authorities at a series of meetings in Paris during 1983 and 1984.

The several bodies already mentioned were joined, to different degrees, by the International Maritime Pilots Association, the International Federation of Shipmasters' Associations and by the International Yacht Racing Union.

IALA were the prime movers because although the various lighthouse authorities in the United Kingdom—Trinity House, the Northern Lighthouse Board and Irish Lights—are generally independent, the lighthouse authorities in many countries are direct government bodies as are the port authorities. Thus, with government money at stake, it was logical that a lighthouse/port body should act.

Early in the VTS discussions it became obvious that the language to be used by a port was a vital part of the whole operation. If the world was to ask a Chinese second mate and a Pakistani second mate to speak to a Dutch VTS operator in English, then it was an urgent priority to agree what type of English they should use.

At first there were plans to extend the existing *International Standard Maritime Vocabulary*, but a vocabulary alone is not enough; it is the way that language is used that matters.

"Seaspeak" itself was about language at sea, but it had little to do with the specialized use that was necessary for ports. Thus a separate research programme was started, to concern itself with port operation alone. Most of the same people were involved, and with finance from several governments, as well as with a grant from the European Economic Commission (EEC), an additional research programme was organized which produced a useful document *Seaspeak for VTS*. It is that which has been the basis for all subsequent development of VTS.

The *Seaspeak Reference Manual* is a book of 120 pages, and it would be silly as well as unnecessary to try to summarize it. It is a discipline for the way sentences are used as well as a vocabulary for use at sea. Nevertheless, it is important to summarize the principle of what are called "Message markers" if the manner in which the language is to be used in a VTS is to be understood.

The central principle of "Seaspeak" is that a man should immediately understand the type of message that is about to follow from the very beginning of the message. It is achieved in two ways. First, by the use of standard phrases and a standard vocabulary; secondly, by the use of what are called "message markers".

In ordinary speech we do much of that automatically. If describing our own boat on an official form we might write:

Length: 9.8 metres
Displacement: 6.3 tonnes

and so on. It is unambiguous. The word length tells the recipient that he is about to hear a figure representing length. Technically it would be just as accurate to say:

9.8 metres, length

but until the word length had been spoken it might not be clear to what the figures referred and it would be that much more difficult to understand.

Multiply that basic philosophy several times over and we have the principle both of the standard format and of the message marker. The *Standard Marine Navigational Vocabulary* recommended format and the basic words to be used. Seaspeak extended that vocabulary and then added the message marker.

If a harbour authority needs to pass a message to a Chinese second mate, does it say "Will you ...", "You should ...", "I would like you to ...", "Could you please ... ", "It would be best if you ... ", "Can you please ... ", or any of the many other variations that are possible? Does a man say "Change to Ch 05", "Switch to Ch 05", "Go to Ch 05", "Let's try Ch 05", "Up to Ch 05", "Down to Ch 05" or "Ch 05. O.K."?

Next, having agreed which words are best—and it must be remembered that the choice of the man with English as his mother tongue is not always the best—the next step is to accept that not all messages can be handled by standard phrases. In fact it would not be desirable to try to handle all traffic in that manner.

The Seaspeak research suggests that nearly everything can be classified as either:

a *question*
an *instruction*
as *advice*
as a *request*
as *information*
as a *warning*
or as the announcement of an *intention*.

They are the seven message markers.

For a VTS a message might be:

"QUESTION. HOW MANY TONNES DO YOU
REQUIRE—OVER."

The word "question" marking the message. Another example might be:

"WARNING. NUMBER 3 BUOY IS UNLIT—OVER."

And to that the acknowledgement might be:

WARNING RECEIVED—OUT."

By including the message marker—warning—as a reply marker, not only did the harbour authority get an acknowledgement of the warning, but it knew that the ship had realized that the message had been a warning.

That is merely a part of the overall discipline for Seaspeak. Some of the initial traffic will be slightly longer, so that it can include the message markers. However, the overall traffic will be considerably shorter—because repetition will be avoided—as well as far less likely to have built-in anomalies.

Compare the difference between:

"CAN I HAVE YOUR CARGO PLEASE?"
"COULD YOU GIVE ME YOUR DRAUGHT?"
"GIVE ME YOUR POSITION?"
"PLEASE STATE YOUR TONNAGE?"

All, in Seaspeak, would have been prefixed with:

"QUESTION. WHAT IS . . . ."

the word "question" marking the message and the phrase "What is . . . " as a standard prefix to that type of question.

Alternatively, compare:

"MY ETA IS ONE SIX ZERO ZERO."

with

"THE WRECK IS ONE SIX ZERO ZERO METRES FROM . . .".

One is time and the other distance, but would that be immediately obvious to the Chinese or the Pakistani?

With Seaspeak, time is prefixed with the word "time" and a position prefixed with the word "position".

For example:

"QUESTION. WHAT IS YOUR ETA?"
"ANSWER. MY ETA IS, TIME, ONE SIX ZERO ZERO . . .".

followed by the indication of the time zone. Said like that, it cannot be misunderstood.

A local ship may assume the time is local time, but a ship arriving from foreign parts may well be working with a different time zone on the ship's clocks. Thus it has to become the norm to specify what time is used. Appendices A and B show details of the standard conventions regarding the representation of time, as well as many other factors, but enough has been written to outline the objective of Seaspeak.

Nobody is suggesting that the maritime world suddenly changes the way in which we use our own language, but Seaspeak will be taught in nautical colleges and the hope is that it spreads throughout the VTS of the world.

An English VTS operator might well say: "Hang on a bit, old chap. I think you have got yourself into a bit of a twist." If he speaks in that manner to a Chinese second mate he will not be understood. Thus the more formalized style will be used for the simple reason—if not for any other—that it works. The more small craft comply, the better will they find they are understood. (See Appendix B.)

Where Do Small Craft Fit In?

In one sense, the way in which small craft fit in to what is mainly a commercial atmosphere—the modern commercial port—is the most important single facet of the whole subject. At one extreme there are ports with a comparatively small volume of shipping and plenty of deep water in which the ships can manoeuvre; the small craft is not really "involved" at all. At the other extreme, as has already been mentioned in Chapter 2 in relation to specialized areas like the Thames Barrier at Woolwich, the small craft of any size may be involved as much as any other vessel; she too has to report in and obtain permission to proceed.

Broadly the small craft involvement can be divided into one of three main headings.

Level 1. Vessels that have no VHF R/T are involved merely by their presence. As has already been stressed, VHF R/T is being fitted by very large numbers of small craft, but, except in a very few highly specialized areas, there is unlikely to be any requirement to carry radiotelephony. Furthermore, even if there was such a requirement, it would be difficult, if not impossible, to make it apply to the smallest sailing dinghy or rowing boat. Thus, in any VTS there has to be an allowance made for such craft.

Their responsibilities are the normal ones of observing the Collision Regulations that apply and any appropriate local bylaws.

Level 2. Some ports will require all vessels (which have the facility) to monitor a particular port operational channel. The requirement might apply only to vessels of a certain type or to vessels of over a certain size, but a requirement to listen—to keep a radio watch—is distinctly different to the responsibilities in category 1.

Level 3. In the third category—the one that will apply only to large ports—there will be a requirement to report in, but that requirement will usually apply only to certain classes of ships. However, for some ports there will be a requirement, or a recommendation, that **all** vessels report in. Thus, from the point of view of the small craft, category 3 is *sometimes* completely different from the requirements of category 2.

Those three basic levels of small craft involvement have been outlined in the *Seaspeak for VTS* booklet published in 1984 as a result of the initial research into how the English language should be used for Port Operation traffic. In addition, the guidelines suggest the possibility of using day signals as well.

The guidelines suggest:

> "In certain circumstances, it might be of assistance to the VTS authority for a small craft participating at level 2 [the listening watch] to indicate that she is monitoring the port operation primary channel, by exhibiting a day signal—numeral pendant 9 for example—from the backstay or where it can best be seen."

In practice that day signal would be interpreted by the harbour master's launch, or other patrol boat, as meaning: "Do not concern yourself with me. I am listening to the Port Radio and I know what is being broadcast." It might apply where the VTS authority employed a launch to hail small craft which appeared to be unaware of an approaching hampered vessel.

Similarly, there might be circumstances when a small craft needed a day signal to indicate that she was unable to comply with a requirement to monitor a particular channel. Whether the reason was the malfunction of a

VHF set or any other reason, a signal—numeral pendant 0, for example—would be interpreted by the harbour master's launch as meaning that the vessel was not able to comply with any requirement to listen and was therefore to be considered to be participating at level 1.

At no time has it been suggested that those two visual signals should be promoted in any way. The VTS recommendations are guidelines, nothing more. But it is possible that a harbour authority might feel that a particular dredged channel or entrance was sensitive enough to require the type of visual signal that has been summarized.

The alternative might well be an outright ban on movement, but if small craft are to be allowed freedom of movement, they must slot into the VTS system with the absolute minimum of additional problems for the VTS authority.

Other minor recommendations in the guidelines include the point that it is the responsibility of the VTS authority to promulgate the requirements of a port by the use of announcements in the yachting press, by posters in local clubs or by similar means. The amateur sailor will not normally have access to the professional mariners' reference books; nor will he have a Pilot to act as "postman".

As has already been made clear, the number of ports where small craft are *required* to report are still small, but there are already a very large number of ports where a listening watch is a distinct advantage.

The Supplement to this book—*Coast and Port Radio* (kept up to date by periodic correction sheets) summarizes all the ports in the United Kingdom and on the near continental shores from Brest to Die Elbe that have port radio. The entries for each port, listed geographically, indicate the size or displacement limit at which a vessel is required to report. The entries also list the times during which the port radio (VTS) is manned, and summarize the services available.

Collision Regulations

CONSIDERING the complexity, as well as the importance, of today's Collision Regulations—or the International Regulations for Preventing Collisions at Sea, to give them their correct title—it seems almost unbelievable that the first time they were even presented in a codified form was as recently as 1863.

Man has been trading, by sea, since at least as far back as 1600 BC, when the Phoenicians started to become the masters of Mediterranean trade, but any rules that existed were established by custom and prudence.

By 1878, 15 years after the rules were first agreed internationally, there is the record of a 239-ton brig, *Tirzah*, which was found at fault, by the courts, because her port and starboard lights were partially obscured by her sails. As far as small craft are concerned, it took another 98 years—until the present Collision Regulations became law in 1977—for that particular problem to be solved by the introduction of masthead-mounted, tricoloured navigation lights.

The use of the masthead for navigation lights on yachts was first tried as recently as 1974. Today the masthead is used extensively, but although it is undoubtedly the best place to mount navigation lights of small sailing yachts when in the open sea, it is by no means the best place in all circumstances in the close-quarters situations in commercial harbours. More about that later; it is the basic Steering and Sailing Rules that matter even more.

Since the first attempt to reach international accord, the Collision Regulations have been rewritten many times; however, it is the relationship between small craft and larger vessels which affects this book most of all. In 1913 *The Corinthian Yachtsman's Handbook*—which was the leading reference book of its day—stated:

"By the rules, a steam vessel has to give way to everything else, but in practice I am sorry to say that she does not always do so."

In the next paragraph the author goes on:

"The small boat owner must remember that often when there is plenty of water for his little craft there may be very little indeed for a big steamer, which consequently could not give way without incurring a

43

risk of running aground. As he has no knowledge of the draught of water of an approaching steamer, it is prudent, when sailing in a comparatively narrow channel, to assume that the steamer is unable to give way owing to lack of water."

That decidedly vague philosophy existed, in different ways, for a long time. The next generation of yachtsmen were brought up to read *Cruising and Ocean Racing*—a magnificent book from the mid-1930s. The editor devotes a whole chapter to the Rule of the Road, and concerning this "grey area" he writes:

"By regulation a steam vessel must on all occasions—except, of course, as modified by the exigencies of navigation—give way to a sailing vessel. Article 20 lays down: 'When a steam vessel and a sailing vessel are proceeding in such a direction as to involve risk of collision the steam vessel shall keep out of the way of the sailing vessel.' This is the hard and fast rule of the sea but it does not imply that a deeply laden tramp ploughing steadily along at 9 or 10 knots, or the *Bremen* moving up Southampton Water, would get out of the way of a small two-tonner."

At that time the rules were clear—steam gave way to sail—except that no one seriously expected the rules to be followed in really confined waters!

We have "enjoyed" two more rewritings of the Collision Regulations, but there is still a degree of uncertainty. In 1913 the editor was merely suggesting that there should be a difference of behaviour in a narrow channel. Twenty years later the advice was still advice even if the assumption was more strongly worded. It was not until the present set of rules—the 1972 version which came into force in 1977—that a more serious attempt was made to define the responsibilities of small craft in restricted waters.

Rules 9 and 10

When considering the rights and responsibilities of small craft, it is important to understand the basic difference between Rules 9 and 10 in the Collision Regulations. Also it is vital to appreciate that both the wording of Rule 9 and the wording of Rule 10 have blown away most of the mist that surrounded the questions of right of way between large and small vessels. Today the difference in size and in manoeuvrability between a small craft and a large bulk carrier have forced the rule-makers to take note. Today the rules that used to apply—or were **supposed** to apply—seem impossibly naïve.

The two rules in question cover the behaviour of small craft in two, somewhat different, circumstances. Rule 10, about which there has been countless hours of discussion ever since it was framed, covers the behaviour of all vessels—but mentions small craft in particular—when using traffic lanes. Thus, Rule 10 is only of passing interest to the question of the behaviour in a harbour. Rule 9, on the other hand, concerns itself with the question of behaviour in narrow channels. It is thus of great importance to virtually every harbour in the world.

Nevertheless, although Rule 10 can never apply to vessels—either large or small—**within** a harbour, there are an increasing number of national administrations which are introducing traffic separation schemes close outside major ports. Thus Rule 10 is of concern within the terms of reference for this book.

Rule 10

Since the 1972 Collision Regulations came into force there has been more discussion regarding the intention of the numerous points raised by Rule 10 than for any other rule in the book. It is a mammoth rule in many respects because, for the first time in the history of rule-making at sea, the behaviour of all vessels is controlled *even when there are no other vessels in the vicinity.*

To highlight the most obvious example, the manner in which any vessel—and particularly a small vessel—may cross a traffic lane is outlined in some detail. Previously a vessel behaved in any manner that she liked up until the time when a risk of collision developed. The crossing of a traffic lane, on the other hand, is now acceptable only if undertaken in a particular manner.

Rule 10 reads:

Traffic Separation Schemes

(a) This Rule applies to traffic separation schemes adopted by the Organization.
(b) A vessel using a traffic separation scheme shall:
    (i) proceed in the appropriate traffic lane in the general direction of traffic flow for that lane;
    (ii) so far as practicable keep clear of a traffic separation line or a separation zone;
    (iii) normally join or leave a traffic lane at the termination of the lane, but when joining or leaving from either side shall do so at as small an angle to the general direction of traffic flow as practicable.
(c) A vessel shall so far as practicable avoid crossing traffic lanes, but if obliged to do so shall cross as nearly as practicable at right angles to the general direction of traffic flow.
(d) Inshore traffic zones shall not normally be used by through traffic which can safely use the appropriate traffic lane within the adjacent traffic separation scheme. **However, vessels of less than 20 metres in length and sailing vessels may under all circumstances use inshore traffic zones.**
(e) A vessel other than a crossing vessel or a vessel joining or leaving a lane shall not normally enter a separation zone or cross a separation line except:
    (i) in cases of emergency to avoid imminent danger;
    (ii) to engage in fishing within a separation zone.
(f) A vessel navigating in areas near the termination of traffic separation schemes shall do so with particular caution.
(g) A vessel shall so far as practicable avoid anchoring in a traffic separation scheme or in areas near its terminations.
(h) A vessel not using a traffic separation scheme shall avoid it by as wide a margin as is practicable.

(i) A vessel engaged in fishing shall not impede the passage of any vessel following a traffic lane.

(j) A vessel of less than 20 metres in length or a sailing vessel shall not impede the safe passage of a power driven vessel following a traffic lane.

(k) A vessel restricted in her ability to manoeuvre when engaged in an operation for the maintenance of the safety of navigation in a traffic separation scheme is exempted from complying with this Rule to the extent necessary to carry out the operation.

(l) A vessel restricted in her ability to manoeuvre when engaged in an operation for the laying, servicing or picking up of a submarine cable, within a separation scheme, is exempted from complying with this Rule to the extent necessary to carry out the operation.

Rule 10 is printed in full, because it can be confusing if individual sentences are quoted, but the clauses to which attention should be drawn are clauses (d) and (j).

Clause (d) has been included in the rule since the Collision Regulations were first introduced, and it stems from discussions with the Department of Trade (now Department of Transport, Marine Directorate) and the Royal Yachting Association that took place when the wording was still in the planning stage.

The whole object of Rule 10 is to require through traffic to use the traffic lane. Nevertheless, it was accepted from an early stage in the planning that to *require* a small craft to use a lane—when she might be making good only 2 or 3 knots—was counter-productive.

The other clause to which attention has to be drawn is clause (j). The wording there has been unchanged since the rule was first drafted, but there has been—and still is—a great deal of discussion regarding the precise meaning of " ... shall not impede ... ".

The point is important. In the Dutch and in the German language the expression was translated so that it was read as " ... shall keep out of the way of ... ", but that was not the intention of the words used. In certain circumstances—in a flat calm, for example—it might be impossible for a small craft under sail to "get out of the way".

Wording which the International Maritime Organization has accepted in relation to the expression " ... shall not impede ... "—which appears in Rules 9, 10 and 18—reads:

"When a vessel is required not to impede the passage of another vessel, such vessel shall so far as is practicable navigate in such a way as to avoid the development of risk of collision. If, however, a situation has developed so as to involve risk of collision, the relevant Steering and Sailing Rules shall be complied with."

The purpose of this book is to write about behaviour and responsibilities in general, not to become bogged down in the minutiae of the precise meaning of words. Nevertheless, with traffic lanes leading up to the entrance of ports, Rule 10 is among the most important rules of all and the implications have to be understood.

In one sense the beauty of the IMO clarification of "shall not impede" is that it has no precise meaning. The words "shall keep clear" mean what they say, but once it has been accepted that there are circumstances when a small craft cannot keep clear, then I believe the wording we have is as favourable to the small craft as can be expected.

There have been attempts by various administrations to be more precise, but I am glad to report all have failed: so far.

The responsibility of the small craft is to try to navigate "to avoid the development of a risk of collision". Precisely what is meant by "a risk of collision" will vary with the circumstances. To a small craft in relation with another small craft, the position *might* not arise until the two vessels were within 25 metres of each other. To the navigating officer of a large bulk carrier a risk of collision might be considered to exist when another bulk carrier came within 2.5 miles.

Rule 9

In many ways Rule 9 is completely different from Rule 10. In Rule 10 a small craft (or any other craft for that matter) cannot be told that she may not cross a traffic lane unless certain conditions are satisfied because, with a lane several miles wide, she cannot know what risks will develop while she is crossing: she cannot see the other side.

Rule 9 (d), on the other hand, uses the phrase "... shall not cross ...". That represents the second major change in the 1972 Collision Regulations when compared with any earlier version. Previously small craft were expected to live with phrases stating that steam gave way to sail, even when there was increasing evidence to show that there were circumstances when it could not. Now the "shall not cross" applies to all vessels if the action of crossing a narrow channel impedes the passage of a vessel which can safely navigate only within such channel or fairway.

Rule 9 reads:

Narrow Channels

(a) A vessel proceeding along the course of a narrow channel or fairway shall keep as near to the outer limit of the channel or fairway which lies on her starboard side as is safe and practicable.

(b) A vessel of less than 20 metres in length or a sailing vessel shall not impede the passage of a vessel which can safely navigate only within a narrow channel or fairway.

(c) A vessel engaged in fishing shall not impede the passage of any other vessel navigating within a narrow channel or fairway.

(d) A vessel shall not cross a narrow channel or fairway if such crossing impedes the passage of a vessel which can safely navigate only within such channel or fairway. The latter vessel may use the sound signal prescribed in Rule 34 (d) if in doubt as to the intention of the crossing vessel.

(e) (i) In a narrow channel or fairway when overtaking can take place only if the vessel to be overtaken has to take action to permit safe passing, the vessel intending to overtake shall indicate her intention by sounding the appropriate signal prescribed in Rule 34 (c) (i).

The vessel to be overtaken shall, if in agreement, sound the appropriate signal prescribed in Rule 34 (c) (ii) and take steps to permit safe passing. If in doubt she may sound the signals prescribed in Rule 34 (d).

(ii) This Rule does not relieve the overtaking vessel of her obligation under Rule 13.

(f) A vessel nearing a bend or an area of a narrow channel or fairway where other vessels may be obscured by an intervening obstruction shall navigate with particular alertness and caution and shall sound the appropriate signal prescribed in Rule 34 (e).

(g) Any vessel shall, if the circumstances of the case admit, avoid anchoring in a narrow channel.

The difference between crossing a traffic lane and crossing a narrow channel is thus fundamental. In one the vessels are required to cross in a certain manner; in the other, vessels shall not cross if, by so doing, they impede the passage of others.

Close Quarters

As has just been explained, the expression "shall not impede" cannot have a precise definition; the question as to whether a vessel is impeding another depends on the circumstances. Similarly, any risk of collision depends on what the navigating officers think of the circumstances of a close-quarters situation. The visibility, the sea state, the speed of the vessels and their relative manoeuvrability may all be factors.

A fleet of sailing dinghies could be perfectly safe in conditions where several were within a few metres of each other. Thus distance apart is not the key question. It is the circumstances that matter, and small craft navigators must always remember that many large vessels are frequently committed to a particular course. Even if they wanted to make a change, the time lag between changed helm or engine orders and the actual change of course is so great that any worthwhile alteration is impossible. (See later in this chapter.)

One of the more obvious examples of a vessel being committed to a particular course of action is when a large VLCC or container ship is rounding the Bramble Bank to enter Southampton Water. Rule 9 was framed to allow for these special circumstances. Not only will a large vessel have to approach a tight turn at a particular angle, she has to approach at a reasonably high speed to allow her to get round at all. In a sensitive spot like the Bramble, a VLCC can do nothing to alter her course once she is committed to a particular track.

A small craft might feel herself to be "miles" clear of the VLCC as she approached, but the Pilot of the VLCC will often have a very different point of view.

A Planned Approach

Later chapters of this book are devoted to the seamanship side of boat handling: coming alongside or picking up a buoy. The seamanship side of manoeuvring within a harbour is also given a chapter of its own. However, this chapter is headed "Collision Regulations", and the way in which the regulations affect the navigator's task on an approach is something that deserves further study.

Those who read Rule 10 carefully will have appreciated that not only does it affect the behaviour of vessels when crossing a traffic lane as well as when entering or leaving, it affects their behaviour from a passage planning point of view. Similarly, a wise navigator will consider the implications of the rules when planning to enter harbour.

Rule 10 (d), which was greatly improved by the 1983 amendments, now makes it crystal clear that small craft are not expected to use traffic lanes, even when the small craft is classified as through traffic. "Under any circumstances . . . " small craft may use the inshore zone and, in precisely the same manner—even if not supported in quite the same manner by the Collision Regulations themselves—small craft should try, whenever possible, to navigate clear of narrow approach channels.

The support from the rules appears in Rule 9 (a):

" . . . shall keep as near to the outer limit of the channel or fairway which lies on her starboard side as is safe and practicable."

To take that to a more forceful philosophy, the sentence might be translated as "Leave all starboard-hand buoys to port." However, before analysing the implications of that interpretation do we know what is meant by " . . . the channel or fairway"?

Lord Denning, when he was Master of the Rolls, made several interesting observations when ruling on a case after a collision between the Dutch ferry *Koningin Juliana* and the Danish coaster *Thuroklint*. He ruled that "mid-channel" is the middle line of the dredged channel: not the middle line of the navigable water as marked by buoys. He went on to state that where there was a dredged channel, it was the fairway. Where there was no dredged channel (indicated by pecked lines on an Admiralty chart), the mid-channel was the middle line of the navigable water.

That ruling may appear of little significance to the small craft navigator, but it settled arguments that had been bouncing back and forward in the courts since 1857. The main reason for mentioning it here is first because it establishes that what is the port or starboard side of a channel is not merely halfway between the line of port and starboard buoys; the dredging of the channel to create a fairway may alter that simplistic attitude.

Secondly, and of greater significance to the arguments regarding the rule in this book, was the statement:

"The regulations were made for seamen to follow and should be interpreted by the courts as seamen would interpret them."

In theory, every manoeuvre for any vessel is covered by the Collision

Regulations. In practice, of course, it is not, and Lord Denning's ruling is a useful stand-by. To put the point more crudely, it is not so much what the rules say that matters, as the way they are interpreted by the appropriate authorities.

As an example, the manner in which a vessel crosses a traffic lane caused seemingly endless discussion when the Collision Regulations first became law. Did "crossing at right angles" mean that the course-made-good was to be at right angles or the heading at right angles. If there is a strong tidal stream and a slow crossing vessel, the difference is considerable. The lawyers, on both sides of the Channel, tried to establish that it was the eventual course-made-good that mattered. From the seaman's point of view, a heading at right angles was not only more logical, it was quicker (Fig. 4.1).

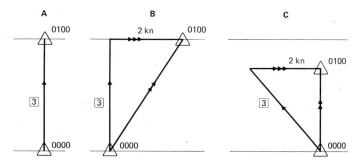

Fig. 4.1. *Crossing a channel: heading not course-made-good. A assumes there is no tidal stream. Thus, at 3 knots a vessel travels 3 miles in 1 hour. In B there is a 2-knot tidal stream, but if the vessel* **heads** *at right angles she still crosses in the same time. If, on the other hand, she heads up into the tidal stream, to bring her course-made-good at right angles, she takes* **considerably longer** *to get across*

A heading at right angles has since been written into the regulations. But that is really an aside. We have established that any traffic lane need not (or should not) be used, but that if traffic has to be crossed, it should be crossed with a heading at right angles to the general direction of flow. Rule 9 also establishes that the small craft should keep as near the outer limit of the channel or fairway as practicable.

Thus, the approach for small craft is as close to the starboard side of any channel as is practicable, and if that channel is marked by channel buoys the expression "leave all starboard hand buoys to port" may now make greater sense than it did on page 49.

But What About Boats Under Sail?

So far, throughout this chapter as well as throughout the Collision Regulations, it has always been assumed that when a regulation requires a particular action the vessel concerned is able to comply. However, for vessels under sail there are many occasions when a particular track or a particular alteration of course are impossible.

What then does "A" do next?

The conflict of interests is not one that is easily solved. Sailing is a sport and one that is extremely popular. It shares with a small handful of other sports—walking, climbing and gliding, for example—an element of challenge to nature. Sailing is fun and it is fun to do-it-under-sail. Whether "it" is rounding up to pick up a mooring, rounding up to anchor, coming alongside or entering harbour, there is greater satisfaction to be had by completing the manoeuvre under sail alone rather than having to resort to auxiliary power.

In open water a large commercial vessel will expect a sailing vessel to behave as a sailing vessel. At the other extreme in waters like the Nord-Ostsee (Kiel) Canal a sailing vessel is allowed to have sail set only if, by doing so, she can keep to the starboard side of the canal and behave as if she was under power.

Much the same policy applies in many of the Dutch waterways, and it would be difficult to argue that it should not. If the regulations require a vessel not to impede and also require her to keep as far to the starboard side of a channel "as is practicable", it would be difficult, if not impossible, to justify making bold tacks right across a channel if, by so doing, there was any possibility of impeding the safe passage of any vessel using that channel.

Motor-sailing

The compromise state, which overcomes many of the problems of using sail in confined waters, is for a yacht to "motor-sail". Even quite a small auxiliary engine will allow a yacht under sail to be handled like a yacht under power in most circumstances. Furthermore, many modern sailing yachts have auxiliary engines powerful enough to allow them to motor in almost all circumstances. Therefore, where does the line have to be drawn?

First the implications of Rule 25(e) must be considered:

> "A vessel proceeding under sail when also being propelled by machinery shall exhibit forward where it can best be seen a conical shape, apex downwards."

Initially that might appear simple. A sailing vessel that is not a sailing vessel should not claim the rights of a sailing vessel. Furthermore, she should make it clear to others that she is not so doing. In practice the problem is not nearly as simple as that.

In the first place there is no obvious position from which to display a conical shape from where it will be seen even most of the time.

One satisfactory solution is to work on the assumption that if an auxiliary engine is running, the foresail can be lowered and the cone hoisted (triangulated in the foretriangle as an anchor ball or an anchor light might be) in its place. Exhibited in that manner, the cone can be seen from almost any angle, and there is the additional logic that a sailing yacht without a foresail set does not appear as a "vessel under sail" in quite the same manner as does a vessel under full sail.

Bear in mind that the objective should be for the vessel "proceeding under sail when also being propelled by machinery" to avoid confusion. She should do all that is reasonable to avoid a situation when she is claiming privileges—the privileges of a vessel under sail—when she is not entitled to them.

The disadvantage of the "lower the jib and hoist a cone" solution is that there are occasions (especially in broken water) when to lower a foresail takes away most of the drive that is available from the sails. Not only will the boat go much more slowly than she might otherwise be expected to sail, she will not be anything like as satisfying to handle. On occasions it can be somewhat like riding a bicycle uphill with the brakes binding.

Another solution, and one that would be particularly suitable for any auxiliary yacht, likely to be both motoring and sailing a good proportion of her time under way, would be to rig a jackstaff to allow a cone to be exhibited without interfering with the normal use of the sails in the foretriangle. The staff would be best if raked forward (say 30 degrees from the vertical) and something about 2 metres long slotted into both the upper and the lower "hoops" of a bow pulpit would be effective (Fig. 4.2).

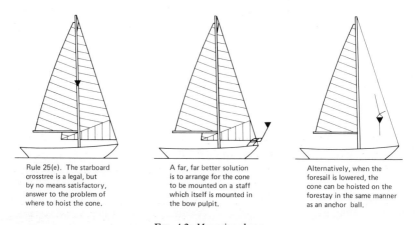

| Rule 25(e). The starboard crosstree is a legal, but by no means satisfactory, answer to the problem of where to hoist the cone. | A far, far better solution is to arrange for the cone to be mounted on a staff which itself is mounted in the bow pulpit. | Alternatively, when the foresail is lowered, the cone can be hoisted on the forestay in the same manner as an anchor ball. |

Fig. 4.2. *Mounting shapes*

In German waters (where the requirement to exhibit a cone when motor-sailing is strictly enforced by maritime police), in Dutch waters (where there are also a large number of water police), in Belgium and in France the practice has developed during the past few years of rigging the cone on a continuous halyard and downhaul in the starboard crosstree. In that manner the cone can be hoisted or lowered with a minimum of difficulty, but the arrangement still does not overcome the basic visibility problem.

Of the three alternatives shown in Fig. 4.2, the cone on a staff is by far the best. Bearing in mind that the need for a cone is enshrined in the Collision Regulations (even if the observance of the rule is rarely seen in U.K. waters), it would be the most straightforward answer if the bow pulpits of motor-sailers, if not all auxiliary yachts, were built to take a tubular staff.

The non-observance of Rule 25 (e) in the United Kingdom is a relic of the days when auxiliary engines were so small that they were rarely used except in a calm, and for that condition the sails were usually lowered. Today the overall scene is very different and if yachtsmen do not learn to comply with that simple regulation they are bound to encourage official opposition to their freedom to come and go as they wish. In many commercial harbours bylaws exist—or can readily be enacted—to control the movements of any small craft which might adversely affect the smooth working of the port.

Hampered Vessels

Vessels at Anchor

The rights of a vessel at anchor are similar to those of a parked car. There are many places where a man may not normally be allowed to "park" his "car"—in a narrow channel for example—Rule 9 (g)—or in a Traffic Lane—Rule 10 (g). However, when anchored he is required to demonstrate that he is claiming the priority allowed to an anchored vessel.

With the exception of really small craft—of less than 7 metres overall—and then only when they are at anchor, "... not in or near a narrow channel, fairway or anchorage, or where other vessels normally navigate ...", vessels at anchor exhibit lights and shapes as required by Rule 30.

The one all-round white light—the anchor light—is surely among the most basic signals in the maritime world. One white light might be the stern light of a vessel under way, it might be the light in a rowing boat and it might even be a shore light, but whatever it is, it is something to be avoided. No man in his right mind would anchor without an anchor light—even if some yachts exhibit lights so dim that they can hardly be seen at any distance. Why is it then that so many ignore the requirement to exhibit the day signal—one ball?

In many harbours yachts share the same waters as commercial craft, and in a river such as the Orwell at Harwich, for example, it is normal to see yachts anchored in the shallower parts and sometimes on both sides of the river. The River Orwell is a good example of the point at issue. There is a well-defined dredged channel and that channel is used by a large number of ships heading for Ipswich.

An anchor ball can be as crude as a dark fender hung on the forestay or even an old sweater stuffed into a string shopping bag. It can be a folding, hinged shape—as used by commercial vessels on occasion—or it can be inflatable. Nevertheless, not more than one yachtsman in three observes the requirement to exhibit.

What sort of logic justifies that behaviour? Why should the pilot of the approaching ship be expected to puzzle out which of the several small craft that he can see are under way and which are at anchor? The failure of so many to comply with the so simple and so basic requirement to indicate that they are no longer under way represents an "I'm all right, Jack" arrogance which is so counter-productive. It breeds an antagonism between the professional and the amateur which is nothing but bad.

A book may not be the right place for a "leading article" type entreaty, but if yachtsmen cannot put their own house in order they must not be surprised if others impose restrictions on their freedom.

Not-under-command

Prior to the publication of the present Collision Regulations it was common to hear yachtsmen claiming that a state like "heaving-to" was something that ought to confer a degree of priority and that a vessel hove-to would be justified in claiming to be not-under-command. However, in discussion in the sub-committees at the International Maritime Consultative Organization (as it was then)—now the International Maritime Organization (IMO)—it was clear that the authorities of the world did not want that type of interpretation.

For a vessel to be entitled to claim the degree of priority that is granted to vessels not-under-command she has to be unable to keep out of the way "through some exceptional circumstance". In other words, a man cannot choose to be not-under-command.

If making way (although not-under-command) a vessel at night exhibits sidelights and a sternlight as well as the n.u.c. signal—two all-round red lights in a vertical line, but when not making way the n.u.c. signal is exhibited "where it can best be seen" without the other lights. By day the signal is "two balls or similar shapes" in a vertical line, but under the clarifications and amendments promulgated in 1983, "vessels of less than 12 metres in length, except those engaged in diving operations, shall not be required to exhibit the lights and shapes prescribed . . . ".

In practice, the "escape clause" for vessels under 12 metres means that practically no small yachts carry n.u.c. lights or shapes—and there is no strong argument why they should. Commercial fishing boats, on the other hand often have the n.u.c. red all-round lights installed permanently. A boat fishing near other traffic—and fishermen are "hunters" not "farmers"—might need an instant means of exhibiting her need for a degree of priority if, for example, she caught her gear in the propellers.

In a lifetime of sailing I have only once needed to show n.u.c. shapes, but, needless to say, I did not have any. It was while motoring down the canal from Amsterdam to IJmuiden on a calm evening. We picked up what turned out to be a cargo mat round the propeller. An auxiliary engine that was unusable might not have been too serious, but the mat, while jamming itself round the propeller, also jammed the helm over and thus made sailing impossible.

Fortunately the Pilot of an approaching ship—into whose path we were drifting—interpreted our antics with boathooks over the stern in a sensible manner (it was long before the introduction of VHF R/T) and all was well. We drifted to a neighbouring jetty and then managed to clear the obstruction.

If we had had two black balls they would have been a signal any professional would have recognized instantly. Now, with the advent of cheap, inflatable anchor balls, I carry two, but by the law of averages I am highly unlikely ever to need them as a n.u.c. signal.

Restricted in the Ability to Manoeuvre

Several degrees of priority are outlined in the second part of Rule 27—Vessels not-under-command or restricted in their ability to manoeuvre—and it is indicative of the changes in the maritime scene that the previous set of rules (as recent as 1965) did not mention the problem at all. Previously there were numerous references to vessels being not-under-command—where the regulations were much the same as they are today (and to the complications of having seaplanes on the water), but vessels restricted by their draught or by the nature of their work are a new phenomenon.

From the port operations side of manoeuvring, the definitions of restrictions are of comparatively academic interest in that small craft are likely to be required to keep clear in any case. Nevertheless, it helps to understand the thinking behind the rule because the right-of-way between one commercial vessel and another is sometimes transformed by "the nature of her work". Furthermore, the importance of the relative priorities can be demonstrated by the fact that the rule in question—Rule 27—has already been largely rewritten since it first became law in 1977.

The essence of the meaning of "vessel restricted in her ability to manoeuvre" is that she is restricted "from the nature of her work". Note also that although vessels of less than 12 metres in length are not required to exhibit special signals to indicate a restricted ability to manoeuvre, they are perfectly entitled to do so if the circumstances are appropriate.

The rule includes lights and shapes for a group of vessels such as those laying cables or navigation marks; dredgers; those transferring persons while under way; and the signal for those "engaged in a towing operation such as severely restricts the towing vessel and her tow in their ability to deviate from their course". (See Figs. 6.2, 6.3.)

What might be called a normal tow—even a major tow of a large vessel—is covered by Rule 24, where the towing vessel exhibits two masthead lights "when towing", or three if the length of the tow exceeds 200 metres. Thus it is only when the nature of the operation "severely restricts" the ability to deviate, that special signals are justified. (See illustrations in Chapter 6.)

Finally, to complete this group of special signals, the vessel "constrained by her draught" has a rule to herself. Whereas the previous degree of restriction might justify the all-round "red-white-red" of the dredger or the unusual occupation, the vessel that cannot deviate because she has insufficient water exhibits "red-red-red". All other vessels, except those "not-under-command" and those "restricted in their ability to manoeuvre", "shall, if the circumstances of the case admit, avoid impeding the safe passage of a vessel constrained by her draught...", and she, in turn, is instructed to "...navigate with particular caution having full regard to her special condition".

Stopping and Turning Distances

There is yet one more type of hampered vessel (and one for which there are no recognized signals); the vessel that is manoeuvring into a berth. Similarly, a vessel manoeuvring in an emergency is probably not "not-under-command". Nevertheless, vessels in either category will be behaving in what may appear to be a very non-standard manner and it helps to appreciate some of the limitations.

The points, or at least some of the main ones, are made by looking at three different categories of vessel. Type I, a small tanker with a top speed of say 15 knots; displacement 25 000 tonnes; and a single screw steam turbine propulsion. Type II, a much bigger tanker of 240 000 tonnes. Her top speed is 16 knots and she too is turbine-driven to a single screw. Type III, a ferry with a top speed of 30 knots. Her displacement is only 1700 tonnes and she is a motor ship.

The first point to look at is what happens if the engines are stopped when the vessel had been steaming full ahead. Type I will travel 2.1 miles before she comes to a stop compared with Type II's 5.5 miles. However, neither figure is of much practical importance, other than to give a sense of scale.

Next, consider how far the ships travel—and how long it takes them to do so—if the engines are put from full ahead to full astern. Type I now travels almost a mile, and takes 9 minutes to come to a stop. Type II still takes 2.5 miles, even with the engines full astern, and she takes 22 minutes to do so.

For comparison the smaller ferry, Type III, travels 0.4 mile when the engines are merely stopped and about 0.2 mile—two cables—if the engines are put full astern. She takes about 1 minute to do that.

Despite all that, the interesting statistics are still to follow. The fact that a ship travels what seems a fantastic distance after the engines are stopped is not really significant because both Types I and II can stop far more effectively—**so long as there is sea room**—by putting the helm hard over.

The turning circle diameter for Type I, from full ahead, is about 4 cables, but, even with the engines still full ahead, her 15-knot speed has dropped to about 5 knots at the completion of the full circle. For comparison, even the big tanker, Type II, with her 240 000 tonne displacement, can turn in a circle with a diameter of a little over 7 cables. That figure—less than 0.75 mile—is an interesting comparison with 2.5 miles for stopping in a straight line.

The loss of speed caused by the resistance of full helm is interesting, but what is even more significant is that the diameter of her turn, if she had started from slow ahead instead of from full ahead, is larger than when she was going twice as fast! Not very much larger, it is true, but the fact that it is larger at all shows how important it is for a large vessel not to let her speed drop too much. By the time the 15-knot Type I tanker has completed the full turn, from slow ahead, her speed is down to about 4 knots.

Further generalizations concerning Type III ferries soon become meaningless because of the question of the effects of twin screw and of bow thrusters. However, before anyone feels at all complacent, think of the implications of having to change the direction of swing.

Our Type II tanker is taking emergency action at full speed and full helm. If, for any reason, the master decided he had to change his mind and swing the other way, it would take 2 minutes 30 seconds before the vessel had even started to swing. 2 minutes 30 seconds at say 12 knots is 0.5 mile; 0.5 mile before she even starts to swing the other way!

No wonder small craft often fail to realize how far ahead the master of a large vessel has to plan. (See Chapter 6 and Fig. 6.1).

Small Craft Lights and Shapes

This chapter opened with a reference to the brig, *Tirzar*, losing a court case because her port and starboard lights were partially obscured. Almost 100 years later the problem for small craft was partially cured by the 1972 Collision Regulations and now, with the changes which were introduced in 1983, we have a really sensible answer.

Right up until the introduction of the 1965 edition of the Collision Regulations yachts were not *required* to exhibit anything until a risk of collision existed even if few were foolish enough to take advantage of the law. That, totally unacceptable, approach was no longer a part of the rule, but there was still no satisfactory way for small sailing craft to light themselves. Equipment we now take for granted—port and starboard lights with a range of visibility of 2.5 miles or so—did not exist until a decade or so ago and a large proportion of small sailing craft still attempted to make do with oil lights hung in the rigging. However the development of the modern rig with overlapping sails in the foretriangle soon made that impossible and the most satisfactory compromise was to use the bow pulpit (the forward end of the yacht's lifelines) as the mounting.

During the late sixties and early seventies many sailing yachts mounted their port and starboard lights on the bow pulpit, the pulpit being the only place where the lights would be clear of the sails. However, the lanterns available were of such poor quality that even when the lights were unobscured the yacht was often at risk because she was not seen.

At that stage in the development there were two basic mistakes. First many mounted both port and starboard lights on the bow pulpit—but so close together that when seen from right ahead the lights merged into one orange "blob". Secondly, those that did use a pulpit-mounted bicoloured light were little better off. The great advantage of the bicolour is that it allows a bulb of twice the brilliance for the same battery drain. However, the bicoloured lanterns that were available had a central pillar between the red and the green glass so that they too were practically useless when seen from right-ahead.

Some lengthy experiments conducted by *Yachting World*, which included "borrowing" Farnborough airfield and turning off all the landing lights for some visibility tests, revealed, for the first time, just how bad was the available equipment. Even the "Admiralty Pattern" bicolour had an arc of confusion dead ahead where the light was virtually blanked off of about 17 degrees.

The results of that research were published in 1971, and that comparatively crude, but revealing, work, coupled with some more scientific research done independently by Ahlemann & Schlatter in Bremen, had a considerable influence on much of the detailed wording in the Annex of the present Collision Regulations.

By 1985 a tiny proportion of yachts still used the pre-1972 lights—illegally —but the vast majority have changed. However, although sensible lanterns are now readily available, there are still many very silly mounting arrangements to be seen.

The essence of the post-1972 lights—and it is illegal in any country to use lights that have not been approved by the appropriate Marine Directorate —is that they have acrylic screens (that let through far more light than did the old coloured glass); they use bulbs with vertical filaments (so that the cut-off is precise); they have an edge-glued joint between one colour and another (so that the "arc of confusion" is almost non-existent); and they have 25 watt bulbs for the coloured lights and 10 watt for the white, instead of 5 watt or 2 watt as used to be fitted.

Today I suspect that most yachtsmen take 25 watts for granted: only a dozen years ago the vast majority did not really expect to be seen.

We have come a long way since *Tirzar*, but the one other transformation in small craft lights was that the 1972 Collision Regulations allowed the use of the masthead with one tricoloured light.

At first that was permitted only for sailing yachts of less than 12 metres in length, but after considerable lobbying by the Royal Yachting Association and the International Yacht Racing Union the limit was raised in the 1983 revision of the Collision Regulations. The tricoloured light is now allowed for sailing yachts up to 20 metres, and one, really bright, light clear above all obstructions soon became the norm.

Ideal Mountings

Following the principle that a picture is worth a thousand words, and remembering that the last page or two have been devoted to praise of the modern bicolour and tricoloured lights, there is one, not uncommon, circumstance when the "ideal" light—that mounted on the masthead—is not good (Fig. 4.3). The circumstance is the precise one most relevant to this book, a small sailing yacht in a large commercial port.

FIG. 4.3. *Lack of visibility from the bridge*

Figure 4.4 shows what might be described as a perfectionist solution. By fitting a combined tricolour and all-round white at the masthead—switched separately—a bicolour in the bow pulpit and a normal sternlight in the stern pulpit, there are three important options available. Light (1) for normal use when under sail, lights (3) and (4) for standby lights in case of bulb failure at the masthead, but also for use in any close-quarters situation such as in a canal or commercial harbour.

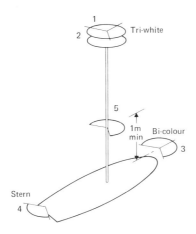

FIG. 4.4. *Positions of small craft lights*

The third option is to use the all-round light (2), with light (3) when under power. However, that alternative, although highly satisfactory for use in open water, does not overcome the problem illustrated by Fig. 4.3. If the stern sector of a tricoloured masthead-mounted light or any part of an all-round, combined masthead and stern light (2) is at or just a little below the height of eye of the Officer of the Watch, there is a distinct possibility that that light will merge with the background lighting of a commercial port.

We now have the strange situation where, having moved lights up to the top of the mast to make them clearly visible at sea, they are occasionally almost invisible in port!

The worst condition is somewhere like the canal leading from the Hoek to Rotterdam. There is a great deal of commercial shipping—much of it large—and a few yachts. From the bridge of a large vessel the horizon is a blaze of shore lights, mostly white. Somewhere among the bright white shore lights the Officer of the Watch has to pick out the stern light of the yacht close ahead of him.

At sea there is not the slightest doubt that a masthead-mounted tricoloured light is the best choice for a vessel under sail. Equally, in a well-lit commercial port—well-lit, that is, from the point of view of shore installations—the masthead can be the worst height for a white light. In a close-quarters situation the Officer of the Watch expects to look down on any small craft in his immediate vicinity and thus a sternlight on a stern pulpit—light (4) in Fig. 4.4—is a far safer answer. Thus, in a commercial harbour, switch to lights (3 and 4) or (3 and 4 and 5)—in Fig. 4.4—depending on whether under sail or power.

Finally, before too many say "But that means two sets of navigation lights", remember that is precisely what most commercial ships are required to have. For commercial vessels the second set is for use in case of bulb failure. For yachts the second set serves the same back-up rôle, but, more importantly, provides an alternative for use in confined waters.

The change-over point will depend on the circumstances, but as both the Royal Ocean Racing Club and the East Anglian Offshore Racing Association require all competitors to have secondary lights—to the full standard—for use in case of emergency, then the doubled-up installation shown in Fig. 4.4 is no more expensive to install than having one set, plus portable, secondary lights. Furthermore, if bulbs or wiring do fail, there is a good chance that the going is rough. The last thing that a busy crew want to be bothered with is crawling around fitting temporary lighting.

Obscured Lights

The overwhelming argument in favour of the use of the masthead for sailing yachts lights is that it is the one place where a light can be fitted where it is clear of the sails. However, a surprisingly large number of yachtsmen fail to appreciate that a burgee, on too short a stick, or even a badly placed VHF aerial, can easily mask a light for long enough for the fault to be of vital importance. A burgee, drooping across a light fitting, may blank it off for several seconds at a time, which makes the light appear to flash on and off. Quite apart from the illegality of the installation, a navigation light that appears to flash is both a danger and an irritant to others.

The Collision Regulations require any masking of a light to be less than 6 degrees. In practice that means that a "broomstick" type of VHF dipole aerial needs to be mounted about 200 millimetres offset from the filament of the light. The flexible "whip" aerials are very much smaller in diameter, and so they do not cause a masking problem, but another common cause of masking is the careless mounting of wind speed and direction indicators. Even the Brookes and Gatehouse unit—which is one of the slimmest—can create an obstruction of at least 3 degrees, and right-ahead too.

There is a definite tendency, in a small boat, to feel secure because the man on the deck of his own yacht is aware of his own lights. He feels that others are aware of them too. That philosophy is as dangerous as the man in a fawn Mackintosh in an unlit country lane feeling that because he can see an oncoming vehicle its driver can see him.

Ideally the man on watch should NOT be aware of his own navigation lights because, if they have been sensibly mounted and are correctly screened, there is virtually nothing to see. On most motor yachts, as well as on some sailing yachts, the masthead light needs to be mounted with a screen beneath it; otherwise, the rays of the light falling on the coachroof top ahead of the wheelhouse, or on the deck, can seriously affect night vision (Fig. 4.5). Similarly, the sternlight of many motor yachts is mounted too low on the transom—where it is partially masked by the vessel's own wash or exhaust smoke—or too far forward where the rays of its light shine on the after deck.

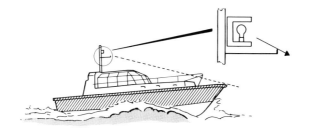

FIG. 4.5. *Shielding against glare*

It is in ports, particularly those with prominent shore lighting that a loss of night vision can be a serious problem. The small craft navigator feels it most because the closer he is to the water the greater the reflection and the greater the interference from the shore.

Almost everything is worth doing to minimize glare. Even the painting of the inside of the lantern itself a matt black is worthwhile. It is not by chance that the Collision Regulations call for light boards (screens) to be painted matt black. The only "piece" of light that does anything really useful is that "piece" from the filament of the bulb that travels to the eye of the observer. Almost everything else is just useless and harmful scatter (Fig. 4.6). It is true that the lens does something towards concentrating the light into a near-horizontal beam, but for small craft the type of dioptric lens used by large vessels is not possible; the small craft light has to have at least 50 per cent of the brilliance still visible at 25 degrees above and below the horizontal. In practice, the better fittings achieve about 60 per cent of the brilliance at those limits. The "big ship" for comparison, which has a magnifying lens system, maintains 60 per cent to only 7.5 degrees above and below the horizontal!

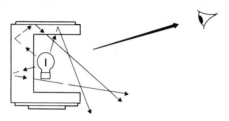

FIG. 4.6. *Shielding against scatter. Reflected light merely illuminates the water droplets in the air*

Finally, in this summary of the way small craft lights can be obscured, the very common practice of hanging anchor lights at a "convenient" head-height on a forestay has one grave disadvantage. The height at which it is easiest to put an anchor light is at about the same height of the greatest bulk of sail of the stowed mainsail. When the anchor light is seen from on board the yacht, the risk of it being obscured is not apparent: the observer is between the light and the sail. However, if it is remembered that the majority of yachts will be anchoring in tidal waters and that the vessels that approach her in the dark will therefore almost all appear from approximately right ahead or right astern, it must therefore be obvious that nearly half will be approaching from a sector that is likely to be masked (Fig. 4.7).

The skipper of the yacht might peer out at his anchor light before turning in for the night and be reassured that it appeared to be burning bright. Little does he realize that, as seen from 0.5 mile down the river, there may be nothing at all or, at most, an occasional short period of light as the yacht yaws in the tidal stream.

The point might seem somewhat academic, but the problem is a real one: even the thickness of a mast is something to consider, let alone a clumsily stowed sail. The solution, on the other hand, is simplicity itself. If an anchor light is hoisted a trifle higher—so that it is above the bulk of a stowed sail—then 90 per cent of the problem vanishes. Alternatively almost all the problem disappears if the light is hung off-centre.

A position in the foretriangle – a little above eye level –
is the traditional place for an anchor light...

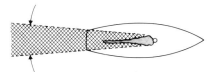

... However, a carelessly stowed mainsail can make that a very
poor solution to the problem of being seen. At the very least,
the light needs to be above the obstruction of the mainsail and,
even better, it ought to be off-centre.

FIG. 4.7. *Danger of anchor lights on centreline*

The custom of hanging an anchor light on the forestay is merely a
convenience: there is nothing in the rules to require the light to be on the
centreline. On the contrary, the rule states it should be: "where it can best be
seen", and a mounting a little off-centre ensures that vessels approaching
from nearly right ahead or nearly right astern—which is by far the
commonest condition—have an unobstructed view. Any approaching across
the tide is extremely unlikely to be on a steady bearing and thus any question
of a masked light becomes virtually non-existent.

Earlier I stated that no one in his right mind would anchor without an
anchor light. Nevertheless, because of the problem of masked lights, which so
few seem to appreciate, a large number of yachtsmen do anchor without a
light that can be seen at all times. Also, because of the greatly improved
charging facilities on a modern yacht, the custom is growing of using an all-
round masthead-mounted white light (light (2) in Fig. 4.4) as an anchor
light, instead of the traditional oil lantern.

From the visibility all-round point of view that is excellent, but
remembering the argument against masthead mounting for small craft lights
in any close-quarters situation (Fig. 4.3) such as a commercial harbour, there

is much to be said against that solution. Electric lights by all means—and there are some available with photoelectric switches to save battery capacity by turning themselves off at dawn—but mount them off-centre and not at the masthead where they become lost in the background lighting of a modern port.

5

The Navigator's Trade

Charts

Navigation has sometimes been referred to as the "haven-finding art". However, for the purposes of this book it is not "finding" the haven that is the primary concern, it is the problems associated with approaching and entering the haven and with manoeuvring within it that matter more.

What the navigator needs is information—lots of it—and in its most basic form the information on the chart is the most needed of all.

For navigation in general, the scale of the charts used could range from 1:10 000 000 for a chart of part of an ocean to one of 1:10 000 (or less) for a port. One is one thousand times as large as the other. Thus the amount of detail that can be shown of any one spot on the chart will vary enormously.

One safe generalization is that few yachts carry enough charts, but a sensible decision about what is "enough" is not easy.

The most useful scale for approach charts for small craft is about is 1:50 000. At that scale the Thames Estuary from Walton-on-the-Naze to South Foreland is covered in two overlapping charts. In comparison, the smaller scale of the general chart of the area—Approaches to the Thames Estuary—is at 1:150 000: it does not include any details of the inshore waters at all.

Each area has to be looked at separately, because the range of charts that are available is so complex. In some of the Scandinavian countries, the range is far more organized. The whole coastline of Norway, for example, is covered with overlapping charts at 1:350 000 and again with overlapping charts at 1:50 000. Even the numbering of the charts has been arranged so that the number indicates the scale used. In the United Kingdom we are not so lucky. Our chart index is extensive, but it has grown over a very long period and the mixture of scales is somewhat confusing, even if recent efforts have been made to rationalize scales.

To give another example of the dual coverage of an area, the Outer Approaches to the Solent extends from Selsey to Christchurch at a scale of 1:75 000, which is rather too small. The area is covered again by six more charts at 1:20 000, and then certain special areas like Southampton and Portsmouth harbours are covered yet again at 1:10 000 and 1:7000. Cowes has a chart of its own at 1:10 000 for the River Medina, with an inset at 1:3500 for Cowes harbour itself.

From that it is obvious that the decision regarding how many constitute "enough" is complex, and that decision is complicated even more by the nature of some of the latest breeds of chart. For Harwich Harbour, for example, there is a recent addition—Harwich Channel—at a scale of 1:10 000, and a harbour chart at the same scale. Both are designed for commercial traffic and neither are "essential reading" for a small craft planning to visit Harwich. At Cowes, on the other hand, the new Cowes Harbour chart is a very useful aid—even if the scales used are so large—because it was specially prepared for small craft and thus contains a tremendous amount of useful data about local services and small craft facilities.

From that it should be clear that even if the initial statement that 1:50 000 is a good scale for approach use, scale alone is not the only consideration.

For the United Kingdom the home edition of the *Catalogue of Admiralty and Hydrographic Publications* is a well-laid out booklet that tells all. For some areas the choice is obvious: for others it is far more difficult.

To use Harwich, again, as an example, the chart of the Approaches to Felixstowe, Harwich, and Ipswich, with the Rivers Stour, Orwell and Deben, at 1:25 000, is an excellent chart for small craft who might use the port. Similarly, for the River Thames there are four charts covering the river from Canvey Island to Teddington, all showing great detail at 1:12 500. Nevertheless, most yachtsmen would find the one chart—River Thames—from Hole Haven to London Bridge at 1:25 000, perfectly adequate.

To summarize, there are places like Cowes, where it is well worth buying the largest scale charts for the additional information they contain, even when the area is also covered at reasonable scales like 1:20 000. In other ports a scale of say 1:25 000 can be enough.

If in doubt, buy. A large-scale chart can make interesting reading and it can allow a safe anchorage to be found or a safe inshore passage well clear of commercial vessels. Furthermore, given reasonable luck, an Admiralty chart can be made to last for many years. The range of charts covering the Harwich approach is illustrated in Fig. 5.1.

Chart Correction

So far only the Admiralty chart has been mentioned, but there are other publishers. Two companies produced so-called "yachtsman's charts", and there are also special charts for special areas such as those published by the Clyde Cruising Club and the Royal Northumberland Yacht Club.

In my opinion the latter can be very useful, especially when they cover small havens that are otherwise charted very badly or even not charted at all.

On the other hand, the overwhelming case for using Admiralty charts, rather than the commercially produced ones, is that the Admiralty chart can be kept corrected.

At the beginning of this chapter I said "What the navigator needs is information . . . ", and information that is out-of-date is almost as dangerous as no information at all. Chart correction is available in two ways. Quarterly correction booklets are published by the Hydrographic Department and include all corrections of interest to small craft. Alternatively, the *Admiralty Weekly Notices to Mariners* are available to those who want to do the chart correction job properly. They can be picked up from any Admiralty chart agent free (or for only a nominal postage charge) and there can be no doubt that that is the best method of all.

For those sailing by day, and then only when the weather is reasonably settled, the fact that a port chart is a few months out of date may not seem particularly alarming. For more serious navigation, on the other hand, when ports will be entered in all weathers and at night as well as during daylight hours, the importance of having information up to date cannot be over-stressed. In really poor visibility the light that does not seem to relate to anything on the chart or even the buoy that does not appear on the chart can be a major hazard.

Almost anyone can enter a major harbour by merely bumbling along in the main shipping channel. However, the navigator worthy of the title ought to ensure that he has the facts he needs at his fingertips so that he can keep clear of main channels. He does not want to spend time trying to make sense of the nonsensical.

The Admiralty chart is the primary "tool" in the navigator's chest: it is more fun as well as far safer if those tools are kept "sharp".

Tides

Second only to a knowledge of the geography of the place, the chart, is a knowledge of the depth of water that is available. In many areas the tidal range is all-important.

While at sea the fact that there is 21 metres or 25 metres indicated on a depth sounder is of interest only to a careful navigator, and then only in certain circumstances. On an approach to a harbour, on the other hand, the difference between 1 metre and 5 metres can be all the difference between success and failure. Couple that with a tidal range of 4 metres for Harwich, 4.5 metres for Southampton, 5 metres for Blyth (in the north-east) or the Yealm River (in the South-West), and up to 12 and 15 metres in the British Channel and Saint Malo, and it is obvious that a knowledge of the precise height of the tide can be vital.

Nowadays there is ample information available to allow a navigator to "work his tides" in the sense that he can take advantage of a favourable tidal

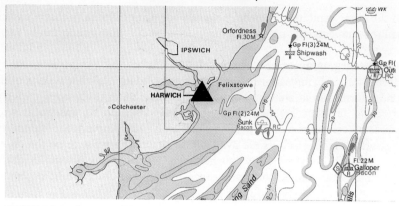

2182a   1:750 000

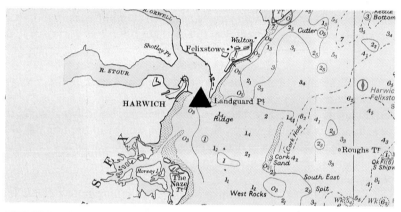

1406   1: 250 000

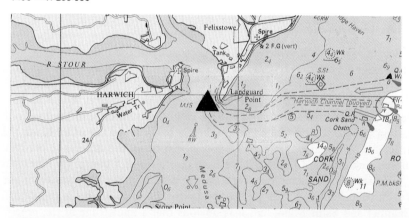

1610   1: 150 000

FIG. 5.1. *Charts 2182a, 1406, 1610, 2052, 2693, 1492. Produced from portions of BA Chart No. 2182a, 1406, 1610, 2052, 2693, 1491 with the sanction of the Controller HM Stationery Office and of the Hydrographer of the Navy*

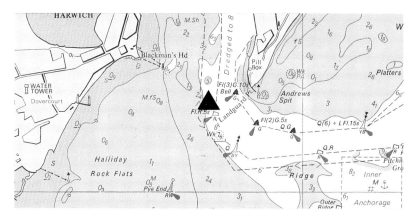

2052   1: 50 000

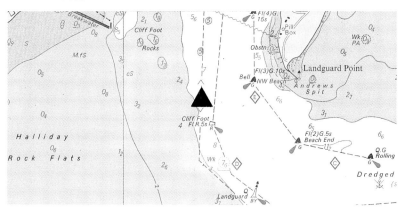

2693   1:25 000

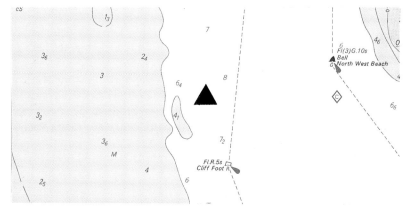

1492   1: 10 000

stream—and it is a sizeable part of a satisfactory passage to have used the natural movement of the water to the best advantage. However, from the port entry point of view, the height of the tide is usually far more important than the direction of any movement. Tidal height and tidal stream need to be thought about as separate problems.

Height

Most navigation books give somewhat general advice about calculating tidal height and many recommend what is known as the "twelfths" rule. That uses the assumption that any tide will rise, or fall, 1/12 in the first hour, 2/12 in the second, 3/12 in the third, 3/12 in the fourth, 2/12 in the fifth and 1/12 in the sixth. As an *aide memoire*—when nothing better is available—that is reasonably correct. However, in certain parts of north-west Europe it is hopelessly wrong, and therefore to use any system that can be misleading is a bad practice.

The professional is taught to use the *Admiralty Tide Tables, Volume 1, European Waters*, and to follow the calculation advice given in its pages. For accuracy there is no better method, but the great difference between a professional navigator, working from a ship's chart room, and the small boat navigator, working from a saloon table, is that the latter is likely to be captain, pilot, look-out, helmsman and (possibly) cook as well.

The difference is enormous, even if the information needed is much the same.

The answer for the small boat navigator is a ruthless adherence to the philosophy that says that as much as possible should be done beforehand. Never should it be necessary to rush a tidal calculation, at the last minute, because the facts that will be used for that calculation are all published beforehand. All that is needed to complete any calculation when actually entering a port, or when coming up to an anchorage, is time. Thus the best way to present any tidal information is with a graph. The most detailed tables in the world are correct for only one time: a graph, on the other hand, has time "built in".

With height on the vertical axis and time on the horizontal one the height of a tide (above chart datum) at any time can be worked out in advance. The only adjustment that might, very occasionally, have to be made is when a port has broadcast that the actual height at any particular place (compared with its datum) is so much more or less than predicted.

That point apart, the tidal height graph ought to become a normal part of every small craft navigator's life.

For great precision, a table, with all the appropriate allowances included, will always remain the best answer. For small craft, on the other hand, the graph is the best compromise, because the *character* of the behaviour of the tide at any particular port can so easily be plotted.

It is the lack of character in the "twelfths" rule that can make it so unreliable. For a standard port like Devonport (Fig. 5.2) the character of the tidal rise and fall is predictable, and all that is necessary is to note the height of high and low water for the day in question and plot a similar character.

For a standard port like Southampton, on the other hand, or Vlissingen (Flushing) (Fig. 5.2b) a "twelfths" rule assumption is a long way out.

The other great advantage of working on a graph, rather than with a table, is that more than one port can readily be plotted on graph paper with the curves superimposed. The curves will be drawn beforehand, of course, and then, when actually entering harbour—possibly 24 hours after the graph had been plotted—the height of tide above chart datum is immediately available at a glance (Fig. 5.3).

Assume a yacht was in Levington marina, on the River Orwell, bound for Blankenberg in Belgium. Assume too that she needed about 1 metre over chart datum to get out of the marina channel. Figure 5.3 shows immediately that she ought to leave by 0500 at the latest to clear the channel; otherwise she might not clear before 0900. Then, if she was looking for 1.5 metres over datum to enter the channel between the piers at Blankenberg, the graph shows that unless she had a very fast passage and arrive off the port by 1830, she will not make a safe entry before 2315.

Once the basic graph has been plotted, it is simple to add extra ports or to check on the depth of water that will be found on off-lying sandbanks. The accuracy is that of the predicted height, of course, not the actual height on any particular day. However, it would be rare for the difference to make a very great difference and the graph—following the character of the height curve for the standard port in question—is many times more accurate that any "twelfths" approximation.

For some ports there is plenty of water at all times, and to enter Oostende, for example, instead of Blankenberg, the precise height is not necessarily significant. However, it is always useful to plot because in poor visibility it might suddenly become important to reduce a sounding to chart datum. Often a bearing and a single sounding can give a position, but only if the sounding has been reduced correctly. With a graph, the job is a matter of a glance lasting 2 or 3 seconds.

I must admit to having "gone on a bit" about tidal height, but the last point is really the significant one. An accurate sounding that can be reduced to chart datum in seconds is an important piece of data. The depth sounder is not merely an instrument to tell you if there is enough water under you to float the boat; it is an important navigational aid.

Tidal Stream

The word "tide" on its own is often confusing. A man might ask: "What's the tide doing?", which probably means is it coming "in" or going "out": in

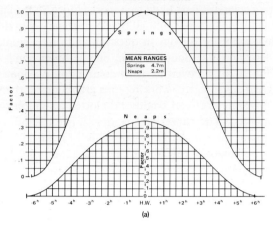

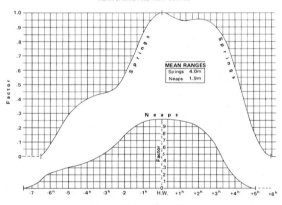

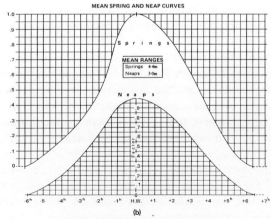

FIG. 5.2. *Tidal height curves: (a) Devonport,
(b) Southampton and Vlissingen*

Time zone: – *0100*   Mid-day

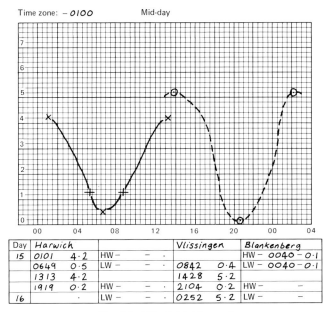

Day	Harwich				Vlissingen		Blankenberg	
15	0101	4·2	HW –	–	·			HW – 0040 – 0·1
	0649	0·5	LW –	–	·	0842	0·4	LW – 0040 – 0·1
	1313	4·2				1428	5·2	
	1919	0·2	HW –	–	·	2104	0·2	HW – –
16		·	LW –	–	·	0252	5·2	LW – –

FIG. 5.3. *BH tidal height graph*

other words, is it rising or falling. On the other hand, the same question might be answered by "It is ebbing", meaning that the stream is going down river. Thus it is less likely to cause confusion if the rise and fall is referred to as "height" and the ebb and flow as the "stream".

So far so good, but there is also the "current" to contend with. In English and in the United Kingdom (but not in the United States) a current is the steady movement of water such as in the upper, non-tidal, reaches of a river or in the Gulf Stream! The Gulf Stream is not a "stream" at all, it is a current.

Generally the strength of the currents around the U.K. coast are such that they can be ignored, but in any river, because the current flow is superimposed on the tidal stream, the apparent ebb stream is always faster than the flood stream.

Obviously a passage ought to be planned to make the best of any favourable tidal stream, and when passing places where tides meet, such as off Dungeness, it is possible to catch two favourable tidal streams in a row if the planning is good and the "gods of the weather" oblige. However, from the port entry point of view, the tidal stream matters most for ports like Lowestoft, where there can be at least 2½ knots off the piers at Spring tides.

For small craft the *Admiralty Tidal Stream Atlas* is almost always the best source of information, even if there is greater detail in the descriptions in the Pilot books. For a tricky approach, like that at Lowestoft, the Pilot is well worth consulting as well, but for all normal sailing the *Tidal Stream Atlas* should be in constant use.

As with tidal height, the tidal stream can easily be predicted by a minute amount of preplanning that can be invaluable in times of stress—later. The *Tidal Stream Atlases* show tidal arrows for every hour either side of high water for a nearby standard port. Thus if high water at Dover is 1119, write that figure, lightly, at the top of the page for high water, and 2 hours before becomes 0919, 1 hour before 1019, and so on. If that is done beforehand, for the whole period of a passage, all that is required is a glance at the time and the appropriate page can be turned up without any hurried mental arithmetic. Similarly, the navigator can so simply look ahead: a mere glance tells him that the stream will be on the turn in $1\frac{1}{2}$ hours, without his having to write anything or to calculate anything.

Obvious perhaps, but by no means is that universally done. I am so wedded to the practice that I keep my *Tidal Stream Atlas* marked up as in Fig. 5.4. I usually mark for 36 hours ahead, because once the high-water time is looked up for "today" you might as well do tomorrow as well, in case the passage is slower than anticipated. My practice is to draw in the box—firmly—in pencil and then cover it with Scotch "magic" tape. By that method the figures for date and time can be rubbed out very easily and the base grid remains for the next occasion.

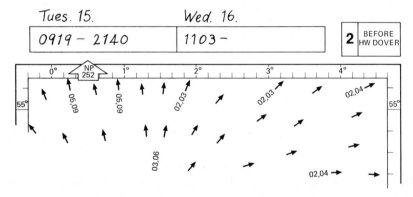

FIG. 5.4. *BH tidal stream atlas time*

When the time comes to enter harbour, a quick glance at the appropriate page and the tidal stream across the entrance can be assessed in a second.

Publications

In most countries in the world—and certainly in the United Kingdom—there are really very few regulations controlling what may and what may not be done. For example, the "Merchant Shipping (Carriage of Nautical Publications) Rules" lay down the requirements for a minimum standard of publications for all vessels " . . . which go or attempt to go to sea . . . ", but there is a realistic exemption clause in the rule exempting vessels " . . . less than 12 metres in length . . . ".

Thus, what is carried by small vessels depends on common sense and the expertise of the skipper. A fisherman—working out of his home port, year in and year out—may not even have a chart on board, and he almost certainly will not have a tide table. He knows where he is and he knows what the tide is doing by an instinct born of years of unconscious learning. The occasional navigator, on the other hand, particularly if he has discovered the joys of cruising to unfamiliar places, needs all the help he can get.

The Royal Yachting Association publishes a *Bibliography of Sailing Directions*. Some of the "yachtsman's pilots", like the Deutsche Segler-Verbande *Hafenhandbüch, Ostsee* and *Hafenhandbüch. Nordsee*, are excellent, and correction booklets are published regularly. Some others, so-called "yachtsmans pilots", were not much good even when first published, and are now years and years out of date. Somewhere between those extremes come useful guides like the *Yachting Monthly* book, *East Coast Rivers* which covers the coast from the Humber to the Swale, and the guides written by Brandon.

Otherwise, let the buyer beware. Look **very carefully** at the publication dates and at the availability of correction sheets.

Another source of basic information about port entry can be found from the current edition of Macmillan's *Almanac* but the emphasis has to be on the basics. With very few exceptions, the chartlets published are not nearly informative enough to allow them to be used as entry charts, but they do give a useful mental picture of a place and they can be invaluable for general planning.

Some yachtsman seem to dismiss the official Admiralty *Pilots* as though they were of use to commercial vessels only. That is far from the truth. Even since the mid 1960s the Admiralty *Pilots* have been getting better and better, from the small craft point of view, and some of the latest to be published are excellent.

Similarly, few small craft carry the Admiralty *Light Lists*. However, if the chart selection is generous, the need for the additional information provided by the official light list is small, even if the serious minded navigator will bless the fact that he carries them on occasion.

Notices to Mariners have already been recommended. Without them the navigator has either to be rich, and repurchase every year, or remain ill informed by having his information out of date. There is no alternative.

Electronic Aids

Nowadays the range of electronic aids with which a small yacht can be equipped is so great that it would have seemed like science fiction only a few years ago.

The first major advance was the use of radio for direction finding, and that began to make itself felt in the 1950s. Today radio direction finding (RDF) is so much a part of the normal small craft navigational scene that it is taken for granted. However, except for one of the latest developments—the Radio Lighthouse (about which more later), RDF is not really an inshore or harbour approach "tool".

Later, in the 1950s, the first small craft depth (echo) sounders made their appearance, and yachtsmen soon realized the importance of having a continuous display of depth. The alternative, for centuries, had been to send a member of the crew in the lee rigging, "swinging the lead". Today that would be almost unthinkable, because accurate sounders are available for all types of boat.

Depth

For inshore and harbour use, when there might be a need to sound to say 20 metres at the most, the choice is almost unlimited. However, the more expensive models also sound to depths of up to ten times that figure and as a navigational aid for use on passage the more sophisticated types are a boon. The ideal answer is to have an analogue repeater—or even two—close to the helmsman. It is he who needs to be able to glance, momentarily, at the dial when manoeuvring in shallow water, and it is quicker for the brain to absorb the position of pointer, on the dial, rather than have to read figures.

The navigator, on the other hand, can benefit from the precision of a digital reading, especially in the deeper water. From the navigation point of view, there is all the difference in the world between 33 metres and 43 metres. However, with a dial marked with a logarithmic scale, the difference between 33 metres and 43 metres might be only a few degrees of arc.

For commercial use, there are numerous echo sounders which plot the depth on sensitive paper, and the inshore commercial fisherman tends to favour the type of sounder where the depth is presented with a revolving LED display. The revolving display is cheap and reliable, in the short term, and is preferred because it (in theory at least) shows an indication of the nature of the bottom. The disadvantage of the revolving LED display is that it is not nearly as easy to see from an angle, as can be done with an analogue meter-type dial. Also it is sometimes very difficult to read the revolving type of dial in bright sunlight.

For harbour sailing a reliable depth (echo) sounder is so important that it is foolish to try to economize too much. Sounders like the Brookes and Gatehouse "Hecta", which are waterproofed, which have variable depth alarms and which can have one or more repeaters and two transducers when necessary, may cost ten times more than the cheapest sounders on the market, but they are at least ten times as likely to be working in 10 years time.

There are many other, commonly used, electronic aids to navigation, with speed indicators, wind direction indicators and wind speed indicators (in that order) among the commonest. However, from the "harbourmanship" point of view, the highly sophisticated wind speed and direction indicators are racing and/or performance aids. They have little to do with boat handling. Boat speed, on the other hand, is of considerable importance, and a good indication of boat speed is a tremendous help.

Speed

Again, as so often, too much economy is unwise. The cheap speed indicators tend to stop working at very low speeds and it is at those low speeds that a check on the actual speed through the water can be valuable.

Until very recently speed has usually been indicated by the use of spinners, of one sort or another, and attempts to use the Doppler effect, and to measure sound waves in the water, have not all been a success. However, the latest speed indication, called "Sonic Speed", by Brookes and Gatehouse, has overcome the earlier problems and for the man who wants the best available it has great advantages. Cost apart, the obvious advantages of using sound waves, rather than spinners, is that sound is unaffected by weed and by stray ropes and with accuracies of less than 1 per cent speed can be a vital input into the computerized display of speed made good (Vmg) and all the other performance indications that are now available.

Integration

Prior to 1983, when the Royal Ocean Racing Club relaxed its ban on the use of hyperbolic aids like Loran C and Decca (about which more later), the idea of linking various instruments together was also banned. The idea of the ban—which was sound when it was first made—was to limit the advantage of the man with the really deep pocket. However, with the cost of electronics falling all the time, the ban was withdrawn and it resulted in a flood of so-called integrated systems.

The idea is simple. Wind direction, wind speed, boat speed and heading can be fed to a computer to produce various performance figures that, at their best, are invaluable to the racing navigator and useful to anybody. However, as they serve little, if at all, in close-quarters manoeuvring, they will not be described here. They are mentioned because of the need to give an important warning. Beware any system which fails to display vital information like the depth of the water if the computer circuits should fail.

By all means supply the navigator's position with "master display units", but try to arrange the installation so that a failure in one part does not blank out everything else.

Despite all the expertise that goes into modern electronic aids, they are NOT infallible. In Chapter 2 I strongly recommended having a second VHF radiotelephone. Here the advice is to provide something as a back-up for measuring depth. Even a smallish lead and line can serve, but allow for something!

Radio Lighthouse

All the main maritime direction-finding beacons operate on medium frequencies, and they have ranges from about 20 miles up to 100 miles, and more for a few. However, the U.K.'s principal lighthouse authority, Trinity House, introduced the radio lighthouse in the early 1980s, and it is now established as a very useful inshore navigation aid. The stations work in pairs, and a true bearing is found by counting audible signals to given an accuracy of about 2 degrees or better.

At present the radio lighthouse is using a VHF frequency, so that no separate receiver is required, but if the necessary support for the system is forthcoming, and if the beacons are installed as originally intended in many parts of the coast, then there would be a strong case for using special, dedicated frequencies with receivers also dedicated to that purpose. If there is one thing that modern electronics do well, it is to count. Thus, with established identity signals, the special—very simple—receivers could display an "ident" group of letters (showing the station) followed by a digital representation of the true bearing. That, in turn, could be followed by "ident" and bearing signals for the sister station with a really reliable position as the result.

A book about the use of harbours is not the best place to discuss the politics of who pays for navigational aids, but the great advantage of the radio lighthouse system is that there are no problems with magnetic variation and no problems caused by the motion. The bearing is accurate, it is true and the installation of the beacons themselves is comparatively cheap.

Hyperbolic Aids

The story of navigational aids for small craft is changing so fast that what follows will be hopelessly out of date in only a few more years. By 1990, or thereabouts, there will be satellite navigation systems available (for those willing to pay for them) which will give a continuous presentation of the position, night and day, with an accuracy of only a few metres. For the moment, and for the next few years, Decca is the pinnacle of development.

The Decca Mark I first came on the U.K. scene in 1983, although other sets using the Decca chain had appeared on the Continent over a year earlier, but by 1985 the Decca Company had reached agreements with two other major manufacturers and there were at least three effective sets on the market. The better sets utilize a master and three slave stations, but even the cheaper Decca Mark III, which uses only two slave stations, is so good an aid that it is difficult not to overpraise it.

When entering harbour in poor visibility, a small craft might expect to be within a couple of cables of her track if relying on so-called conventional methods. With Decca she can expect to be within 100 metres or less in most circumstances. Thus, with emphasis on the phrase "in most circumstances", a Decca receiver relieves the navigator of much of his anxiety.

One small problem with Decca is that it is at its best in bright sunlight, when accuracy is least necessary, and at its worst at night. Furthermore, Decca is susceptible to what the meteorologist calls "static precipitation"; the signals can fail if there is thunder about. By the "nature of the beast", the receiver normally finds its position again, after an interval of perhaps 20 minutes or more, but that warning alone should be enough to add emphasis to the often repeated—but often ignored—warning that electronics are a navigational aid: they ought not to be the means of navigation.

The purpose of this chapter is to summarize what the navigator needs and what is available to him. It is not to teach him to navigate in the first place. However, for harbour entry, as much as for any normal navigation, the essential lesson to learn is not only to know (or to estimate) where you are, but to plot ahead.

In normal coastal navigation that is summarized by the expression to "DR on". My recommendation for small craft navigation is to write most of what is required on the chart itself, rather than in the log. In a dry, and probably warm, chartroom on the bridge of a stable ship the professional will enter everything that happens in his log. In a small yacht, where the navigator may well be helmsman and look-out as well, there is less chance of error if positions, log readings and the time is actually written on the chart.

And if that practice is firmly engrained in the mind, the problems caused by Decca receivers that suddenly, and without warning, switch themselves off, or any other malfunction, is not anyway near as serious as it might otherwise be. If the entry on the chart tells you where you were "x" minutes ago, and where you had expected to be in "y" minutes time, it is comparatively straightforward to calculate where you are now. Without that past and future position actually written down, the problem can be very different.

Navigational Warnings

For coastal waters navigational warnings—buoys out of position or lights malfunctioning and the like—are available on either MF or VHF frequencies from Coast Radio Stations at prearranged times, every 4 hours throughout the 24 hours. For warnings concerning harbour entry, the harbour radio VHF service—summarized in Chapters 2 and 3—is the source. However, yet another and extremely useful system was started in 1984—Navtex—which is likely to prove the most useful of all for small craft, even if it was originally designed with a totally different purpose in mind.

The navigational warnings from Coast Radio Stations are broadcast on the primary working frequency of the station—after a preliminary announcement on Ch 16—every 4 hours. The stations are the same as those used for ship-to-shore radiotelephone traffic.

For U.K. and North Sea waters, navigational warnings are broadcast:

Collafirth	Ch 24	A	Cardigan Bay	Ch 03	A
Shetland	Ch 27	A	Anglesey	Ch 26	A
Orkney	Ch 26	A	Morecambe Bay	Ch 04	A
Cromarty	Ch 28	A	Portpatrick	Ch 27	C
Buchan	Ch 25	C	Malin Head	Ch 23	A
Stanehaven	Ch 26	C	Clyde	Ch 26	C
Forth	Ch 24	C	Islay	Ch 25	C
Cullercoats	Ch 26	A	Skye	Ch 24	A
Whitby	Ch 25	A	Hebrides	Ch 26	A
Grimsby	Ch 27	C	Lewis	Ch 05	A
Humber	Ch 26	C	Wick	1706–1827 kHz	A
Bacton	Ch 07	C			
Orfordness	Ch 62	A	Brest–Le Conquet	1873 kHz	D
Thames	Ch 02	A	St Malo	2691 kHz	D
North Foreland	Ch 26	A	Boulogne	1694 kHz	B
Hastings	Ch 07	A	Oostende	Ch 27	C
Niton	Ch 28	C	Scheveningen	1939 2600 kHz	D
Weymouth Bay	Ch 05	C	Nes	1862 kHz	D
Start Point	Ch 26	A	Norddeich	2614 kHz	B
Pendennis	Ch 62	A	Blåvand	1813 kHz	D
Lands End	Ch 27	A	Farsund	1750 2635 kHz	
Scillies	Ch 61	A	Ch 05 21 25 26 27 61 82		B
Ilfracombe	Ch 05	C	Rogoland	1729 2965 kHz	
Severn	Ch 25	C	Ch 18 24 25 26 27 28		D
Celtic	Ch 24	C	Bergen	1743 kHz	
			Ch 05 07 18 25 85		B

with the following transmission times (all UTC):

A	0033	0433	0833	1633	2033
B	0133	0533	0933	1733	2133
C	0233	0633	1033	1833	2233
D	0333	0733	1133	1933	2333

For the warnings broadcast by harbour authorities, the times will vary from port to port. The Coast and Port Radio Supplement summarizes the services offered. They vary from regular and detailed broadcasts to occasional, unscheduled announcements. However, important warnings will be repeated regularly and warnings such as dredgers working in an approach channel are often transmitted to every ship that checks in to the VTS system.

The third source of navigational warnings is that supplied by the new Navtex system which came into operation in 1984. Coast Radio Stations, from northern Norway to Land's End, now broadcast throughout the 24 hours, but apart from the need for a dedicated receiver (which is expensive), the system has the overwhelming advantage of unattended operation. Once switched on—and the current consumption on stand-by is only about 200 milliamps—the Navtex warnings (as well as weather messages and other important traffic) are printed by dot matrix on thermal paper and, to save expense, the receiver is programmed to receive only the stations in the immediate vicinity.

A Navtex receiver can also be programmed to receive only the types of messages that are of interest. Ice warnings on the Swedish coast are obviously of little interest to a small yacht cruising off the Isle of Wight. Similarly, Pilot vessels off station are of little interest to a yacht anywhere. However, every vessel can benefit from navigational warnings in her area, and the Navtex receivers also print weather messages, gale warnings (accompanied by a warning buzzer) and any other urgency traffic.

The Navtex system is not primarily designed for small craft, nor for inshore and harbour navigational warnings, but because it has the facility of printing messages without the navigator having to be present, it has obvious advantages for short-handed vessels. With plans to extend the system worldwide and with no problems of licensing or charging for the service, Navtex has to be of interest despite the initial cost.

Weather Messages

As has just been mentioned, weather messages are included in the Navtex system, but apart from gale warnings only twice a day. For more frequent reports there are numerous other sources, most too well established to need detailed description here. The BBC Radio 4 broadcasts on 200 kHz are the primary source when cruise planning. They are repeated by local Coast Radio Stations twice every day. In addition, there are numerous local radio stations that feature weather forecasts on a regular basis—especially in the summer months—and, as was mentioned in Chapter 2, many port VTS stations also give current weather, including visibility, when appropriate. Finally, for U.K. waters, HM Coastguard will give advice regarding weather and there is a special VHF frequency—Ch 67—which, in the United Kingdom, is designated for that traffic.

Since 1985 HMCG has begun using the new Marineline Coastal Waters Forecast as a regular forecast service, and the same service, which is excellent, is available on tape from land line stations throughout the country. Thus, in addition to the availability of the main Sea Area Shipping Forecasts, the Marineline inshore forecasts are also available throughout the 24 hours.

The Compass

Finally, in this summary of the navigator's "tools", the most important single item of all, the compass, must never be forgotten.

Amateur sailors tend to abandon compass courses when they get into harbour areas and to rely on sight. To a degree that is inevitable. Once a man can see where he intends to go, his instinct tells him to head for it. In practice, the more the helmsman can be persuaded to be aware of what course he is steering—even if he is steering by eye rather than by a compass course—the less likely he is to allow the boat to drift off the track he had intended to take.

The problem is one of degree, and the experienced helmsman will achieve the necessary corrections by keeping a transit (in his mind) between, say, the buoy for which he is steering and something prominent in the background.

In harbour areas the tidal stream is likely to be stronger than it is in open water, and the actual speed through the water likely to be less. Thus the crab-wise progress of the small slow boat is at its commonest.

Earlier the advantages of the Decca system of position finding was empha-sized, but it is in large commercial harbours that yet another advantage of the system is evident. Instead of presenting the position by Latitude and Longi-tude, a Decca Navigator is equally at home presenting the distance to port or starboard of a predetermined track. Thus, once a track has been programmed into the Navigator, and any one track takes a matter of 30 seconds or so to "tap" in, the display presents distance to go and distance off track.

That feature of the system is useful for general passage-making, but in certain conditions it can be invaluable in harbour. The worse the visibility, the nicer it is to know, at a glance, where the boat is in relation to where she ought to be. Of course a plot of Latitude and Longitude is equally reassuring, but the beauty of using the position-off-track facility is that no plotting is necessary. When motoring down the edge of an approach channel, for example, an unintentional drift to either side of a predetermined track could be highly undesirable.

And All the Rest

If trying to list everything a navigator needs, we would have to include pensils, erasers and even the chart table itself. However, although a chapter on its own might be written about the navigator's "office", there is one more item of particular help in harbour, a large transparent envelope to take a folded chart.

If skipper and navigator are one and the same person, there are occasions in harbour, or while approaching a harbour, when the chart itself needs to be hand-held. For that purpose a plastic folder and a chinograph pencil is the answer. The folder needs to be about A2 size, and certainly no smaller than A3. Several firms make them, but even a sheet of suitable material and a roll of masking tape will make something that serves.

The occasions when a folder is really necessary are very few, but when one is necessary it can become essential if a safe passage is to be made.

6

Restricted Visibility

Sailing at Night

The expression "bad visibility" conjures up visions of men on the fo'c's'le head, peering forward and trying to penetrate the fog. However, the commonest form of bad visibility is night: it occurs every day.

How much light?

Sailing at night is really exactly the same as sailing by day except that it is colder, it is much more difficult to judge distance, the crew is more likely to be tired, there is a far greater risk of being frightened and, above all, you cannot see. Virtually all those problems are caused by a difference in the environment.

Our ancestors had many skills that we have forgotten. There is evidence that Neolithic peoples fished (by hand, of course) in waters up to 200 metres deep. Since the Middle Ages, charts have shown soundings up to 200 metres. Our ancestors judged the time of the turn of a tide by the change in the shapes of the waves. They navigated by using the formation of clouds over mountain tops. They use a mirage effect to increase the distance over which they could take bearings. They used birds to aid navigation. Above all, they memorized dozens of clearing lines in their home waters: they knew that if they kept the second cottage clear of the last tree beyond it, the transit would keep them off the shoal.

Even more important, our ancestors were not used to having their streets lit. At sea they did not expect to see lights.

The key to the problem is what is called "night adaptation". The human eye is an enormously complex organ and it adapts to the ambient light level to a remarkable degree. In a house, a landing or hall needs about 100 lumens per square metre (l/m^2); a kitchen at least 200 l/m^2; and close work, like sewing, requires 600 l/m^2 locally. The eye automatically adjusts to the level required. By day there are hundreds of lumens available from the sun, but the light is so evenly spread that the eye is not disturbed unless looking directly at the sun itself, or unless it catches a direct reflection from some glass or other reflecting surface.

By night too the eye is relaxed as it adjusts to the level of ambient light: it is the unexpected direct bright light that causes the problems, and it is they that must be avoided at all costs.

The problem of night vision is aggravated, for some, because their rate of night adaptation varies enormously. I happen to have a very slow rate of change and thus I may be more aware of the problems than others. However, because I have that poor rate of change, I was forced to try to do something about it: with care, a great deal can be done.

What follows applies to all night sailing, but in case anyone feels that the objective of the book has been lost, remember that it is in port that the problem is at its most acute, and the larger the port, the greater the problem.

The Human Eye

Our eyes have two different groups of receptors (nervous systems in layman's terms) called the "rods" and the "cones". Rods are highly sensitive to light and to movement, but they are completely insensitive to colour. Cones, on the other hand, are what we need for accuracy (sharpness), as when we read words or distinguish colours.

From that it follows that because the rods are highly sensitive to light, it is they that we use to pick up the unlit buoy or to see the silhouette of the anchored ship. For that type of vision it is not precise information that is required, it is an awareness. It is that type of vision that is so important in harbour and it is that type of vision that is most easily spoilt by stray white light.

The first point to establish is that not one yacht in one hundred is properly lit below, because the lighting required for use in harbour and that required for use at sea are completely different.

A cheerful page or two might easily be written about interior lighting and decor for small craft, but that would be outside my remit. For night time under way there are two, quite separate, needs. First, the whole cabin area is best if lit by a very very dim deep red glow. To have the minimum effect on the rods—and thus to retain nearly full "night vision"—the red needs to be a **deep** red and it is amazing how little light is required.

In my previous yacht, 10 metres l.o.a., I fitted four 2-watt torch bulbs, with deep red screens, to illuminate the whole boat. That was unnecessarily bright! We stuck tiny squares of black tape on two of the screw cap screens to reduce the amount of light shining into the eyes of an off-watch man in the quarter berths.

There is no need for any light at all in a cabin, until well after sunset. As a generalization, I found that if there was a need for a compass light, there was a need for some light below. To save wiring (and cost) I wired my four, 2-

watt bulb-holders to the compass light switch. On passage, when the compass light went on, the cabin lights came on.

With that deep but dim red glow, a man can dress without *needing to switch on any other lights at all*. When he goes on deck he has full night vision: he can see. Similarly, a man can come below to find that bar of chocolate he has been thinking about, or to pick up a clean handerchief and, again, this does not affect his ability to see.

The fittings I used were the standard 12-volt bulb-holders used for the lights on life rafts or life jackets; red screw filter covers are available as standard for instrument lighting.

Next comes the lighting of special areas. A galley or a lavatory compartment will need more than the background glow of red, and for that the standard cabin lights from Aqua Signal are available with red covers; 5-watt festoon bulbs are ample, and so long as they are mounted so that they cannot be seen from on deck, the standard interior light with the red screen will serve for the permanent red lighting as well. However, remember that very very little is needed for the all-night background light.

Next, the chart table needs more than the background glow, but, contrary to much that is written on the subject, the latest thinking suggests that a **very** dim white light is better for a chart than the use of red. Red light distorts too much of the colouring of a chart and **so long as the chart light has its own dimmer switch** white is best. For a full-sized chart table—large enough to take an Admiralty chart unfolded—two lights, on arms, are better than one. One arm will not cover the whole area, and it is important to keep the level of light to the lowest possible level. With two arms—switched separately—a glow of light the size of a small dinner plate can be concentrated where it is needed and everything else kept dark.

The alternative so often seen—one bright white light over the chart area—is exceedingly dangerous. The skipper may be unsure of something as he enters harbour. He slips down below to have a glance at his chart, and when he returns to the cockpit he is "blind".

Compass lights also need very careful attention. Again the latest research suggests that red lights are wrong for the job. The brain takes longer to focus on red, and it takes longer for the brain to absorb the digital information from a red light. Again, white is the answer.

Even more important than the chart light, a compass light **must** have its own dimmer switch. All the numerous experiments with "Beta" light and similar devices failed because the amount of light needed at dawn and dusk and the amount needed in the middle of a pitch black night is about 5:1. The light needs to be as dim as can be found comfortable at any one moment, and it must be concentrated precisely over the figures to be read, nowhere else.

Already the advice given here goes far beyond the norm, but there is more to come. Nowadays the helmsman expects a continuous presentation of depth and speed, and many yachts offer wind direction information as well. So be it.

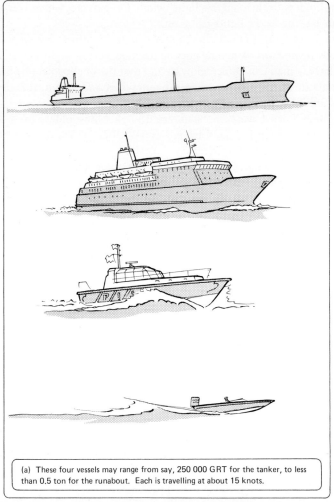

(a) These four vessels may range from say, 250 000 GRT for the tanker, to less than 0.5 ton for the runabout. Each is travelling at about 15 knots.

FIG. 6.1. *Deceptive speed of large vessels*

Chapter 5 stressed that information is the vital ingredient, but the supply of that sort of information must not prevent the helmsman from performing what is his primary function on all but large racing boats; he is the principal look-out. In other words, all instrument lighting must also be treated as was the compass; it, too, must have a dimmer switch.

Finally, beware of stray light from torches and the like. Even a second of bright white light in the helmsman's face can incapacitate him for a couple of minutes. If there are smokers in the cockpit, ensure they turn away and give a warning before lighting a match. Everything helps. Spreader lights that shine downward are so dangerous to night vision that I would recommend they should be banned by clubs organizing racing.

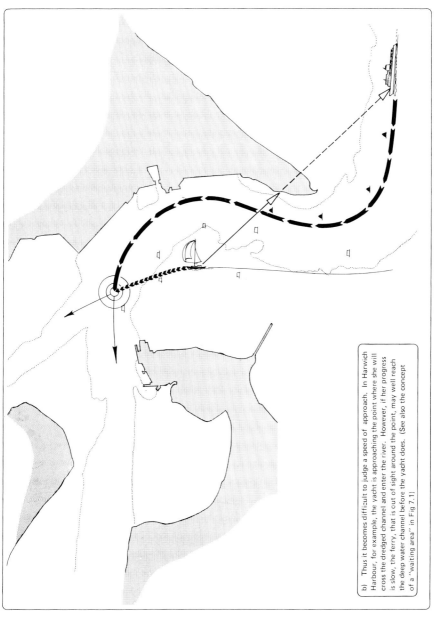

b) Thus it becomes difficult to judge a speed of approach. In Harwich Harbour, for example, the yacht is approaching the point where she will cross the dredged channel and enter the river. However, if her progress is slow, the ferry, that is out of sight around the point, may well reach the deep water channel before the yacht does. (See also the concept of a "waiting area" in Fig 7.1)

Fig. 6.1b

Commercial ports are a blaze of light on shore, and the lower the height of eye, the more those lights cause problems. Harwich Harbour Board's *Shipmaster's Guide* wisely states: "Unscreened deck lights should be kept to the minimum so that the navigation of other vessels is not adversely affected." Unfortunately, few seem to take heed.

Rule 30(c) of the Collision Regulations reads: "A vessel at anchor may, and a vessel of 100 metres and more shall, also use the available working or equivalent lights to illuminate her decks." That too creates many, many problems for small craft. Few shipmasters seem to appreciate the problems that can be caused by carelessly screened lights. At least I must assume that they do not realize this because it would be difficult to imagine that their actions are deliberate. To sail past an anchored "super-tanker" at close quarters can mean almost complete loss of all vision, and the only advice that is at all helpful is to say "Try not to look." The problem is somewhat akin to the passenger in a car who exclaims: "Just look at that idiot's badly adjusted lights." The one thing the driver should try **not** to do is to look at them.

Chapter 4 had a good deal to say about the screen of small craft lights. The subject is important at all times, but especially so in bad visibility. Water droplets in the atmosphere can reflect any light. Thus everything that avoids the production of stray light is worth doing, especially the screening of masthead lights and the use of matt black paint as recommended.

Fog

Having written so much about night affecting visibility, it is fair to summarize fog by saying it is the same as night, but more so.

If you cannot see properly, then behave as does a poorly sighted person on land; do everything possible to improve the other senses.

Can you hear properly? Auxiliary engines that have exhaust pipes at water level, so that they "gobble-gobble-gobble" all the time, are a menace.

A look-out in the bow can usually hear far better than those in a cockpit. However, before sending a man into the bow make sure any signalling system is agreed and understood. On a large yacht with a noisy exhaust a call from the bow may easily be misunderstood, or even not heard at all. It is best if a look-out points towards danger—whatever it is—not towards where he wants the boat to head.

Sound cannot be trusted in fog. Sound travels best in a homogeneous atmosphere, in clear air or in thick fog. It is patchy fog that is the worst problem, and even the loud fog signals used at pier head signal stations can be difficult to identify.

Apart from the ability to hear, the knowledge of where you are is the next sense to concentrate upon. It is astonishingly easy to loose all sense of direction in fog, and in light winds (which are common in fog) there is even

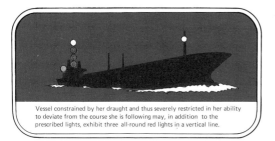

Vessel constrained by her draught and thus severely restricted in her ability to deviate from the course she is following may, in addition to the prescribed lights, exhibit three all-round red lights in a vertical line.

Vessel making way, but, by the nature of her work, restricted in her ability to manoeuvre.

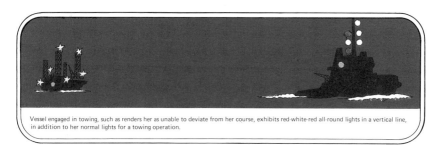

Vessel engaged in towing, such as renders her as unable to deviate from her course, exhibits red-white-red all-round lights in a vertical line, in addition to her normal lights for a towing operation.

Power driven vessel when towing, when length of the tow is less than 200 metres.

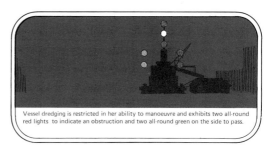

Vessel dredging is restricted in her ability to manoeuvre and exhibits two all-round red lights to indicate an obstruction and two all-round green on the side to pass.

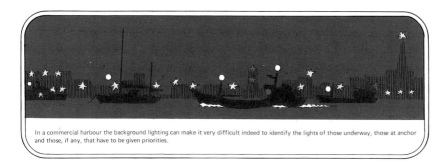

In a commercial harbour the background lighting can make it very difficult indeed to identify the lights of those underway, those at anchor and those, if any, that have to be given priorities.

FIG. 6.2. *Vessels restricted in their ability to manoeuvre, constrained by their draught and night confusions*

more of a problem because the helmsman does not have the steadying effect of the wind on his face to give him his general sense of direction.

In Chapter 5 the importance of having an approximate compass course "in the mind", even if steering by eye, was stressed. In fog a compass course becomes a necessity. Motor boats that are steered from within a wheelhouse have even greater difficulties. The helmsman has no "feel" for the weather and often he has pretty poor visibility as well. On the other hand, motor yachts are likely to have the advantage of an autopilot to keep the course steady.

Much is written, and rightly so, of the dangers of sailing along under the control of an autopilot and not keeping a proper look-out. However, although the warning is important, I submit that a short-handed motor yacht is far better off if the helmsman steers a steady course under his "pilot" and keeps all his senses available as look-out.

Those with radar as an additional aid are in a different category—and more about that later—but for normal, low visibility navigation those with an enclosed wheelhouse are well advised to arrange the controls so that they can stand just outside the wheelhouse door, on occasion, and keep an "outside" look-out while the autopilot is holding the course.

Heavy rain—or even light rain for those who wear glasses—is another hazard, and for that, as well as for general rest for the eyes, I use ski-goggles. Clear ski-goggles (designed to fit over spectacles) can be wiped clean (or reasonably clean) far more readily than can the glasses themselves.

It is while entering harbour that these points matter most. The skipper/navigator often needs to go below—for a momentary glance at his chart. It is then that details like clean spectacles really matter. I keep a spare pair of reading glasses by the chart table. With that system, at least I know my reading glasses are clean!

Signals

The Collision Regulations are perfectly clear regarding what sound signals a vessel should make. What is not so clear is whether the modern shipmaster makes them and whether he would hear those made by small craft anyway.

The lack of regular signalling by sound is regrettable. In one sense it is the "man-walking-with-a-fawn-coat-in-the-country-lane" syndrome over again. The shipmaster is in touch with the harbour authority VTS. The VTS may have just broadcast the fact that "so-and-so" is about to turn round to approach berth "such-and-such". Thus the shipmaster seems to feel that those that should know, do know. He forgets that small craft need to hear sound signals to help to identify "who" is doing "what".

It will be a long time before sound signalling is no longer needed. It is not the regulations concerning sound that are wrong, it is the fact that harbour authorities do not enforce them.

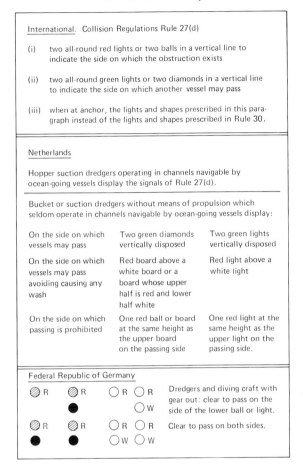

International: Collision Regulations Rule 27(d)

(i) two all-round red lights or two balls in a vertical line to indicate the side on which the obstruction exists

(ii) two all-round green lights or two diamonds in a vertical line to indicate the side on which another vessel may pass

(iii) when at anchor, the lights and shapes prescribed in this paragraph instead of the lights and shapes prescribed in Rule 30.

Netherlands

Hopper suction dredgers operating in channels navigable by ocean-going vessels display the signals of Rule 27(d).

Bucket or suction dredgers without means of propulsion which seldom operate in channels navigable by ocean-going vessels display:

On the side on which vessels may pass	Two green diamonds vertically disposed	Two green lights vertically disposed
On the side on which vessels may pass avoiding causing any wash	Red board above a white board or a board whose upper half is red and lower half white	Red light above a white light
On the side on which passing is prohibited	One red ball or board at the same height as the upper board on the passing side	One red light at the same height as the upper light on the passing side.

Federal Republic of Germany

Dredgers and diving craft with gear out: clear to pass on the side of the lower ball or light.

Clear to pass on both sides.

FIG. 6.3. *Dredger signals*

For small craft themselves, the position is complex. In the first place, there are very few foghorns on the market that are capable of making a signal likely to be heard by commercial vessels. Nevertheless, there are electric, compressed air horns that are suitable, and the Swedish-made "Tyfon" foghorn is available as an electric or hand-pumped horn. It is eminently suitable for a marine atmosphere (I had one on my previous boat for 17 years without more attention than an occasional drop of oil), and it gives a blast of over 125 decibels. At that level the sound is likely to be heard at least 0.5 nautical mile—by someone outside a wheelhouse. Thus there are answers to the problem, even if they are not always easy ones.

Most small craft use the type of hand-held horn mounted on a small aerosol can. They are reasonably cheap to buy and are convenient. However, they are not much use as a fog signal, even if they do serve a purpose for signalling in a close-quarters situation. A hand-held "aerosol" horn is highly unlikely to be heard at more than 2–3 cables in even a moderate wind.

The rules require vessels of over 12 metres l.o.a. to be equipped with whistles (fog horns) capable of being heard at 0.5 nautical mile. Vessels of less than 12 metres are required to have "some other means of making an efficient sound signal". The subject is complex. It is discussed in greater detail in *Yacht Signalling*, and the specifications for the volume of sound required are given in the appendix to the Collision Regulations.

Those that wish to equip small craft so that they have a good chance of being heard at something approaching 1 nautical mile should remember that the horn part of the unit is most efficient if mounted well above the deck level. Also, it is far better to have two horns, sounded together, so long as the frequency difference is at least 2/3 octave. To achieve a comparable range with one, the sound pressure level has to be at least 6 decibels higher than with two.

The fact that most small craft owners turn a "blind eye" to the details of the Collision Regulation requirements does not remove the fact that on rare occasions the ability to signal "loud and clear" in bad visibility is a major safety factor. Also, despite the "aerosol can" convenience, the propellant—freon gas—is likely to freeze up at the trigger if used repeatedly in a cold atmosphere.

A vessel under sail, in restricted visibility, is allowed the privileges of a vessel not-under-command or a vessel restricted in her ability to manoeuvre (among other categories). Thus, without an efficient means of signalling, that privilege cannot be claimed.

Another privilege that can be claimed by any vessel is that of a vessel at anchor. The normal day and night signals were discussed in Chapter 4, but in fog the situation is different.

A vessel at anchor, except those of less than 12 metres l.o.a., is required to "... ring the bell rapidly for about 5 seconds ... " at intervals of not more than 1 minute. But that too is a regulation which is rarely observed as it should be. However, before commenting further on that aspect of the problem, it is useful to note that a vessel of less than 12 metres may make "some other efficient sound signal ... "!

The previous clause requiring the bell goes on to require a gong "... sounded rapidly for about 5 seconds in the after part of the vessel ... " (which again would greatly help the safe passage of any other vessel trying to "feel her way" past), but the rule then continues with: "A vessel at anchor may, in addition, sound three blasts in succession, namely one short, one prolonged and one short blast to give warning of her position and of the possibility of collision to an approaching craft."

There, in my opinion, lies the reasonable answer for small craft. Traditionally the small fishing boat used to bang a spanner inside an iron saucepan (and I have once seen, and heard, that done), but the days of heavy iron saucepans have gone too, so it is a little difficult to advise. If a bell is used, it has to be one with a diameter of about 200 millimetres to give a worthwhile sound. The "toys" so often seen on the after bulkhead of a wheelhouse are really decoration.

On the other hand, the sound signal—"R"—is best thought of as the answering signal (Romeo being "Received" in radiotelephony). In effect, it is telling an approaching vessel that her approach has been "received", audibly. A blast on a foghorn signalling "R" might not be understood by all, but it is most certainly "...some other efficient sound signal...".

Radar

One of the greatest difficulties for the small craft navigator in poor visibility is his inability to judge distance. He might see a light, or the loom of a light, but there will rarely be any reference points to help to tell him how far off it is. However, although small craft radar is usually considered a collision-avoidance "tool", it is radar's ability to give an accurate distance off that is really far more important.

In theory, as well as in practice on larger vessels, radar is also a highly efficient collision-avoidance "tool" because it is comparatively straightforward to calculate if a particular blip on the screen is on a collision course or not. In practice, in a small craft life can be very different.

In the first place any calculation concerning risk of collision must depend on a steady course and speed. Thus, to be of any use at all for the necessary calculation of a risk of collision, the helmsman must hold an accurate course or the vessel must be under the control of an accurate autopilot. Secondly, the small craft navigator rarely has the facility to plot the blips that he sees because, especially in a harbour environment, there are likely to be too many "possible" targets to plot.

Next, it has to be remembered that, even if the helm is being controlled by an efficient autopilot and the skipper is occupied plotting on the radar screen, there is still the urgent need for someone to keep a visual look-out. It is all too easy to assume that everything will show up on the radar scan, but for the usual types of small craft radar in use in 1984, that is far from the case. Small yachts, without large radar reflectors, and small fishing craft often do not show at all.

Finally, when assessing small craft radar, the problem of the ambient level of light must be considered. There are conditions when the sky above is still bright—although the fog, at sea level, may restrict visibility to a cable or so. In those circumstances, a navigator using the Decca 060 type of small craft radar will find that when he buries his face in the screen's visor he may need half a minute or more before his eyes adapt to the light on the screen. Similarly, when he removes his face from the visor, the bright, overhead light almost hurts his eyes, because he has emerged from almost total darkness.

Furthermore, while peering at his screen and trying to assess the approach of a "target" a mile or two away, he has not been keeping a proper look-out at short range.

None of what has just been written is intended to decry the value of radar as an aid. In certain conditions it would be foolish to try to make a passage without it. Nevertheless, radar is by no means the automatic solution that some seem to believe.

Fortunately, science is fast coming to the aid of the small craft navigator. The latest sets, particularly the Mars RM radar which has an excellent daylight viewing screen (as well as other interesting features), eliminates most of those problems. There is still just the same need to keep a steady course and just the same difficulty in plotting "risk-of-collision" triangles. However, the facility to glance at the screen, rather than have to bury one's face in a visor, is a major improvement.

At night the advantage is not so great, because the older type of screen can be used more effectively to glance at. But for all small craft radar there is still the need to proceed with caution. Prior to the introduction of small craft Decca position fixing receivers, I would have placed the ability of a small craft radar to give an accurate position at the top of any list of advantages. Now, with Decca available, the priorities are different.

To summarize: small craft radar is still an extremely important aid in bad visibility, and it allows a man to shift a berth or to make a passage in conditions when it would otherwise be very hazardous. However, what it does not do is provide a simple and foolproof collision-avoidance display.

Radar Reflectors

Unfortunately many small craft owners still look upon a radar reflector as something which (if he remembers) he will hoist in the rigging in bad visibility.

What he fails to appreciate is that a merchant ship is likely to be "looking", from the radar scan point of view, at a range far beyond that which the small craft will consider necessary. Thus, just because visibility is still say 5 cables, does not in any way imply that a reflector is not needed.

In broken water a yacht could have disappeared into the clutter at the centre of a poorly adjusted set at half a mile and if she had not showed up at say 2 miles, or more, she might never be "seen" on the screen at all.

Sailing in a commercial environment, in any type of poor visibility, without a good, large reflector hoisted correctly, is like riding a bicycle on a main highway in thick fog. It *might* be legal, but it is highly dangerous.

Unfortunately, because of the nature of the science, small reflectors are almost useless. The echo varies as the fourth power of the size of the reflector, and thus an octahedral reflector of less than about 400 millimetres across a diagonal is highly suspect. Nowadays there are good reflectors to be had which are clusters of more than one corner reflector, encapsulated in a g.r.p. skin. But even with them the smallest one available is somewhat suspect.

For cruising boats, for large racing boats and for all motor boats the only satisfactory answer is a permanent mounting aloft. Small sailing yachts **might** justify having to hoist, when necessary, to cut down wind resistance. Everyone else ought to mount permanently and unless there is an obviously suitable position, such as between twin backstays, for the permanent mounting, I believe the answer is a direct mounting on the mast—without risk of chafe or fouling—and an acceptance of the fact that there will be a very limited echo in one direction because of the blind sector created by the mast itself masking the signal.

Remember, too, that in these days of harbour radar surveillance, a well-positioned reflector can be a useful aid, even in bright sunlight. In ports where the VTS asks for small craft to report—as at the Hoek of Holland—it is a great deal easier for the operator to identify those showing a reasonable echo.

Aid Memoire for Bad Visibility

Remain especially alert.

Cut out all stray lights at night.

If sailing, keep the auxiliary ready for an instant start.

If motoring, remember that a look-out forward can help, because he can hear so much better than in the cockpit.

Use an autopilot to hold the course steady when possible.

Keep an especially careful check on the position.

Listen to the harbour radio all the time.

Remember that a change of plan that introduces a few hours at anchor—until the fog clears—might easily be the wisest course if there is a suitable anchorage well clear of any fairway. But if anchoring in a harbour because the fog is too thick to make it safe to proceed, consider the possibility of reporting your position and intention to the harbour office. In some places it would certainly not be necessary, but in others a report could be of assistance.

Seamanship at Close Quarters

SAILING, like all other sports, attracts a multiplicity of "how to" books. How to build, how to maintain, how to convert, and how to improve are some of the commoner subjects, but without question the commonest theme of all is how to make the boat more efficient, how to make her go faster.

To a degree that is as it should be. Sailing is largely a competitive sport because even if boats are not competing against each other they are competing against the elements. However, there is one overriding feature of all sailing in a close-quarters situation. It is often more important to learn how to keep full control **while the boat is going slowly** than it is to make her go faster.

In one of the classic cruising books of all time—Claude Worth's *Yacht Navigation and Voyaging*—the author, writing in the 1920s, summarizes the entry to a port with:

> "Unless it is a large natural harbour where there will be plenty of room, it is usually advisable to take in the gaff topsail and perhaps one of the headsails while still outside. But almost invariably the mainsail should be carried right up to the anchorage in order to have the yacht well under command."

There is a lot of good sense in that, even if the best advice today would be completely different. The key phrase is contained in the last nine words.

It is common to see a man drop too much sail so that he hardly has control and may lose all steerage way. It is even commoner to watch a man with far too much sail. He cannot see properly under a genoa. The crew cannot move about on deck properly because of the angle of heel. Nothing is ready. There are no sail tiers on the boom, in readiness for when the mainsail will be lowered. If the fenders are on deck at all, they are probably not secured in the right positions and certainly not at the right height. The warps are not at-the-ready, and the anchor (which should always be ready to let go within a few seconds) may not even be shackled to its chain!

To make a film of that scenario it would not be necessary to set up any special arrangements: merely take a camera to any crowded berth or anchorage on any windy day.

The advice in Worth's book about lowering sail is still sound, even if the reduction is unlikely to be the lowering of a gaff topsail. The guidelines for any entry into any area where close-quarters manoeuvring is probable is much the same as it was then: it is the circumstances and the equipment available that has changed.

Harbours where small vessels under sail can press on under full sail and then round up to an anchorage—once inside the harbour mouth—shoot up head to wind, to lose way, and drop an anchor are rare. Of course, there are still many natural harbours where, like in Plymouth Sound, Falmouth Road, or Milford Haven, there is plenty of water, clear of any dredged channels or commercial fairways, and where it would be unwise **not** to carry adequate sail until well into any anchorage area. On the other hand, there are far more harbours where, today, the only prudent course to take is one of extreme caution.

Boats rarely become damaged at sea: it is manoeuvring at close quarters that causes most damage, and it is low-speed manoeuvring that this chapter is all about.

Crossing Narrow Channels

Chapter 4 explained the implications of Rule 9 of the Collision Regulations. There are occasions when any small craft must wait until there is time for them to cross a particular channel without impeding the passage of another vessel. And if anyone feels that that is unjustified, he should look to the skies. At any busy airport an approaching aircraft is required to proceed to a "Holding" facility—London airport has no less than four "Holding Stacks"—and the aircraft is then allowed to proceed, as a result of a highly complicated control system where the particular navigational system onboard an aircraft, her type, her speed, and so on, is taken into account before she is given permission to land.

At sea we already have the beginnings of that type of "control" in that in many large commercial ports a shipmaster will be asked to time his arrival at a particular place so that the pilot, the tug or the berth is free. Equally, in rivers and canals like the Niew Waterweg to Rotterdam or the River Thames to London, ships will adjust their rate of progress to avoid meeting others at awkward moments when a channel is blocked by a ship swinging or when a lock gate is closed. Small craft, on the other hand, are their own "traffic controllers". It is the skipper, in most circumstances, who has to assess a situation, and the principle of the aircraft "holding area" is one that deserves attention.

Chapter 4 explained the implications of Rule 9 in some detail. We have the situation where certain classes of vessel " ... shall not cross ... " and that is why a "holding area" concept needs to be introduced into the yachtsman's thinking. It is not suggested that there will be many, if any, actual marked areas, but, just as we already have recommended, routes for small craft marked on a chart, it is not unreasonable to consider recommended areas designated for waiting while some larger vessel passes.

Once again Harwich is a useful example of that type of thinking. Charts Nos. 2052 and 2693 both mark a small craft recommended route across The Shelf, off Harwich Town. There is plenty of water for even the largest yacht—and, as it happens, the small craft route is actually shorter than the deep water channel. However, having crossed The Shelf, any vessel bound up the River Orwell must cross the east–west dredged channel used by all the passenger ferries bound for Parkestone Quay, between the Guard Buoy and Shotley Spit.

In view of the implications of Rule 9, it makes sense to consider the area immediately to the south of the Guard Buoy and the area to the north-west of Shotley Spit beacon as "waiting areas": stretches of water where a small craft might pause before crossing (Fig. 7.1).

In practice there would usually be no need to wait at all in nine passages out of ten. It is a state of mind that recognizes that there will be occasions when waiting is necessary that matters.

Slowing and Stopping

Our forefathers looked upon heaving-to as a normal part of sailing. Today the art of stopping, which still under sail, is almost lost. However, before describing the art itself there are many other ways of "stopping" in a close-quarters situation that deserve consideration.

Assuming a small craft was about to cross a dredged channel and the skipper realized that he might not have enough time to cross without impeding the safe passage of another vessel navigating within the channel. The most practical manoeuvre of all is to appreciate the situation long enough beforehand so that his speed of approach—to the point when he actually crosses—is reduced: in other words, he slows down.

In the regulations any action by a give-way vessel has to be " . . . positive, made in ample time and with due regard to the observance of good seamanship".

Rule 8 (which is really very sound) goes on to stress that any alteration of course or speed " . . . be large enough to be readily apparent to another vessel . . . ". However, although that obviously applies to two merchant ships, it is not so obviously relevant to a large passenger ferry steaming at say 12 knots—even in harbour—and a sailing yacht sailing, at most, at a quarter of that speed.

The key to the sensible answer lies in the next paragraph of the rule, Rule 8(e). It reads:

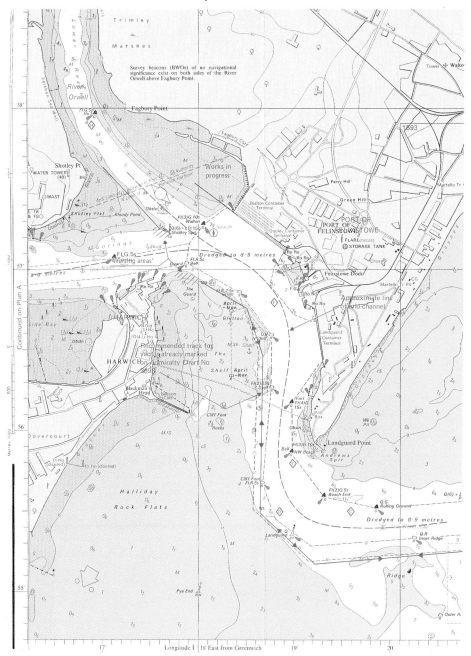

FIG. 7.1. *The concept of a waiting area. A recommended track for yachts entering Harwich keeps small craft clear of the channel. However most continue north up the River Orwell and thus the shaded areas suggest a "Waiting area" that yachts might use while double-checking that it is safe to cross the dredged channel between Shotley Point and Harwich Guard buoy*

"If necessary to avoid collision or allow more time to assess the situation, a vessel shall slacken her speed or take all way off by stopping, or reversing her means of propulsion."

The situation under review is when a sailing yacht might want to pause to allow another to pass ahead. The only worthwhile advice is to try to make it obvious to the other vessel what action is being taken. A genoa sheet let fly, for example—or a genoa lowered to the foredeck while the yacht "jogged along" under mainsail only—would be perfectly obvious "signals" to the Officer of the Watch of the larger vessel that the yacht was not pressing-on trying to cross ahead.

Whether the sailing yacht—the give-way vessel—was actually sailing or was motor sailing makes little difference. When the action of giving way implies an alteration of course, that alteration is in itself a signal. However, when the action is merely slowing down, then let that too be recognizable for what it is.

The objective should be to avoid causing doubt or confusion in the mind of the skipper of the stand-on vessel. Sound signals do not apply when there is no alteration of course (or no question of applying astern propulsion), and sound is highly unlikely to be the answer for the circumstances being considered. There is no question of hand signalling—as there might be on the road. There is no question of looking to radio as the means of signalling for these circumstances; as has already been explained. Thus, all that is left is to make it as clear as the circumstances permit that the intention is to act as a give-way vessel until the danger has passed.

If sailing with a foresail slacked away, so that it has lost all drive, is the first step towards slowing down, lowering the foresail is the second step. A bold alteration of course—say at least 60 degrees—might be considered the next stage. A motor-sailer or a motor yacht might make such a bold alteration and then steam slowly straight into wind or tide for the few minutes that it might be prudent for a pause. However, do not forget Claude Worth's advice " . . . to have the yacht well under command".

In light to moderate conditions almost any manoeuvre will be comparatively easy to perform. In fresh to strong winds, on the other hand, it is surprisingly difficult to slow down and yet still keep proper control. It is here that heaving-to comes into its own.

Heaving-to

Like picking up a man overboard or riding out a storm, heaving-to is an operation that everyone has heard about but remarkably few have ever experienced. The first two undertakings are of a type that will probably not have to be "enjoyed" by more than one in a hundred yachtsman, but heaving-to is something that can serve a useful purpose many times a season. The circumstances will not always be the same, but the method of achieving the state of being hove-to is nearly the same, regardless of wind strength or sea state.

For those who have never experienced the manoeuvre, the objective is simple and the effect remarkable. The objective is to steady the boat by keeping the wind on one side, or the other, of the sails—so that there is no flogging or change of direction—but at the same time to cancel the drive from those sails. The affect is remarkable, because the difference in the motion of the boat "before" and "after" has to be experienced to be believed.

In the days of sail, heaving-to was a necessary part of life. In shallow water a vessel can usually anchor, if she needs to stop, but in deep water—or in any depth when the need to stop is short-lived—heaving-to was the norm.

For traditional rigs the manoeuvre meant backing the sails on the main mast but leaving the sails on the foremast to fill. Sail "A" cancels sail "B" while (still with tradition) the fore and aft sails on the mizzen would have kept the ship heading in a steady direction on a close reach, even though progress was very slow.

Everybody with any deep love for the sea must have a mental picture of the scene—so loved by artists—and usually captioned "Waiting for the pilot" or some such wording. A three-masted barque lies, hove-to, with a sailing pilot cutter in the foreground—also hove-to—and the pilot's "gig" rowing across between the two.

Romantic stuff. Pilots today are more likely to be transferred by helicopter without the ship having even to do more than slow down, but the principle remains.

To heave-to without a major alteration of course usually means hauling the foresail aback and slacking away the main sheet. However, a modern foresail is often a large, overlapping sail and it is not always as easy as it sounds to haul it to weather. A far easier method, when the circumstances permit, is merely to put the helm down, come about, but not to alter the foresail sheets at all. Thus the yacht is tacked, but, because the foresail remains where it was, it is now fully aback.

The amount that the mainsheet might have to be slacked away (to reduce its drive) and the amount that the helm might have to be held down (to reduce unwanted speed) will vary from vessel to vessel. In general, the longer keeled, heavier displacement yacht will lie more quietly than will her lighter, more lively, and more fin-keeled younger sister. However, I have never yet found a yacht that would not lie *reasonably* quietly, even if some seem to need the attention of a man in the cockpit to "tweak" this or that, and others seem to lie as if glued to the sea bed.

Another way of sailing slowly, and one that is very rarely practised except by racing dinghies before a start, is to lie—across the wind—with both main and foresail sheets slacked right away. The sails will flog, of course, so that it is not a method to be practised for more than a short period at a time, but it is surprisingly effective.

Almost all vessels, from the *Queen Mary* to a tiny rowing boat, will lie across wind and waves if left totally to their own devices. Our forefathers called that laying a-hull, and to this day it is a recognized procedure for extreme conditions. In really strong winds, when further attempts to make progress become difficult, the manoeuvre is similar to that of heaving-to. There is little or no propulsion—because the sails are not set—and the pressure of the wind on the superstructure and on the mast and rigging acts to dampen what would otherwise be a very violent motion indeed.

In harbour, the idea of taking off all sail and lying across the wind would not have the same effect, because, without the steadying affect of a strong wind in the rigging, the boat might "dance-about" too much. However, in the version just described—with all sail set, but flogging—progress is minimal and the motion usually acceptable. To recover way, even a slight adjustment, to haul in one or other sheet, will immediately restore steerage way.

This manoeuvre can be very useful as a means of taking off all way, but still keeping control immediately after an anchor has been weighed; but more about that later. Here the object is to slow down while approaching a waiting-area, a buoy or a marina berth.

Earlier in this chapter the idea of a waiting area was mentioned in connection with a crossing of a channel or fairway. However, the principle of slowing down applies equally as well for many other circumstances. If the crew, or the helmsman, have to rush about on deck with ropes, fenders or a boat hook, the manoeuvre has failed.

Of course it is occasionally necessary to act very quickly, but it is really the reaction time that is important. So long as the approach to any buoy or berth is **under control**, the slower the approach, the greater the time there is for the crew to react.

Picking Up a Buoy

Once upon a time every manoeuvre had to be undertaken either under sail or under the power of a man's arms. Today most yachts have engines of some sort or another and those that do not—such as dinghies and day-boats—can resort to a paddle for the final stage of coming alongside a jetty or a slip. However, anchoring and the picking up of a buoy are still manoeuvres that can often be undertaken under sail, even if the somewhat more hazardous business of coming alongside a berth is usually undertaken under power.

Almost everything that has been described about sailing slowly—but still keeping control—applies to the manoeuvre of picking up a buoy. The objective is to arrive at the buoy with practically no way on at all: it is as simple as that. However, remember that there are still two types of mooring buoy and they need to be approached in a slightly different manner.

The older type of small craft mooring consisted of a ground chain with another (usually lighter) chain attached to which the yacht will ride. However, that riding chain will lie on the bottom when not in use, and there will be a rope attached to its upper end leading to a small buoy at the surface. With that arrangement the mooring buoy will be small—it merely supports the rope that leads to the riding chain—and it will have to be picked up as the yacht approaches.

That method of arranging a mooring was common until recently, but it has the great disadvantage that, even when the actual buoy is on deck, there is still a length of rope to be hauled aboard. Not only does that hauling aboard occupy time—and the weight of the riding chain has to be taken as well—the buoy will usually have been lying down tide on the buoy rope. Thus the yacht would still have to be moving up tide at the moment the buoy was picked up on deck to allow time for the next stage of the operation.

Today that type of mooring is rarely seen. Synthetic materials, both for the buoy and for the mooring, have superseded the traditional arrangements. The riding "chain" (and it might itself be all or part synthetic) will be shackled directly to the underside of a large buoy to which the yacht will lie without having to pick the buoy on deck. Whether there is merely an eye on the top, to which the yacht makes fast her own lines, or whether there is already a short length of suitable rope attached (waiting to be picked out of the water) makes little difference to the speed of approach. The buoy will be lying in the water at almost the same spot as it will be after the yacht has made herself fast to it. All the helmsman has to do is to adjust the speed of approach to bring the yacht to a position where she is stationary over the ground at the moment that the bow reaches the buoy.

Note that the position is in relation to the ground. In tidal waters that position may well be when the yacht is still moving through the water at a knot or two. That is the great challenge in the manoeuvre. To be able to round up to a buoy in fresh conditions, to bring the bow exactly to the position of the buoy at the moment when the yacht is stationary over the bottom and to have time for the helmsman to **walk** (not run) to the bow to pick up the rope on the buoy without effort, and without rush, is among the most satisfying operations of all.

In contrast, the foredeck panic-parties that are so common need little description. Do not send a crew forward until a few moments before he is going to be needed there.

The "harpoonist" exhibitions, with crew crouched in the bow pulpit—boathook at the ready—merely block the helmsman's view. If there is a job to do on the foredeck, let it be done, but only one person should ever stand there, his position with his back to the fore side of the mast, facing forward.

Stood there, his bulk makes little difference to the arc of obstruction to forward vision that the helmsman has to suffer already.

Another common mistake is to use boathooks that are far too short. On a small family cruising boat a pair of boathooks each 2 metres long should be the absolute minimum, and to have two 3 metres long—when a suitable stowage can be found for them—is a blessing.

Boathooks MUST have a proper stowage, and they so rarely do that special thought needs to be given to the problem. The Dutch—sailing most in semi-sheltered waters—frequently stow really long hooks vertically in the shrouds with a small hoop top and bottom to retain them. However, for sea-going, a more rigid stowage is better and for the length of boathook recommended a position on deck may be the only answer.

"U"-shaped wooden chocks are the most likely answer, but not merely at say one-quarter and three-quarter lengths along the pole. That leaves both ends as potential "rope catchers" and, in any case, the "U" chock needs a rubber "shock cord" grommet to hook over the top of the pole to keep it in place at all times.

One answer is to use the spike at the end of the boathook as one of the stowages and let the other end also have some form of masking.

It must be possible to drag a rope or a sail across the deck without picking up snags. At the "other" end—the end normally held in the hand—a rubber cap, such as is manufactured for the bottom end of an invalid's crutch, is ideal. Then, when fending off, the boathook can be end-for-ended and used without risk of damaging the finish of another boat.

There is yet one other type of mooring buoy that has not been mentioned, the commercial ship steel buoy which, on occasion, is almost as large as the yacht that wants to lie to it. Rarely will there be an opportunity to use such a buoy, and they are far from ideal "bed-fellows" anyway. Such a buoy may have a displacement as great as the yacht, so that even a slight "nudge" can cause considerable damage.

The best answer is to avoid any buoy of that type. However, when it *is* necessary to lie to anything that might cause damage if the yacht rubs against it, a drogue—hung over the stern—can transform a situation. The problem occurs in tidal waters if the tide and wind are from opposite quadrants. Each time the wind picks up, the yacht will be blown on to her own mooring, but the addition of a drogue makes the influence of the tide that much greater.

It is not a total answer, but with a drogue of say 0.6 metre diameter the difference is remarkable.

Drogues at Harbour Mouths

Logically this chapter would now consider slowing down to come alongside a berth. However, with slow speed as the theme and harbour behaviour as the subject it is worth dwelling on the use of drogues for the purpose for which they were intended. A drogue to keep a yacht from blowing up on to her own buoy is merely a convenience. A drogue for use on harbour entry, on the other hand, can make all the difference between life and death.

Drogues—or sea anchors—have such a mixed reputation that there will be much misunderstanding if the definitions are not clear. For what follows a "sea anchor" is a device used in very bad weather and in deep water and hung from the bow. In theory, a boat can "anchor" herself in the sea and make slow progress "crabwise" and partially stern first with the bow to the wave crests. Few have ever experienced that state, and of those that have few have much that is good to say of the method.

A "drogue", on the other hand, is something streamed from the stern and, as used by the heavier Royal National Lifeboat Institution vessels, towed astern, even if they are still using power ahead. The objective, therefore, whether lying to a drogue under greatly reduced sail, lying to a drogue under bare poles or steaming ahead against a drogue "towed" astern, is twofold. It is to keep the stern steady, towards the seas and to slow down what might occasionally be a dangerous "spurt" of speed.

Here too drogues have had a very mixed reception, and it was not until some very extensive research was done by the National Maritime Institute (NMI)—following the loss of life in the 1979 Fastnet Race—that the behaviour of a drogue was properly understood.

As chairman of a small advisory committee, set up by the Department of Trade and Industry to advise on some small craft research, I was in an unusually good position to assess the importance of that research. The research was into the behaviour of small craft life rafts—a subject not a part of this book—but the spin-off that is highly relevant concerns the behaviour of drogues themselves.

In really bad weather offshore I now am convinced that, subject to certain provisos, a drogue (of a particular design) on a really long warp would be an enormous advantage in slowing down a small craft which was otherwise running down the face of advancing waves too fast. The use of a drogue for those conditions (which have nothing to do with this book) might prevent the danger, in those extreme conditions, of being "bowled over" as the bow buries and the stern is picked up by the advancing wave crest. However, the reason for mentioning the phenomenon here is that in certain weather conditions and in certain ports a very similar condition arises.

The "certain weather conditions" refers to fresh to strong onshore winds, especially on an ebb tide. The certain ports refer to harbours like Whitby and Salcombe where there is a shallow bar but deep water close to seaward of it. In those conditions a really dangerous short steep sea can build up—over a short period—and the most dangerous part of the situation is that, as seen from seaward, short breaking seas on a bar often look comparatively harmless until you are among them.

In the conditions described, the crest of these waves—waves that are generated by the bulk of the water being forced up on to the shoal area by the wind when the tidal stream ebb exacerbates the situation—moves remarkably fast. Fifteen knots would be no exaggeration when the waves further offshore were still comparatively harmless.

It is for those—specialized—conditions that I believe a drogue can make an enormous difference, but even then it must be made clear that "any old thing" will have little effect.

To summarize months of model and full-scale trials of drogues in a few sentences, the drogue—a cone-shaped "canvas" device held by a four-part bridle—is still today much the same in general appearance as the type used for generations of seamen. In fact, it is different in one of two vital ways .

In the past drogues have been sworn by and sworn at by different groups, and the true facts were difficult to assess because so very few had worthwhile experience of using them. All my life I had been mystified why some men should feel so strongly one way and some so strongly the other. The reason I now know is that unless made in a particular manner the drogue is "tripped" in the wave crest and rendered useless. However, the phenomenon is further complicated by the fact that, having been tripped—and tangled—by one wave, the same drogue may well be returned to its former "efficiency" by a wave or two later (See Fig. 7.2).

The problem, shown in Fig. 7.2a, is that the apex of the "canvas" cone is picked up by the rotational movement of the water particles, in the crest of a steep wave, and thrown back over itself. The apex is thrown into the bridle, at the mouth, and an efficient breaking device is instantly converted into a small bundle of tangled canvas. That, naturally enough, has practically no breaking effect on the vessel's forward progress.

It is a steady load on the drogue warp that is required, not an intermittent one. That is available only if the drogue is doing its job **all** the time.

The difference between the traditional canvas cone and the type of drogue now fitted to Department Approved life rafts is that the latter are manufactured from a porous material—which steadies the cone as it is dragged through the water—and the bridle is fitted with an anti-tangle "barrier" around the four-part bridle. For mine, I followed the advice given by the Icelandic Coastguard, and put a mesh around the bridle. Anything will do so long as the apex can never become entangled in the bridle itself. Undoubtedly porosity helps, but I believe that for the type of family cruising yacht that is under review, with a displacement of 5 to 7 tonnes, a cone of about 0.6 metre diameter would be the minimum to say 1 metre diameter for the larger boat.

With that, loads of up to 500 kgf might be generated. Thus the warp needs to be led to a winch, and it is a vital part of the arrangement that the drogue is streamed well aft, ideally in the back of the second wave astern. There is no "magic" length for a drogue warp, but a nylon drum of multi-plait of say 75 metres might be an absolute minimum to consider.

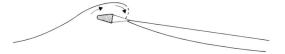

There is an orbital motion of the water in the crest of a wave and the apex of a drogue can be picked up and "thrown" up-and-over, so that the drogue becomes tangled in its own bridle.

(*a*)

Recovery line

Towing warp

Icelandic Coast Guard trials of drogues for liferafts not only confirmed the overwhelming importance of having proper drogues but proved that a piece of netting, or a light line spliced in as a spiral (as shown here), prevents the cone from becoming tangled.

(*b*)
FIG. 7.2. *Drogues:* (*a*) *in wave;* (*b*) *anti-tangle cone*

Of course I am aware that practically nobody carries a suitable drogue, few carry a suitable warp and the occasions when it might be needed are very rare. The only logical alternative is to stay away in the conditions described. If equipped with high speed, such as in an Atlantic 21 lifeboat, and if the necessary skills are available, it is possible to "skate away" from advancing waves for the comparatively localized areas when a drogue might be used. However, family yachts do not have high speed, nor do the crews have skilled training.

I believe a drogue is highly desirable for any sailing boat likely to meet the conditions described and a necessity for any motor yacht. The RNLI crew do not stream drogues as a matter of course in their slower speed lifeboats, and for the conditions I have described, without having good reason.

Few, if any, chandlers stock the type of drogue that I believe is desirable. It need not be nearly as clumsy as some ship's lifeboat "sea anchors". The mouth needs to be held open with a "hoop", but the hoop need not be particularly strong because it carries little load. The bridle on mine is made from 7 millimetre nylon, because, by definition, it carries load only when the load is spread four ways. Any "friendly" sailmaker, who still does some hand work, could make something suitable, but I do *not* believe that precise dimensions are critical.

The RNLI (and tradition) says that the apex has a tripping line attached, which can be used for recovery. However, discussions with those who have used a drogue "in anger" suggest that the tripping line itself can be a hazard and that the moment while transferring the load from warp to tripping line can cause tangle problems.

For use on ocean voyages the advice might be different, but for harbour entry, when the conditions suggest there might be a dangerously steep sea on a bar, my choice would be to heave to, or slow right down, while outside and stream a drogue *without* any tripping line, then gather way again and sail in towing the drogue on as long a line as possible. You will lose a couple of knots of course, but that is what it is all about. Something has to generate the load on the warp, and it is the reduction of speed that does it.

Perhaps I have written too much on such a specialized subject, but for harbour entry, in the circumstances described, I am convinced the use of a drogue can convert a really hazardous operation into a safe one.

I have never had to use my drogue "in anger", but I have used it in strong following winds as an experiment, both under sail and under power. The effect is staggering.

Coming Alongside

As was mentioned earlier, there are not many occasions today when our family cruising boat will want to come alongside under sail. With a well-drilled crew and with reasonable room it is more than possible, it becomes a part of the challenge of sailing. However, the norm is to drop the sails when still clear of the berth itself and make the final approach under power.

As a young boy I still have a clear memory of walking down to the end of The Cobb, at Lyme Regis, and standing fascinated as a big trading ketch sailed up to the harbour mouth. She rounded up and dropped anchor close off the end of the pier. Two men rowed ashore in her clinker dinghy, towing a big "grass" warp, made it fast to the granite bollard on The Cobb (which is still there) and then rowed back to haul themselves alongside, with the warp led to a windlass.

That was how sailing ships around our coasts had been handled for centuries. It was slow but reliable. In those days, if conditions of wind or tide were not right, you waited until they changed.

Today the method of propulsion has changed, but there is still more than one lesson to be learnt from that traditional way of coming alongside.

The first part of the lesson is to take things in a logical order. It is amazingly common to see a yacht round up, to go alongside, and then for the crew to start dashing about looking for the warps or fenders. Next would be the problem created by not assessing the predominant force, wind or tidal stream.

Almost always it is best to approach against the stream, because the tidal stream then becomes the natural brake. The point that few seem to appreciate is that in a strong stream (or current) the boat can be stationary over the ground but still moving through the water and still having reasonable steerage way.

A wise man will always glance aloft as he approaches a berth, because an important factor is the effect the wind will have on his mast. With a motor yacht, the wind direction is not quite so vital, but it will still have a considerable effect as the speed drops to a knot or less. Motor yachts with out-drive propulsion are something of a special case, but most other forms of propulsion have particular characteristics and they need to be learnt because there are few hard and fast rules.

In the first place there is no standard direction of rotation of the propeller. Thus, for a single screw installation everything described for a right-handed propeller is exactly the opposite for a left-handed one. The problem is not only that all engines are not always rotating in the same manner, the numerous types of reduction gear available means that a right-handed engine will have a left-handed shaft and propeller with one model reduction gear but the right-handed version for another. In other words, two boats with identical engines might still have opposite rotating propellers.

Even twin-screw installations can vary with some having both propellers outward-rotating and others inward-rotating. Further—and to make comparisons even more difficult—a modern motor yacht with twin installations has little to worry about in a low-speed manoeuvre, whereas a modern auxiliary sailing yacht, with one propeller tucked away close abaft the keel and well away from her rudder, may well find it almost impossible to manoeuvre under power at low speed without a degree of anxiety.

Thus everything that follows has to be a generalization. The simplest type of installation is a single screw with a propeller working in an aperture close ahead of the rudder. If the propeller is left-handed rotation [right-handed] when looking forward, there will be a slight, but comparatively unimportant, tendency to steer to port [starboard] at all times when going ahead. This slight tendency is hardly noticeable and can very easily be counteracted with a little rudder. When going astern, on the other hand, there is a very noticeable tendency for the stern to swing to starboard [port] when the engine is first put into gear. If the boat speed is low and the engine revolutions high, this tendency can be marked, but more often than not it can be used to advantage.

Leaving aside, for the moment, any effect the rudder may have, this sideways thrust from a propeller rotating astern—a paddle-wheel effect—is best understood if it is realized that the blades are comparatively close to the surface. However, each blade, each time it revolves, is "gripping the water" far more in the deeper water at the bottom of the rotation than it is at the top.

To take the extreme example, a propeller at the surface will have the blades doing little more than blowing bubbles when they are near the top of the revolution but working much harder at the bottom.

That "paddle-wheel" effect applies to all propellers in all ships, but in most installations it is noticeable only when the shaft first starts to go astern at a time when the forward motion of the boat is small. The propulsive efficiency of the propeller is also low, but the "paddle-wheel" (sideways) effect is at its highest.

The other great influence on the manoeuvrability of a small craft at low speed is the effect that a short burst of engine speed has on the blade of the rudder. Some rudders are almost useless at low speed, others still surprisingly effective, but all are greatly improved if a jet of water from the propeller can be directed on to them.

Boats with out-drive installations are still a special case, and boats with well-organized twin installations have virtually no problems. The former achieve the thrust required by turning the helm one way or the other and then applying a short burst of power. The twin screw installation achieves her manoeuvrability by her ability to go slow ahead on one engine but astern on the other. With care, the twin installation boat can be turned almost in her own length, but she still has to approach her berth in a sensible manner.

Wind and Tide

Apart from the question of propeller thrust, and the way it may affect the final stages of any manoeuvre to come alongside, it is still the effect of the wind and tidal stream that matters most.

It has already been mentioned that, if possible, it is always safest to approach "up-tide", and if it is possible to approach a berth up-wind as well your problems are minimal. However, in the real world it is the occasions when tide and a gusty wind are opposing each other that stick in the memory. They are the awkward occasions and the skipper's job is to try to assess beforehand the influences that are likely to be the greatest.

Will the tidal stream still be flowing right in close alongside the berth? Will the wind be blanketed by those buildings nearby? Above all, will the influence of wind or tide be carrying the boat on to the jetty or holding her off. Couple those thoughts with the fact that almost every boat is affected in a similar manner when she loses her way in a cross-wind—her head blows off—and the facts that have to be assembled before a decision can be made are almost complete.

On some occasions it is best to carry a good way right up to the berth, because otherwise you may suffer the indignity of having the head blow off before any lines are ashore, thus having to "go round again". In other circumstances the more cautious the approach the better, because, even if the boat comes to rest when still a few metres off, the influence of wind, tide or both will soon close the gap.

Within a Marina

Shortly after leaving the sea, as a profession, I was working in a yacht designer's drawing office and I remember feeling somewhat overawed by the size and complexity of a job I had just been given. The advice I was given by the senior draughtsman was something that applies to many situations. He said: "Don't worry, a big job is just the same as a small one; except that it is bigger."

The advice can be applied to the job of manoeuvring within a marina. The degree of difficulty is just the same as when manoeuvring in any other close-quarters situation, except that, within a marina, the space available is likely to be even less.

A part of the problem is that too many seem determined to try the impossible. They see somebody else round up with a flourish, give a short burst of astern power, and then step quietly off on to the jetty and they forget that the circumstances may be totally different when they try to do the same. The tide and wind combination may not be the same; the manoeuvring characteristics of the two boats may be completely different; and (although they may not want to admit it to themselves) the other man's experience may be far greater.

The manoeuvre that I always try to remember is that of the two elderly crew of the ketch I watched off Lyme Regis. They could not have sailed straight up to their berth—or even if they had succeeded the manoeuvre would have been extremely hazardous. They did what they knew they could do without taking unnecessary risks.

There cannot be any hard and fast rules on marina behaviour. The twin screw motor yacht with good all-round visibility from the helmsman's position and with a skilled man at the controls can be manoeuvred into a space little bigger than the boat herself, whether that berth is up-wind, down-wind or even across the wind. The short-handed, single screw, auxiliary sailing yacht with a high superstructure, on the other hand, might find a similar manoeuvre totally impossible and the skipper would be highly irresponsible to attempt it.

The prime objective must be to know your boat. Experiment to discover what happens if you apply full astern power. Can the boat be steered when going astern? Can the amount of "paddle-wheel" effect be predicted in different conditions? Can the point at which steerage way disappears and the bow falls off the wind be assessed?

The answer to all that type of question is probably "Yes", but only to a man who has learnt his trade.

If the marina berths are tidal, in the sense that there is a strong tidal stream affecting the berth at certain periods, then admit to yourself that certain manoeuvres are unwise, or impossible, without proper precautions. Proper precautions might entail a manoeuvre that included rounding up and putting a temporary warp on another boat or berth, up-tide, and then dropping back to the chosen berth under the control of the warp. Alternatively, it might mean ensuring that plenty of fenders were in position, that all the crew knew precisely what was intended and that someone on shore was ready to assist.

Fendering and the use of mooring warps are subjects for the next chapter, but having mentioned assistance from somebody on shore it is necessary to make one point of principle. It is the ship, not the shore, that decides what is to happen. In helping another boat in a marina—or in any other circumstances for that matter—there are numerous occasions when the man on shore, or on the other moored boat, will be thrown a line. Unless requested otherwise, it is his job to make the end of that line fast as quickly as possible—so that those on board can haul on it or whatever. It is not the shoreparty's job to start heaving on that line.

The man on the yacht should indicate (point) to where he would like the warp made fast—if not already obvious—and the man on shore makes fast.

The logic of that advice is irrefutable. The approaching boat may weigh 5 to 10 tonnes, but the lightly built person on shore, or on the deck of the adjoining boat, can pull only a tiny fraction of the load that might come on that warp. Nevertheless, when throwing a warp to a man on shore he seems to feel some strange need to "do" something with it and more often than not starts pulling.

The rate of approach might already be too fast, yet it is common to see the man "helping" by heaving like mad, then he may drop the rope as he tries to assist in fending off. Having heaved on the warp (when his job was to make it fast), he then leaves it lying on deck while he pushes against the lifelines of the new-comer.

In contrast, if there is a nice big "shore party" waiting and willing to assist, a boat can be "parked" by the shore party with those on board muttering their thanks. Circumstances change, but the norm has to be to let those on board make the decisions.

Slip Ropes

One of the difficulties concerning generalized advice is that the best action almost always depends on the circumstances. What is right for a boat with four strong men on deck and two more waiting ashore is completely wrong for a man and a wife and probably impossible for someone single-handed.

However, there is one "trick-of-the-trade" that helps in many situations, the use of a slip rope. All that the expression means is that instead of having a warp which is led, as a single part, from point "A" to point "B", the warp

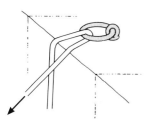

Pull on the part leading under the
ring to minimize the friction of
the rope passing round the ring

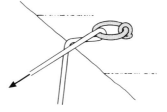

Wrong: the upper part of the rope
is pressing the ring down on the
lower to cause maximum friction

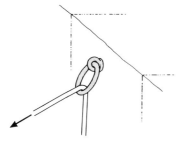

Right: no problem so long as the
rope is not jerked so that the
bitter end flicks over the top

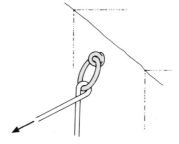

Wrong: the rope is being dragged
all the way round the ring to
create the maximum friction

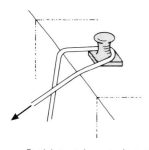

Good: but not always easy because of
the friction of the rope on the edge
of the jetty

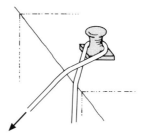

Bad: the hauling part is dragging
across the top of the tail and
maximizing the friction on the
jetty

FIG. 7.3. *Use of slip ropes*

leads from "A" (the boat) to "B" (the shore or another boat) and then back
again to "A". That is the simple geometry of the slip rope; the practicality is
that it should be led in such a manner that when one end (on "A") is let go,
the other end (also on "A") can be hauled back aboard.

To pass a slip rope is child's play, but to pass one that will always "slip" can take a little thought. Figure 7.3 tells the story. All that is necessary is a little common sense when first passing the warp—remembering that the angle that the warp will assume when it is being slipped is not necessarily the same as it will take in use. Secondly, it is important to pause for a moment and think about which part of the slip rope to haul in. Finally, try to avoid jerking the last metre or two of the tail as it passes through the ring or round the bollard. Rope tails have an awkward habit of flying about all over the place, and if they take a turn round the hauling part the result can be highly embarrassing.

The point of using a slip rope should be obvious; it is to allow the warp to be let go from on board the boat. There are countless ways in which that can be useful. Some will be described in Chapter 8, when mooring and making fast is considered, but slip ropes are occasionally also invaluable for a manoeuvre.

If approaching a difficult berth, for example, it has already been mentioned that to put a temporary warp on another berth or another boat up-tide and then drop back can be very useful. However, if the up-tide point where the warp is to be made fast is on the *opposite* side of a main marina channel, your temporary warp can be an embarrassment, or even a danger, because it blocks the free passage for others. Thus, if a slip rope is used, the "obstruction" can be removed immediately the slip rope has done its job and without having to send a man round to release it.

There is yet another form of quick-release that is useful for manoeuvring and it, too, can apply to the type of temporary mooring just described. If the warp ends in a bowline or an eye splice with a largish eye, it is surprisingly easy to flick that eye off a bollard or post. Slack away until the warp makes a gentle catenary and then one bold up-and-down movement of the hauling part—while keeping the load fairly slack—will flick the eye off the bollard. The "trick" can be useful, and it is reasonably fail-safe because it cannot cause problems: either it works or it does not.

If it is important to be able to free the warp without going ashore, use a slip rope. Alternatively, if there is a convenient bollard at the end of an arm of the marina, an eye will usually serve and a warp with an eye has the advantage over a slip rope in that only half as much warp is needed.

8

Mooring, Anchoring and Making Fast

To the purist in the use of language, to moor is to lie to two anchors—and thus restrict the swinging room—and to anchor is to lie to one.

In common use "anchoring" means lying to an anchor and the word "mooring" is used primarily for when the boat is lying to her own—or a borrowed—buoy. The mooring buoy will be secured with chains laid both up and down tide. Thus a boat on a mooring buoy will behave as if she was moored in the traditional sense; she will not move very much, up or down tide, as the tide turns.

Furthermore, there is often confusion about the expression "tying-up". Some use it for the more traditional expression "make fast". To me the latter is far more useful. A man might tie a knot or he might tie up a parcel. However he makes fast his boat and whether he is made fast to the ground with his anchor—anchored—or made fast to a jetty with warps, the boat is fast even if he merely tied a bowline in one of his warps in the process.

Thus having defined the heading for this chapter, we must accept that the traditional "moor" is something rarely practised.

In the most classical sense a sailing yacht beats up to a position above where she intends to lie at anchor and above that position by a little less than the length of the chain to which she is about to lie. She then slacks away about twice that length, until she is well down wind of the final position at which she will lie. At that point she lets go the second anchor and hauls herself back on the first chain while slacking away on the second. When she has placed herself approximately equidistant between the two anchors, she is moored.

One of the reasons why mooring was considered the "right" way to come to rest was that the traditional fisherman anchor does not like being pulled first one way and then the other. For most bottoms the fisherman is not nearly as efficient as some of the anchors developed more recently. Thus, having "set" a fisherman while mooring, the skipper could be reasonably satisfied his anchors would stay put.

Mooring remains an excellent way of anchoring, but the manoeuvre is appropriate only for extreme conditions of weather or for anchoring in places where there is very little room to swing. Nowadays, if sailing up to any anchorage where there are already other boats at anchor, it is reasonable to assume that they are anchored, not moored, unless there is any evidence to the contrary.

Anchoring

When coming up to an anchorage there are several points that have to be considered. If there is a choice of position, then the first has to be the degree of shelter that the chosen spot will provide. That will depend on the surroundings, the nature of the bottom and the weather forecast.

Next, having chosen a likely spot, the depth of water will be the key point. What is the state of the tide and therefore how much scope will be required?

In Chapter 5 the use of a graph for tidal height was strongly recommended. When coming to an anchorage it can be invaluable. A glance at the time and a glance at the graph is all that is needed to tell the skipper (a) how far the tide will go down before it turns: in other words what the depth will be at low water, (b) what the depth will be at high water: in other words, how much scope will be necessary.

The next point to consider is how much room will be needed. The commonest fault by far—so common that it is almost the norm—is to anchor too close to the yacht astern.

The sequence of thought seems to be: "Ah! That looks a likely spot." As soon as he has reached it, the newcomer to the anchorage lets go his anchor, forgetting that he will then drop astern several boat's lengths. If there is not much room to spare, he will then be almost on top of the boat astern and "miles" away from the boat ahead.

Another hazard is that "unlike" boats swing in different ways. A shallow and high-sided motor yacht will lie to the wind far more than to the tide, whereas a heavy displacement, long keeled cruising boat will be almost totally controlled by the tide unless it is blowing hard.

Thus, even from that introduction, it is easily appreciated how confusing an anchorage can become, especially as nearly everyone lies to too short a scope for safety anyway.

Tradition dictates that chain is the only correct method of attaching the boat to her anchor and that there should be a minimum of at least three times the depth of water AT HIGH WATER in the scope. Unfortunately, as so often happens in a fast growing pastime, tradition is not always followed. Even if it was, recent research suggests that the traditional "×3" advice is unsound; for a given strain on an anchor, the "correct" scope varies with the depth of water.

For example, for a given strain on an anchor if it was correct to lie to a scope of 3 in a depth of say 17 metres, the load would be the same only if the scope was 3.8 in 12 metres and as much as 6 in 7 metres. The shallower the water, the greater the scope: strange but true.

Couple the need for generous scope with the fact that many small craft today lie to a comparatively short length of chain and then rope, and we have a perfect recipe for the dragging of anchors.

Arithmetically the problem can be shown by the formula

$$\frac{L^2 - D^2}{2D} \times W = \text{load (kgf)}$$

where W is the weight in kg per metre of chain,
  D the depth of water and
  L the length of chain.

Diagrammatically it can be shown (as in Fig. 8.1) or pictorially, for one depth (as in Fig. 8.2). In Fig. 8.2 the two boats are each in 7 metres of water. One lies to 8 millimetre chain with a scope of 3.5: to achieve an equivalent load on the anchor, the other, if lying to rope and a length of 7 metres of 8 millimetres chain, needs a scope of 6.5. Many small yachts attempt to anchor with even less chain than that, but the diagram illustrates the problem. Not only do boats lying to rope need a swinging circle with twice the radius, there is practically no chain dragging on the bottom to keep them in one spot. Thus in certain conditions they roam about and the kinetic energy that builds up before the rope becomes taut makes the anchor far, far less likely to hold, even if the scope appears to be enough.

Until comparatively recently all yachts carried at least 30 fathoms of chain, and the size was laid down in good, cautious advice from *Lloyd's Register of Shipping Rules*. Today, once light displacement became so important to so many racing boats and once the racing authorities (led by U.S. influence) no longer required offshore racing yachts to carry chain, the whole attitude to anchoring has changed.

The problem is exaggerated by the fact that modern nylon anchor warps are nice to handle, they stow well and, IF ENOUGH ROPE IS USED, they are very effective in a blow. For anchoring *in extremis*—to hold a boat off a lee shore in a severe blow—a really long length of rope is very good practice, so long as there is also a certain amount of chain at the lower end.

The problem is at its worst when yachtsmen—used to the erroneous ×3 traditional scope for use with chain—start to use rope in a tidal anchorage in a similar manner. It can be very anti-social as well as dangerous. Boats in tidal waters when lying to rope will charge about all over the place, in certain conditions of wind over tide, and the momentum of that "charging about" builds up a kinetic energy that far exceeds the load that would be put on the anchor by an all-chain arrangement.

Thus a compromise is necessary. I believe a minimum of 40 metres of chain

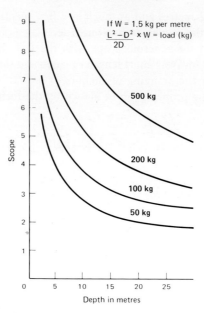

FIG. 8.1. *Anchoring scope. Theoretical loads achieved with 8 mm chain*

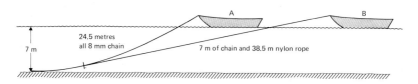

FIG. 8.2. *Rope and chain*

(of a size ranging from say 7 millimetres for boats of 7 metres l.o.a. to 10 millimetres for boats of 33 metres l.o.a.) should be aimed at and to that 75 metres of nylon multiplait would cover most situations. The unusual twist to that recommendation is that when considering chain the heavier it is the better. However, the opposite is true for the anchor warp! It can be shown mathematically (and has been confirmed by some full-sized tests done at sea) that, when using nylon or other rope that stretches, the thinner the rope the better (within reason).

Traditional thinking might suggest that the rope needs to be as strong as the chain. However, the point about having thin rope is that the thinner it is the stretchier it is and the stretchier it is the longer it takes to absorb the strain from any particular wave. Thus, by the laws that govern these things, if a given load at the bow of the boat is spread over a longer interval, then the load at the other end (at the anchor) is less.

Never forget, however, that for an anchor to work, the load at that anchor must be horizontal, or very nearly horizontal.

The Anchor

Before considering what might be termed the "art" of anchoring any further, think for a moment of the anchor itself.

Just as the formula already shown proves that the traditional thinking about scope is bogus, there is also a great deal of highly suspect (to say the least) thinking about anchors. It arrives, I suspect, because so rarely do we actually see what the anchor is doing. It works—or it appears to work—if the boat stays where she was put. It does not work if the boat drags.

Since earliest times anchoring has been a problem. Many centuries ago man used a stone, bound into a sort of shank, with two crossed (and curved) pieces of wood for the anchor itself. It was a crude grapnel—a killick—and was quite effective in rocky bottoms.

Next, historically speaking, came the big fisherman type of anchor which is still in use today. The larger versions—popular as exhibits outside maritime museums or the town halls of seaside resorts—had a wooden stock and the problem, in the past, was to make the anchors strong enough. Then, as far as small craft are concerned, the present type of plough anchor—the CQR—was developed in the 1930s, originally as a seaplane anchor. It was followed in the United States by the Danforth type, and those two, the CQR and the Danforth (and the many copies), held sway until research work for the offshore oil industry created the type of anchor known, in the smaller sizes, as the Bruce.

Thus, to summarize, small craft still have a choice of the fisherman or the grapnel—best described as surface-piercing anchors—and the CQR, the Danforth and the Bruce—best described as burying anchors.

Summarizing again—and there have to be numerous assumptions—a fisherman might be expected to hold up to fifteen times its own weight before it starts to drag. The burying anchor, on the other hand, will usually hold up to twenty-five or even, occasionally, fifty times its own weight before it drags.

By no means is that the end of the story.

A fisherman's efficiency varies a great deal on the angle at which the flukes are made. Most are far too flat and some work done (by Brian Grant for the Department of Trade and Industry) a few years ago suggests that the ideal angle of the flukes should be about 30 degrees to the shank. At the commoner angle of about 60 degrees to the shank, the efficiency drops by about 50 per cent.

Next comes the general assumption that fishermen and grapnel anchors are probably the best in rocky bottoms—despite their lower holding power in more sandy bottoms. They are good because they have a chance of hooking under a rock. How else can the continual use of fisherman anchors by the

RNLI be justified, and why else should the weighted grapnel type of anchor be so popular in Norway?

A heavy fisherman anchor is also reasonably efficient in heavy kelp—where the burying type of anchor is almost useless—but the other point to realize about the "surface piercing" anchor is that when it has pierced the surface (not hooked itself on a rock) it will drag *through* the surface, when overloaded, at a reasonably constant load.

The burying anchor, on the other hand, behaves in a totally different manner. Many yachtsmen assume that it digs in and then goes on burying. This is not so. The research already referred to indicates that a burying anchor will bury below the surface but invariably, as it is then loaded more, it will rotate and come back to the surface, only to bury again. It might have rotated through 180 degrees and then back again, or it might have rotated through 360 degrees in the process, but rotate it will—always.

Obviously, if not overloaded, it will stay put, but the fact that once the limit has been reached it will start to rotate out (in comparison to the fisherman which drags through) alters the whole concept. Put another way, the efficiency of a burying anchor is the speed at which it will dig in, and then dig in again after having rotated out.

This concept is certainly not the usual one, but it is based on quite extensive model and full-scale research into anchor design.

The fundamental difference is thus that a graph for an overloaded fisherman anchor, under load, is a fairly constant horizontal line, unless the anchor happens to snag on a rock. The graph for an overloaded burying anchor, on the other hand, is a regular series of peaks and troughs.

The point being made concerns overloading. If not overloaded, *anything* will "hold"; it is what happens when the load increases that is of interest.

Earlier the CQR, the Danforth and the Bruce anchors were grouped into the one type; the so-called burying anchor. However, there is still one important difference. The CQR and the Bruce both behave in a very similar manner. When they reach the surface (after having been overloaded and rotated back to the surface) they will both dig in again. In fact it is the ability of a CQR and a Bruce to dig in *quickly* that makes them so popular. The Danforth, on the other hand, has flukes that hinge back and forward across the line of the shank. Thus, a Danforth can often rotate back to the surface in a "fluke uppermost" manner. It will dig in again only if the flukes are free to drop down on the hinge and resume the position that the anchor was in at the beginning. If, on the other hand, there is a stone—or even a lump of clay—wedged between the shank and the flukes, the Danforth may not dig in again at all; it may skate across the sand with its flukes jammed, pointing above the level of the bottom!

That is not guesswork. It has happened to me on two occasions, and the research to which I have already referred duplicated the same behaviour.

For soft bottoms a Danforth holds well. It is popular for what the

American yachtsman calls a "lunch hook": an anchor to lie to for a short period. However, I do not believe a Danforth is the right configuration for an anchor for use in tidal waters where there is a distinct possibility that it will be overloaded and pulled out of the ground on the turn of the tide and then have to rebed itself.

Many people use them and many like the easy manner in which they can be stowed, but I am now convinced that the CQR and the Bruce have overwhelming advantages, they dig in again so much more readily.

Finally, to weights. I am cynical enough to believe that many products establish themselves because of the claims in their advertisements. Tidy little tables equating recommended weight with overall length tend to be believed—regardless of the amount of research (**if any**) associated with their production—and they then become folk-lore after having been reprinted over and over again in magazine articles and books.

Quite apart from the dangers of following the recommendations of advertising copy, there is little logic in using l.o.a. as the guideline without stressing that light displacement boats with low freeboard might need less weight in their ground tackle and heavy boats with high superstructures more.

As a starting point for CQR or Bruce anchors see below.

L.O.A. (m)	Anchor (kg)	Chain diameter (mm)
7	7	7
8	9	
9	11	8
10	13	
11	15	–
12	17	
14	22	10
16	27	11

For those sizes I would recommend 30 to 45 metres of chain as a minimum, and a good deal more for the larger boats, particularly if they can handle the weight with power winches.

Handling the Ground Tackle

Another of Claude Worth's sayings that has stuck in my mind is that the limiting factor in the size of boat that any man, or men, can handle is the weight of her ground tackle. Of course he was referring to what can be handled by muscle power, and he would turn in his grave at the suggestion that a boat should anchor to anything other than chain.

Thus, to deal with chain first, remember that when chain starts to run out it gathers momentum and can become very difficult to stop. Rule 1 must be to ensure that the bitter end is fast, but on this subject tradition gives poor advice. Countless times in the past I have seen recommendations that the bitter end should be made fast in the chain locker. The worst policy of all is to shackle the bitter end there. Not only can it not be let go in a hurry, the shackle might seize so that it cannot be let go at all! Next is the recommendation that the bitter end is *seized* to an eye in the chain locker. Assembled like that, the chain could, at least, be cut adrift, but the key point is not only that the arrangement chosen should enable the chain to be let go (one day that might be really important), but the letting go operation *must be done from on deck*.

The answer is simple and cheap. The bitter end of any anchor chain—or chain and rope—assembly must be made fast to a short length of rope that is itself long enough to reach from the chain locker to the deck.

Some chain lockers open directly to the deck anyway, but the objective is simple, to prevent the chain (or chain and rope) running out, out-of-control, and to allow the whole "caboodle" to be cut adrift in a hurry. If a large vessel was drifting down on to another smaller boat, at anchor, or if it was ever necessary to get under way **immediately** (say because of a man overboard), the whole chain might have to be let go. Preferably there would be time to buoy the bitter end, but that point is secondary. There must be the possibility of converting a vessel at anchor into one that is under way within moments.

Thus, having established the need for an emergency procedure for letting everything go, the normal method of recovering an anchor is far more time-consuming, and, as Claude Worth stressed, it can also be strenuous.

At one extreme, small craft can be fitted with power winches or capstans—driven by electricity or hydraulics—which, if the anchor chain leads through a hawse pipe or special bow rolled, can be totally self-stowing. At the other extreme, not only does somebody have to pull the anchor in, it has to be lifted aboard as well.

The anchor pawl (Fig. 8.3) is another device adapted from an idea of Claude Worth's. It is so valuable that it is amazing to me that it has not been copied almost universally in small craft. Below about 7 metres l.o.a. a *fit* man can handle the ground tackle alone—in most circumstances—but around the 9 metres l.o.a., with heavier anchor chain and anchors of, say, 12 kg, a good pawl—rigged as shown—is worth *at least* another strong man, occasionally two.

That is no exaggeration. The idea of holding a pawl firmly against the links was devised for my boat—*Barbican*—and in 16 years of anchoring, on what must have been many hundreds of occasions in every sort of condition, I never once needed assistance in recovering my anchor by myself. Worth's pawl was gravity fed and relied on a bolt (in single shear) through the side of the stem. Mine was loaded by shock-cord and was held with a drop-nosed pin which passed through **both** arms of the stemhead roller guard.

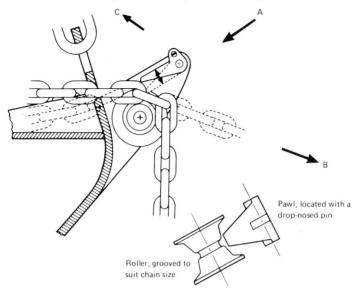

FIG. 8.3. *Pawl. A: Main force when chain is bearing on the roller but not being held by the pawl. B: Alternatively, while lying at anchor the force is in the opposite direction if the load is held by the pawl, instead of transferred to an anchor bollard. C: Light force of a short length of rubber shock cord used to hold the apex of the pawl on to the links of the chain. Gravity **might** be enough, but a piece of shock cord makes certain that the pawl engages properly, every link*

Nobody makes them as standard, but the principle is so good that it is worth making a considerable effort to modify a stemhead fitting to adopt the idea. Note that when "at anchor" the load on the stem is aft and down ("A"), but when the pin is in use the load is almost opposite ("B"). If the stemhead fitting is really well secured, there is no problem, but the point must be taken: few stemheads are secured to withstand an outward force.

The pawl needs to be "custom made" to fit the chain. Mine was deliberately made a trifle too long so that it could be filed away to fit. However, it is the principle of use that matters most.

Normally, with a hand-held chain, those doing the hauling spend perhaps three-quarters of their energy merely holding what they have just achieved. With a good pawl, the pawl does **all** the holding.

In anything of a sea, the boat actually helps. If the anchor is well bedded, a few links can be gained each time the bow dips. A second or two later the chain is held while the bow rises. It is magic.

Finally a thought about the stowage of the anchor itself. There is a tendency nowadays to sail with an anchor resting in its bow roller. If the arrangement has been well thought out it can be excellent: very few are. The whole bow structure has to be planned for it.

In a small boat there is no real problem, because one man can pick up an anchor weighing say 12 kg and stow it where he thinks fit. However, above about 16 kg the operation becomes a bit more of a problem and there is a lot to be said for stowing an anchor well aft of the bow; It makes recovery so very much easier.

Keep a few metres of line fast to the crown of the anchor and then, when weighing, haul away on the chain until the line on the crown is just within reach of a boathook. Then, once the line has been brought on deck, the anchor can be hauled up, and aft, by a man standing well aft of the bow in the position occupied by the traditional "cat head". In that position the anchor is raised up to deck level, but it does not have to be raised up and over a stemhead where it is impossible to get a sensible place to stand.

The anchor can also be dropped overboard from that position, because it will hit the water before it swings back on to the bow. Then, having dropped the anchor itself, the chain can be slacked away in the normal manner.

Finally, the anchor must be **stowed**—whether it is in a bow roller or in chocks on deck. I say again, stowed: not placed in little chocks and forgotten. To reinforce the point, think of the feelings of a friend of mine—an experienced seaman—with a well-found "Twister", about 9 metres l.o.a. He had hove to, for lunch, in a bit of a blow in mid-Channel, when the wind force was about 6. He was sitting in his cockpit making up his mind whether to carry on to Brittany or turn back when, without any warning, a rogue wave broke aboard. A second or two later he realized that his 11 kg CQR was lying against the cockpit coaming, alongside where he was sitting!

The anchor had been "properly" lashed to carefully made wooden chocks on the foredeck. Nature has all sorts of tricks up her sleeve.

Down below it can be perfectly satisfactory to stow something with wooden chocks or eyes screwed to a bulkhead; on the foredeck "stowed"—for anchor chocks—probably means either through bolted or at least screwed through into deck beams or into under-deck chocks.

Fast Alongside

The Collision Regulations' definition of "under way" is that she is not at anchor, or fast to the shore. In other words, there is a clear distinction between making way and being under way. On breaking out an anchor, or when the mooring ropes are let go, a vessel is then under way—as far as the rules are concerned—whether she is making way or not.

Obviously there is a "grey area" when changing from one state to the other—in particular when the anchor and chain are still to be recovered—but when about to go alongside and therefore to become "made fast to the shore", the intentions are usually obvious.

Chapter 7 described some of the manoeuvres when making the approach. The objective here is to consider the various ways of making fast.

Making fast, quickly and sensibly is an art that needs to be learnt, because there are numerous factors that must be taken into consideration.

(i) If there is any wind at all, or any wash from passing small craft, the boat will be on the move and therefore the arrangement of mooring warps must allow for that movement and not attempt to prevent what nature will not allow you to prevent.

(ii) If making fast in tidal waters, what is right for one tidal direction must also be right for the other.

(iii) If making fast in tidal waters to a jetty or other structure that is not going to float with the tide, then a knowledge of the exact range of the tide is vital.

(iv) If there is any risk of a wash from a passing ship, then the fendering as well as the arrangement of warps needs care out of all proportion to that which might be perfectly acceptable in more sheltered surroundings.

(v) Finally, always remember that it is not only your own boat that is to be made fast. In many circumstances you might find half a dozen other (and possibly larger) craft outside you, made fast to you, and thus hanging on to your warps. It ought not to happen, but it does.

Figure 8.4(a) shows the principle of making fast. A boat is an awkward shaped object and the mooring problem is best solved if the boat is treated as if she was a rectangular box. It needs to be held in the quay, and it needs to be held to prevent it moving along the quay.

The warps holding the "box" from moving fore and aft are called "head ropes" (at the "head") and "stern ropes" at the stern. Similarly, the ropes holding the "box" in to the quay are the "breast ropes" (abreast, meaning side-by-side). In calm conditions those two forces—B and S (or H) in Fig. 8.4(a)—can be satisfied with a resultant load at, say, 60 degrees or so—Fig. 8.4(b), but if there is any likelihood of encountering movement, such as the wash of a passing boat, that single-rope solution is far from satisfactory.

Study Figs. 8.4(c) and 8.5 together, and the main point is obvious. The roll in Fig. 8.5 is only 15 degrees either way, with a wash of waves about 0.5 metre from crest to trough. Nevertheless, even with those small figures the distance between the fixed point on the floating pontoon and the fixed point on deck at the fairlead is doubled as the boat rolls. In fact it is slightly more than "times two", as drawn.

That point needs to be engraved on the heart of the man responsible for mooring, because the implications are so great.

If a mooring like Fig. 8.4(b) was attempted, the warps would snatch like demons. Assume a tidal stream. Assume, therefore, that at least the up-tide warp is reasonably taut. Along comes the wash; the boat rolls against a warp that is already taut and the result is inevitable; there is a snatch which can jerk the boat back against the roll and against the jetty. Sometimes the jerk can be really alarming and, apart from the discomfort, the chafe, the risk of breaking something and thus the downright danger, the jerk also pulls the poor boat hard against her fenders so that she then tries to bounce off again.

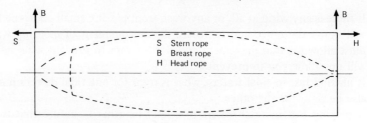

Think of the boat as if she was in a rectangular box. It would need "breast ropes" at each end to hold it into the quay. Also it would need a "head rope" to hold it ahead and a "stern rope" to hold it by the stern.

(a)

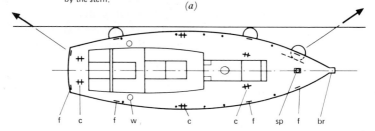

In settled and gentle conditions the job of holding the "box" both close to the jetty and fore-and-aft alongside the jetty, can be achieved with merely one mooring warp at each end.

(b)

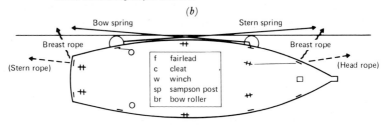

However, in a tidal stream, it is far more comfortable to lie to two "breast ropes" - which can be adjusted so that they are usually slack - and two "springs" - which should be taut.

(c)

FIG. 8.4. *Alongside: (a) basic geometry; (b) lay-out of fairleads and cleats; (c) warps and fenders*

There is only one answer to the "jerk-and-bounce-off" cycle, and that is the golden rule. Bow and stern springs (or head and stern warps led well ahead and astern) can be taut because neither wash nor swell has any major tendency to move the boat fore or aft. However, breast ropes MUST be adjusted initially so that they are slack.

Nothing is gained by trying to hold the boat close to the jetty. In fact there is a lot to be said for deliberately adjusting the warps so that the boat lies a little off the jetty (see later).

I say again: springs can (and should) be taut, but breast ropes must have some slack in them.

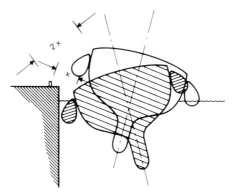

FIG. 8.5. *Fenders and slack breast ropes*

The main objective is to hold the boat in position, without jerking at the ropes or putting undue pressure on the fenders. Forgetting for the moment the question of the size, position, or the type of fenders to use, consider the effect of a tidal stream on the arrangement shown in Fig. 8.4(c). The fore-and-aft position work is being done by the springs and because the point of attachment is off-centre there is a slight outward turning force on the hull. Thus (for one direction of tidal stream only) all that is essential is one spring and one breast rope; the other pair are doing little or nothing. Take that arrangement a stage further, and it is usually child's play to adjust the warps so that the tidal stream effect is actually holding the boat **off** the jetty.

Figure 8.5 illustrates the advantage of so doing. Not only does a wash jerk the breast ropes in an alarming and dangerous manner, if they are taut, the movement can easily deposit the fenders on top of the jetty itself. Thus fenders need to be positioned as low as possible—to minimize the effect. That, in turn, dictates that they need to be as large as possible.

Remember that it is not the deck (in plan view) that is being fendered when lying to a pontoon, it is the side of the boat at the height of that pontoon. When approaching the berth it is comforting, as well as good practice, to have a fender in position well forward on the bow—as shown in Fig. 8.4(b), but note where it lies. The flare in the bow sections means that a fender for that purpose needs to be about 0.5 metre diameter at the least. The fenders in the illustration are about that size, but that is about two and a half times larger than is the norm.

The habit of trying to use little "sausage-shaped" fenders may stem from the days of the coir fender, or the little canvas bags filled with cork, that our forefathers tried to use. Today there are plenty of manufacturers making the right tool for the job and the bigger the better. A large fender, with little or no pressure in it, absorbs the load slowly, and two really big ones are worth half a dozen small.

Note where the two "working" fenders are positioned in Fig. 8.4(c). They should be as far forward and as far aft as possible; the further they are from the centre of the mass of the boat, the easier it is for them to do their job.

On practically all yachts fendering is an afterthought. Somebody once went to a local chandler and bought four little "sausages" and they were then hung on the lifelines amidships. When a boat is stationary, alongside, the life lines *might* be used for fenders—if nothing else serves—but it is never good practice. A fender should, at the very least, be hung with a half hitch around the *base* of a stanchion, before taking a turn around the lifeline at the top of that stanchion: never lead the fender line directly to the top itself. The point at issue here is that as the boat approaches her berth there is always the chance that the fender will catch on another boat or be jammed at the end of the pontoon. If that happens, the fender line will try to stop the forward motion of the boat—suddenly. If made fast to the lifelines, either the lifelines or the stanchions are almost certain to be damaged.

Ideally fenders should be purchased to suit the position where they will be used. To achieve a fore-and-aft line on the boat that is parallel to the pontoon or lockside, a fender to be used well forward will almost certainly have to be larger than one in a corresponding position aft. The difference in cost between small and large is not great, but the difference in comfort and convenience between adequate and inadequate fendering is enormous. Furthermore, the avoidance of damage to the topsides will more than compensate for the extra cost of the larger fenders.

The best type of all is the pear-shaped fender made as a net buoy for commercial fishing. They do not need to be blown up hard, but they do need a decent length of light line spliced into the eye at the top. Ideally, in my opinion, the deck ought to have robust eye-plates especially for the fender line, if there is not a convenient stanchion socket or fairlead around which to take a turn. But in any event, always take a round turn around something—the top of a closed fairlead, or a hitch around the base of a stanchion—before leading the fender line to wherever it will be made fast. Even if *you* never come alongside a berth carelessly, somebody else will come alongside you in a silly manner.

Even "huge" fenders need not be heavy and therefore they are not really as difficult to stow as some seem to believe. There is usually space for one really large one at the foot of a quarter berth; above the occupants' feet of course. Also the "eyes" of most boats are unused and are therefore ideal for light objects like the modern inflated fender. Motor yachts often arrange stowage on the foredeck, in racks, but I have rarely found that an attractive answer, although it can be convenient.

Finally, having recommended the pear-shaped fender as the best way to achieve size for a given bulk and weight, it has to be admitted that they are not ideal for use when lying against posts with fender boards. Thus, if there is space for a couple of "sausages" as well, so much the better.

Chafe

In any chapter of a book on any subject connected with small craft there has to be reference to chafe. It is at its most dangerous aloft, when halyards or sails can so easily become damaged, but chafe on mooring warps is easily overcome with a little care. Traditional seamanship advice often refers to the use of spirally split hose lengths, to twist on to warps where they pass through fairleads. I have never found that satisfactory. Hose—yes—but do not split it. Any thick gauge plastic hose will serve if it is slightly larger in the bore than the warp itself. The procedure is simple. Forget all about chafe while coming alongside, but once settled spend a few minutes feeding a short length of hose on to each warp, in turn, and then sliding it along to the point where it will be needed.

It is as simple as that. In 16 years' cruising with my last boat, I bought odd off-cuts of plastic hose on two or three occasions, but when she was sold she still had the original mooring warps on board and in good condition. I had had to splice one of them once, and that was when the chafing piece had shifted.

To secure the hose, cut an eye at one end of each piece and splice a short length of small stuff into it. Then, once slid into position, a hitch around the parent rope will do all that is necessary.

Fairleads

It should be enough to say that a fairlead should give a "fair" lead. Unfortunately they rarely do.

The commonest type is made from a long, thin casting which is then cut up like slices of a Swiss roll. It is shown on the left side of Fig. 8.6 and it is horrid. A better type is like a pair of crossed fingers, but note that the "base" of each finger *must* be circular, not square.

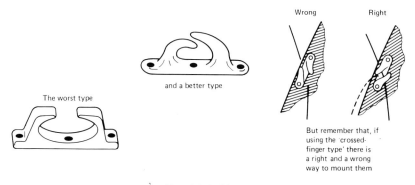

FIG. 8.6. *Fairleads*

The object of a fairlead is simple. To give the fair lead already mentioned and to prevent the rope jumping out. Thus there is a right and a wrong way to mount the crossed-finger type and they have to be bought in pairs. Best of all are those that are totally enclosed, ropes never jump out of them. However, some crews need a little time to get used to them because, of course, the rope has to be led through each time. Even so, I would not use anything else, even if they have to be at least 100 millimetres, fore and aft, in the mouth to avoid the difficulties that might arise if another man's ropes were too big to pass through your leads.

Tidal Height

Finally, and possibly most importantly of all, Fig. 8.7 illustrates the problems that arise when making fast to a wall in a harbour with a good rise and fall. As drawn, the range of the tide is somewhat larger than average but by no means exceptional. The lesson is obvious. Breast ropes are almost useless, because they have to be adjusted all the time. Thus the boat must use springs, as in Fig. 8.4(c), and a head and a stern rope (as shown dotted in Fig. 8.4(c)), and they must all be really long: all of them.

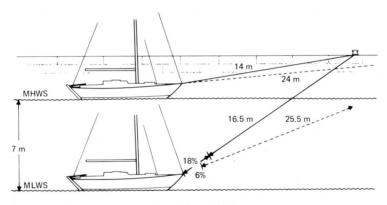

FIG. 8.7. *Effect of tidal range*

If trying to use warps as shown by the shorter warp in Fig. 8.7, the extra length needed at low water is about 18 per cent. On the other hand, if using nice long warps, as shown dotted in the illustration, the "extra" needed at low water is only 6 per cent more than at high water. With that arrangement, the warps would not need much adjustment, if any at all.

In real life there never seems to be a bollard in the ideal spot, and thus it always seems necessary to use even more rope than shown in the illustration. However, the longer the warp, the less the percentage change.

Beware the edge of the quay, however. In anything of a swell, the warps are moving back and forward across the edge the whole time and 2 or 3 metres of the warp must be covered by hose if that type of protection is to be tried.

Vigilance is probably the best answer, but beware. The one warp that I had to resplice, as mentioned earlier, was after a night in a Danish harbour where, despite the lack of tide, there was a bit of a swell running into the harbour mouth all night. A perfectly sound warp was chafed almost through in about 8 hours. When checking before turning in, I had not appreciated that the movement, although slight, was "gently" dragging the warp back and forward across a join between two of the granite blocks!

Alongside Others

Nowadays, the idea of berthing to a pontoon is so common that we are sometimes apt to forget that there are ports where there is also the need to lie alongside other boats. If there are to be difficulties, they are more likely to be found when lying alongside others than when lying in a berth of one's own.

In the ideal world, the largest boat is alongside the pontoon, with progressively smaller and smaller boats outside her. In other words, there is a convention that the newcomer always lies alongside someone larger than himself. In practice, of course, despite the quite amazing goodwill that is usually to be found in a crowded harbour, it is often necessary to lie outside boats that are smaller than one's own. Sometimes smaller boats that are already made fast will shift—or even prefer to shift—to allow a larger boat to come on an inside berth. On other occasions the owners of the smaller, inner boats may not even be on board. Thus the latecomer may not have much choice.

In a group of boats there are two main conventions. It is the newcomer who must be responsible for fendering the boat that was on the outside; in other words, each boat looks after the fenders on her own "inside". If she also wants to put fenders on her own "outside", that is a bonus, but it is not expected of her.

Secondly, the newcomer must put lines ashore—at a sensible angle well ahead and well astern—as well as any breast ropes and springs that may be called for to secure her to the boat outside which she is lying. In practice, the observance of that "rule" will depend a bit on the sizes involved. If a small boat lies alongside another which is much larger, it is reasonable for her to lie to the other's mooring warps: all she is expected to do is to put out breast ropes and springs.

On the other hand, when there is a tier of boats, all lying alongside each other, then, at the very least, every other boat should put out head and stern ropes and if there is any sea running at all every boat should do the same.

The reason should be obvious. First, without head and stern ropes from those on the outer berths—and they must be put out at a sensible angle to do their job—those on the inner berths will have a far more uncomfortable night than is necessary. Secondly, without head and stern ropes from the outer boats, those on the inner are unable to "wriggle" clear when they wish to leave.

Figure 8.8 tells a part of that story. There are many ports where it is common to see yachts lying six or eight and more abreast, at regatta times, and if there is any tidal stream at all the use of head and stern ropes by those on the outer berths is vital.

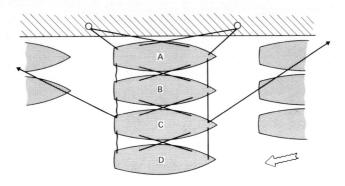

FIG. 8.8. *Warps for a tier of yachts*

The figure shows near perfection, but note that C's head and stern ropes are led at a wide angle. They will have to lead across the decks of others—and sometimes it is necessary to do that with care—but without that type of "geometry" the load on the warps of the inshore boat, and the pressure of her fenders, has to be experienced to be believed.

When leading head or stern ropes across the decks of other boats, do not make them fast to those boats. The object is to prevent fore and aft movement of the tier in which your boat is lying, not to try to lock everything up. Sometimes it can help to lead the head and stern ropes across the top of the other boat's lifelines, or to make up a little "lift" with a piece of small line to raise your head rope off his varnish. The point is that the two tiers should and will move independently.

Do not be fooled by a lovely quiet evening. It is far less trouble to put out head and stern ropes in daylight than to have a scramble to do it in the rain and at night.

Ideally the tier "dissolves" in the morning, with the outside boats leaving first. In practice, of course, those that arrived after the shops shut are the least likely to want to leave early.

It helps everyone when any boat is to be left unattended if those "inside" her know when the crew are likely to return. Common sense dictates that those outside must be prepared to help those inside to leave, and the general rule is to allow an inside boat to "wriggle" herself clear while the rest of the tier are lying to the up stream (or up wind) head or stern ropes. If there is any doubt about which way the tier will swing, then pass another (light) warp ashore, but by-passing, by circling around, the boat that wants to leave. In that manner it is safe to let go the head or stern ropes of the outer boat—while the inner boat is manhandled clear. As soon as the inner boat has dropped down tide and been manhandled clear, the remaining boats in the tier can be brought under control as the slack in the new (temporary) head or stern rope is taken up.

Given a generous dose of goodwill, it is amazing how many boats can lie in one "block". I have seen small Danish harbours when it would have been almost possible to walk across from one side to the other. Also, in a port like Zierikzee, in the Dutch Ooster Schelde, where there is commercial traffic at any time of day or night, there can be several tiers of eight to ten boats occupying one alongside berth at regatta time.

Making Fast in Locks

Of all the ways of making fast, the procedure for lying alongside in a lock can be the most complicated of all. Figures 8.9(a) and 8.9(b) tell part of the story.

At all times it is necessary to remember that if a warp is to do its job without being too over-loaded then the angle must be right. The point was stressed for the head and stern ropes, in Fig. 8.8, and it is even more important to get things right in a situation like the one shown in Fig. 8.9. From the lock-keeper's point of view, he is trying to help by allowing yachts to fill in some of the gaps left by the commercial traffic. By and large, the professional barge skippers in Holland and Germany are amazingly tolerant. Nevertheless, it is possible to find yourself close astern of some "giant" Rhine barge in a situation when it is she who will have to get under way before you. She cannot (or will not) bring her bow away from the lock side by merely pushing with a boathook—she might weigh 2000 tonnes. She will take it as a matter of course to use her springs and her engine power. It is up to you to have made sure that your head rope is at an angle where it can do its job.

Similarly, there can be considerable difficulties when using small locks such as in the Caledonian or the Göta Canals. When going "down" there is no problem; all that is required is the slack away head and stern ropes as the water level falls. However, when going "up", especially in an old-fashioned lock, the turbulence as the water runs into the lock can be considerable.

The worst locks I know of are the locks at the Stockholm end of the Göta Canal when the canal is busy. There is **just** room for six yachts in some of these locks, only just. Those who enter first have to put out head ropes that lead not far off the vertical. Then, when the gates have been closed and the water begins to sw.l around at the top end of the lock, the water rises, causing the head rope to slacken. In turn, that allows the bow to fall

(a) In locks used by large commercial vessels a yacht may be directed to occupy a berth close astern of a ship. Usually small craft are directed to leave the lock first but in the circumstances shown, make sure that the yacht's head rope is led as far forward as possible. The turbulence when close to a commercial ship's propeller can be severe.

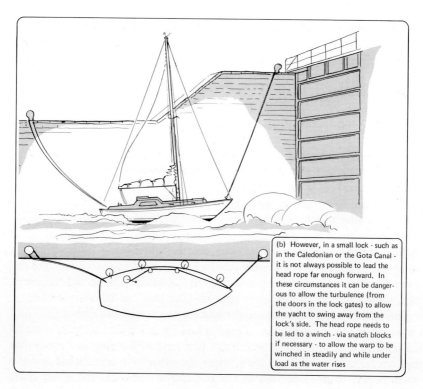

(b) However, in a small lock - such as in the Caledonian or the Gota Canal - it is not always possible to lead the head rope far enough forward. In these circumstances it can be dangerous to allow the turbulence (from the doors in the lock gates) to allow the yacht to swing away from the lock's side. The head rope needs to be led to a winch - via snatch blocks if necessary - to allow the warp to be winched in steadily and while under load as the water rises

FIG. 8.9. *Warps in locks*

off—away from the lock side which, in turn, makes the effect of the eddies even worse.

The answer is reasonably simple, but proper precautions must be made beforehand. Either there must be about three "gorillas" on the foredeck to take in the slack in the head rope as the water rises, or the head rope should have been led to a winch. The latter is the better alternative, and a block at the stemhead (or near the bow) and another one or two around amidships will allow the head rope to be led to a cockpit winch. A motor yacht might have to lead it to an anchor windlass, but both power (of some sort) and strength are essential.

The point is not that the initial load is so great—it is not. The point is that the load becomes great if the bow is allowed to fall off across the turbulence of the water rushing into the lock through the "doors" in the upper gates.

In a modern lock the water gushes in via ports in the sides and in the bottom, so that there is practically no turbulence at all. All that is required is to have a man forward hauling in the slack of the head rope as the water rises. In the older type, on the other hand, beware—and anyone who has been through the Caledonian Canal or the Göta Canal in fresh conditions will understand my liking for closed fairleads.

In addition, canal work, more than anything else, reinforces what was said about the need to lead fender lines with a turn round a stanchion base—or some other strong point—before taking a turn around the lifelines themselves. With a large crew, one or two can be allocated the job of standing-by with a fender, but if shorthanded the fenders should be positioned beforehand and that will require a little thought. What is right for a pontoon is not necessarily right for lying against a lock wall and quite likely to be unsatisfactory for lying alongside another yacht. However, for all those alternatives, large fenders are better than small ones and note, in particular, the bow fender (shown dotted in Fig. 8.4(b)). A large fender well forward can save many an embarrassing moment for a short-handed boat, but it needs to be large to do any worthwhile work, because of the flare.

Leaving a Berth

The procedures for letting go are really much the same as for coming alongside, except that they are usually easier. Chapter 7 recommended the carrying of much longer boathooks than is the norm, and one of the reasons why they are useful is the way the head, or the stern, can be swung away from a pontoon with a nice long pole.

In the first place the spike on the boathook should be a spike, pointed. Then, either the rubber "inner" end can be used if bearing off on another boat or the spike comes into its own if it can be jabbed into the wood of a lock post or jetty. That is what it is for, and the type of boathook end without a spike is just silly. I prefer one hook and a spike, not two hooks and a spike.

With the former it is less likely to become caught accidentally. However, one tip that I learnt the hard way, recently. Screw a small roundhead wood screw into the "inner" end of the pole, in line with the hook at the "outer" end. In that manner your hand can tell on a pitch black night in which direction the hook is pointing.

Remember the absolute minimum length would be 2 metres; 3 metres is far better.

Small commercial ships—and also large ones that do not have the benefit of bow thrusters—use their springs to advantage when leaving a berth. If the engines are put slow astern when the stern spring is still fast, the bow will steadily swing out from the jetty. The same is also true the other way round. Go slow ahead against a bow spring and the stern swings clear. Nevertheless, it is a manoeuvre that applies more to larger craft than small because up to say 12 metres l.o.a. the displacement is such that the same effect can be achieved so much more surely with the use of one man leaning on the boathook.

The main reason why getting under way is so much easier than coming alongside is that the timing is more in the hands of those who have to undertake the manoeuvre. What is the tidal stream doing? What is the wind effect likely to be? Is the channel clear? Is everything that will be needed ready, and to hand? When coming alongside a last minute problem might be a problem because the boat was already committed to what was about to happen. When leaving the berth, on the other hand, the timing is normally in the hands of those who are about to leave.

Another similarity, however, is the use that can be made of slip ropes. Remembering at all times that a slip rope must be led so that it will slip, when required, a slip rope led to another boat, or to another pontoon up tide or up wind, can easily transform an almost impossible manoeuvre into a perfectly straightforward one. The point is really that with a slip rope to windward the skipper can do whatever has to be done in two stages. If preparatory to motoring out of a leeward berth, the bow is pushed out into the wind, the engine must be put ahead and the boat must be made to gather steerage way, otherwise the effect of the wind will be to blow her back onto any obstructions to leeward. With a slip rope to windward, on the other hand, the same operation can be done without rush and often without any risk of falling off before that vital commodity—steerage way—has been gathered.

Other tricks of the trade, when leaving a berth, include allowing the tide to swing the boat right round while still in her berth. So long as the tidal stream rate is moderate, it is amazing how easy it is to swing a yacht; usually with just one man standing on the pontoon and "walking" one end up wind or tide as the wind or tide carries the other end round in a half-circle.

Yet another useful dodge is to "walk" the whole boat to a more advantageous position before actually letting go of the shore. In a marina it can be far safer to manhandle a boat in or out of a tight corner rather than to have to use the engines.

Finally, when planning to leave a marina berth, pause a moment and think. Have you told somebody where you are bound? As Chapter 11 will explain, a frighteningly large proportion of rescue services' time is spent looking for somebody who was thought to be "overdue" when in fact plans had been changed and nobody had thought to mention the fact to others who might be anxious.

Also have you paid your harbour dues? Many harbours still run on a system of trust. If yachtsmen are not willing to co-operate and to take some initiative themselves, we shall end up with armies of dues-collectors in every port, with the obvious increase in the dues themselves that goes with that type of collection.

We still live in an era where, in most parts of the world, visiting yachts are welcome. In some places there is no charge at all, in others the charge may seem exorbitant, but mainly exorbitant by comparison. The more we show a willingness to pay what is expected, the longer will we enjoy the truly amazing "open-house" tradition that most ports follow.

9

Harbour Authorities and the Law

WHEN planning the original synopsis for this book I had intended to include summaries of the bylaws from selective, major ports. In practice, when a representative handful were examined, it was found that some were not applicable, some were rather out-of-date, some were about to be rewritten and some hardly mentioned small craft at all: they were there to give "teeth" to the laws affecting commercial vessels.

Although it may seem strange, the law that affects most of U.K. ports is based on the Harbours Docks and Piers Clauses Act of 1847, and although many ports have additional bylaws it is somewhat unrealistic to imagine that visiting small craft skippers will be familiar with the ramifications of all local legislation.

In general the bylaws in a commercial harbour give the harbour authority very wide-reaching powers, and the all-too-common feeling that: "It's a free country. I have as much right to be here as he has" is far from the truth. In reality some bylaw or other usually covers speed, track, mooring, anchoring, the disposal of rubbish, or even the state of health of the Master. Thus, from the small craft point of view, it is more important that the "spirit" rather than the "letter" of any bylaw should be observed.

In that connection, it is appropriate to stress that in a commercial harbour—and Harwich is a good example again, because of the high volume of both commercial and private small craft traffic—what may seem like open water to the small vessel may be a highly restricted channel to a VLCC. The fact that a ferry might have sufficient water to allow her to alter course to avoid a small craft by no means suggests that it is her duty to do so; nor is it wise that she should be required to do so.

The point at issue usually revolves around the interpretation of what is meant by a narrow channel in Rule 9. To use the Southampton area as another example, a laden VLCC inward-bound in the area to the north of the Nab Tower—several miles from land—is in a narrow channel in one place where the channel is dredged whereas the same piece of water might be as far out into the "open sea" as a particular, half-decked day-boat had ever travelled. Both might be perfectly equipped and adequately crewed, but the relatively responsibilities towards the Harbour Authority as well as towards each other would be completely different.

With many harbour bylaws dating back 30 years and more, it is obvious that none were phrased with the present explosion of small craft in mind. Nevertheless, most harbours have bylaws covering the need to " . . . inform the Board's Signal Station on entering . . . " or some such phrase. Also clauses such as: "The Master shall moor, anchor, place, load, unload and move, and shall cease to moor, anchor, place, load, unload, or move such vessel in accordance with the directions from time to time given . . . " are about as all-embracing as they could be.

On the other side of the coin, even if commercial port authorities have powers to do almost anything within their own authority area—and they even have powers to move sunken vessels and send the owner the bill—there are remarkably few examples of those powers being abused.

It is easy for any authority, anywhere, to say: "Go away." In practice, any organization knows that unreasonable restriction would soon lead to enquiries, protests, petitions and all the paraphernalia associated with living in what we like to think of as a "free country".

Today the RYA Regions have representation, of various types, on Water Authorities and Harbour Authority committees throughout the country. The RYA is also represented on numerous Fairway Committees and on ten Water Authority Recreation and Conservation Committees.

Some are useful; others less so. However, the principle of consultation is well established and as far as yachtsmen are concerned the feedback is via the Cruising and General Purposes Committee of the RYA to the RYA Council.

The Association also has two representatives on the Department of Transport, Marine Directorate, Safety of Navigation Committee and the same two men (1985) serve on the U.K. Search and Rescue Committee. Neither of those committees is concerned with the problems of any particular harbour, but both have considerable say in the overall liaison between the commercial maritime world and small craft.

Special Signals

Since the adoption of the present Collision Regulations, when dredger signals were included for the first time, the number of "special" signals that apply to a particular harbour is far less than it was.

The Netherlands Authorities still have special signals for some bucket, non-self-propelled, dredgers working in their inland waters, but that particular anomaly is no particular problem.

The Thames has certain special signals that differ, somewhat, from the Collision Regulations. Code "D", for example, when made as a sound signal, is restricted, in the Collision Regulations, to use " . . . in restricted visibility".

The Port of London bylaws permit its use in clear visibility and, in practice, the signal is used frequently by tugs while towing.

London also uses a signal for a vessel turning round: "four short and rapid blasts, followed, after a short interval, by one further short blast, if turning to starboard or two if turning to port".

That particular "turning signal" is used in a number of other ports, including The Medway, but there is conflict. Milford Haven, for example, uses "four short blasts" to mean "not-under-command or unable to give way to an approaching vessel".

In practice any small craft should treat any multiple-blast signal to mean they should keep clear—particularly as the Collision Regulations Rule 34(d) states that " . . . at least five short and rapid blasts . . . " shall indicate that a ship fails to understand the intentions of another or is in doubt whether sufficient action is being taken by the other to avoid collision.

In practice, sound signals are not used, nor heard, nearly as much as they used to be. The modern ship's bridge is enclosed, and if the officer of the watch wishes to "signal" to another ship—or even to someone on his own forecastle—it is more likely that he will pick up a telephone handset than use a whistle signal. Nevertheless, especially from the small craft's point of view, that trend is greatly to be regretted. The fact that a small craft is required to keep clear, in many circumstances merely accents the need for proper signalling.

Four short blasts plus one in the Thames means "I am about to turn round to starboard." Four short blasts, in Milford Haven, is a signal requiring the approaching vessel to keep out of the way. Of the two I would prefer to see the four plus one and four plus two recognized internationally and to reserve the "five or more" signal from Rule 34(d) for the circumstances described in the Milford Haven bylaws.

One of the sillier anomalies concerning special port signalling—and the problem is world-wide—is the use in many large ports of a special signal to indicate an explosive cargo—an all-round red light. What action any other vessel is supposed to take, other than that already covered by the collision regulations, is not clear. However, the most confusing aspect of the use of that particular signal is that from certain angles an all-round red light will be vertically above the vessel's port light. Thus she will be indicating a state of "not-under-command". On seeing that, another vessel might take action that would not be justified and the very signal that is supposed to avoid a collision might well cause one.

It is to be hoped that common sense will let that particular piece of "nonsense" die a natural death soon. If a ship is manoeuvring with difficulty because of her draught, there is already a special "deep draught" signal. Possibly there is a need for another "special consideration" signal. However, I am sure "one, all-round red light" is not it.

Moorings

For reasons that must be buried in history, the arrangements for small craft moorings differ widely from port to port. At Burnham-on-Crouch, for example, all the moorings are owned by the local boatyards. Only a few miles away, on the Medway, almost all are owned privately or by the clubs. In another large yachting centre, Poole, there is a mixture, the Harbour Commissioners having moorings, the clubs having them and local yards and marinas having yet more.

The rights of way and the rights of navigation are similar on both tidal and non-tidal waters and there is generally a right (subject to Collision Regulations and bylaws) temporarily to "stop". However, there is no right to lay permanent moorings.

"A man may not use the highway to stable his horse", but what his rights are is not so easily expressed. (See *You and the law*, RYA G 10.) Generally the rights to the sea-bed and the foreshore rest with the Crown, but there are exceptions based on some ancient charter: Beaulieu River is one. The "Crown" in this context is the Crown Estate Commissioners, and they control the "rents" of many "landlords".

Furthermore, moorings can often be affected by planning authorities, because a mooring may be a "development" in the eyes of the law. The suggestion that if there is no statute to prevent him, anyone can lay a mooring where he likes has been described by a U.K. judge as " . . . little less than fantastic".

The question of the right to charge rates on a mooring are less obvious, but the fact that many mooring holders do not pay rates is usually more a question of small sums being too expensive to collect individually rather than that there is not the right to do so. If a boatyard controls a block of moorings, the local authority can charge the boatyard the rates; they are then passed on to the occupier. If, on the other hand, there is no overall "owner" of a cluster of mooring buoys, then rates may not be sought.

Insurance

Few yachtsmen appreciate that statute law overrides the detailed terms of any marine insurance, and the most difficult aspect of all for the layman to understand is the question of the ability of a man to limit his liability.

The principle of the limitation of liability was first introduced to protect the shipowner from the full consequences of the behaviour of his crew. However, the problem is so complex that too short a summary can do more harm than good. For example, a Master who was also the Owner—as in a yacht—might, in law, be acting as the Owner or be acting as the Master: the two responsibilities are not necessarily the same!

To try to explain how the law can work, an extreme example was reported in *The Times* in 1984 when a Liberian tanker anchored off the River Tees and her ground tackle damaged an oil pipeline from Ekofisk Field. Thirteen oil companies claimed from the ship for a sum exceeding 25 million dollars. The shipowners admitted liability, but sought the right to limit their liability to under a million dollars.

The subsequent court case revolved around whether the Master *ought to have known* of the existence of the pipeline. He was navigating on a very out-of-date chart, but the case finally went against the owners because it was shown that the owners knew that the ship's charts were very out of date, but that they had ignored a report to that effect. To put it bluntly, it was their fault too and therefore "... as a matter of law, the actual fault of the Shipowners".

Thus, although the principle of the limitation of liability is more "good" than "bad", there is some doubt regarding the amount that is applicable. New laws were introduced in 1984, and the new "platforms" below which limitation cannot be claimed are (1985) about £200,000 for personal injury and about £150,000 for property damage.

From that it should be obvious that any insurance policy needs to have a "third party" clause for a sum that may bear little relation to the market value of the vessel herself.

Another area of misunderstanding regarding insurance concerns the value of the vessel insured. There is no point in over-insuring. If a 20-year-old boat is written off as a total loss, the owner may be entitled to claim a vessel of similar type and age; underwriters are not required to build him a new boat! It is the true market value of the boat that matters, and yachtsmen must bear in mind too that when filling out the proposal form they must make a full declaration. If incorrect information about the vessel or the way she will be used is given, the insurance company can seek to deny liability.

Other points to watch are the periods of validity, the geographical area covered by the policy and special features such as Excess Clauses. In my experience a careful man, with a well-found boat, is well advised to carry a sizeable excess clause. The insurance company then know that they will not be bothered with small claims and the resultant reduction in premium can be significant.

As with buying a car or a house, a good insurance broker is almost as important as a good insurance company. And, as a generalization, fancy "special offers" in the insurance world are as suspect as they are in any other market.

Salvage

There is a well-established custom that yachtsmen do not ever claim salvage against their fellows—and long may it remain—but the law of salvage is almost as complex as the law affecting insurance.

First, it is important to distinguish between any moral right for reward, and the law. If a man finds another's property he is obliged, in law, to take reasonable steps to discover the identity of the owner and to return it.

On shore, if a man risks his belongings in trying to help another in difficulties, there is no legal responsibility on the owner of the car that was broken down, or the house that was on fire, to compensate or repay. At sea the law is different.

First, the action must be voluntary. Next, the property, or part of it, must be saved, and thirdly, the vessel, or someone on it, must be in real danger. For example, a man would find it difficult to claim he was not in real danger if he had already fired distress signals.

Salvage services might include towage, pilotage or even merely standing by, but salvage cannot be claimed by anyone acting in an official position. If a police launch offered assistance, there is no problem.

Ideally any acceptance of a tow, in difficult circumstances, should be preceded by the signing of a Form of Salvage. In practice that is likely to be difficult, if not impossible, and the advice has to be to try to ensure that at least the crew of the vessel seeking help are witnesses of what is arranged. If it is merely a tow that is required, make that clear. If salvage is mentioned, the services should be accepted under the Lloyd's open Standard Agreement "No cure, No Pay", and the payment for the claim will then be settled, in the event of success.

That summarizes the law, but there are countless "myths" about what is involved. In the real world most seamen are willing to help each other, and I know of numerous occasions when commercial fishing boats have helped yachtsmen in serious trouble and "settled" for a couple of bottles of whisky and a handshake.

His Honour Judge Phelan, whose chapter on salvage in the RYA booklet G 10 has been referred to here, summed up the position well.

> "Yachtsmen should not become churlish in their caution. Adequate thanks and a round of drinks do not prejudice either party if a matter later goes to law."

One of the strange features of human behaviour is that after a period under stress, when the wind and waves die down, the seasickness vanishes, and when the idea of drowning has passed into oblivion, a man is rarely willing to admit to himself, let alone to anybody else, that he was in real danger.

The Royal National Lifeboat Institution has countless examples of people who did not even want to say "Thank you" after being rescued.

That is rather sad, but something we have to face up to. I know first hand of one couple with a newly purchased yacht that came ashore off the Dengie Marshes in most unfriendly weather. The local Coastguard offered them shelter for the night in her own home. She then spent several hours helping to recover the more valuable property. There was no question of salvage; the initial help had been while the Coastguard was on duty and later everything was from goodwill. The coupled went away from the Coastguard's home the following day without a word!

Those who work professionally for our rescue services and those who work voluntarily for the RNLI, or for yacht clubs, do not do it for acclaim; but common courtesies can help.

Club Custom and Behaviour

Finally, under a general heading of "other laws", the complexities of planning permissions for yacht clubs, of local bylaws and of licensing laws are outside my brief. Nevertheless, the relationship between the yacht club and the harbour authority must not be ignored.

A Milford Haven bylaw sums up the position well.

> "The organizer of any boat race, regatta or other occasion when a number of vessels is expected to assemble ... shall give ... notice thereof ... ".

Generally the liaison between recognized clubs and harbour authorities is good. At Southampton the Cowes Combined Clubs have excellent relations with the Southampton Authority and for many years past special racing buoys have been laid by the Harbour Board, to avoid the possibility of confusion by having yachts using navigational buoys as turning marks. The local racing rules themselves also take note of the problems, and all courses are laid to make the need to cross narrow channels as infrequent as possible.

Consultation is the key. Warn pilots beforehand if there is to be a regatta. Ensure that visiting competitors are made aware of any local problems. Discipline the club's own members if they cause annoyance to other users of the harbour. Even invite the Harbour Master to the club's annual dinner!

With common sense, we will not run out of water on which to sail for a long time yet!

Other Rules and Regulations

A GLANCE at the subject headings for this chapter might given an impression that there are a large number of government authorities and quasi-authorities affecting the freedom of a small boat to come and go. In fact that is not true. Yachtsmen generally enjoy a remarkable freedom and in the United Kingdom our freedom is considerably more pronounced than that of most of our neighbours.

From the national point of view, almost the only requirement—apart from the obvious need to observe the Collision Regulations and any local bylaws as outlined in Chapter 9—is the requirement under the Merchant Shipping Act to wear an ensign. However, in home waters there is no legal requirement, in the Act, to do even that if under 50 GRT.

Ensigns

In practice, most small craft do wear an ensign in home waters, even if there is no actual requirement to do so, because it is a pleasant custom and is a means of showing that the Master is "in charge"—in the technical sense—even if he is actually ashore.

Overseas, while in the territorial waters of another nation, all vessels **must** wear an ensign, and there is also the very well-established custom of wearing a courtesy ensign of the country being visited as well (see later).

The ensign is worn from 0800 to sunset or 2100 (which ever is the earlier) local time or from 0900 in the winter. The times, as with practically everything else to do with the use of flags at sea, are a custom, the reasons for which are buried in history. Note that an ensign is referred to as being worn. All flags are hoisted. All flags are then flow, before being lowered, but an ensign, by tradition, is worn.

The purpose of the legal requirement to wear an ensign when overseas is obvious. A port authority needs to know the origin (allegiance) of the visitor. Nowadays there are many other ways of announcing one's intentions, but the requirement to wear an ensign remains.

The courtesy flag, mentioned previously, is a miniature of the maritime flag of the country being visited. Note that where there is a difference it is the *maritime* flag. Vessels visiting U.K. waters wear a Red Ensign, not the Union flag. However, for U.K. yachtsmen visiting our neighbours, there are no special maritime courtesy flags.

It needs to be made clear that there is no legal requirement whatever to wear a courtesy ensign. Nevertheless, some of our near-neighbours—especially Holland and the Scandinavian countries of Norway and Sweden—are very much more flag-conscious than we are in the United Kingdom. Needless and considerable offence can be caused by ignoring the custom.

In the days when International Code flags were used for conversation, it was normal to have several flag hoists in use at the same time. Thus the various hoists had to be read in the right order. All that is now history. In today's International Code, each signal is made with one hoist. However, the old order remains. The starboard (outer) crosstree is the primary position, followed by the port (outer) crosstree and the starboard (inner) and so on. Thus the established custom is always to wear a courtesy ensign in the starboard rigging: no other flag is "superior" to the ensign.

To recapitulate, the only requirement for small craft is to wear an ensign in the territorial waters of other states, but to show how deeply the regulations are buried in history, the actual wording of the Act (at present under review) refers to the use:

> " ... if there is sufficient light for it to be seen ... on falling in with any other ship, or ships, at sea or when within sight of or near land and especially when passing or approaching forts, batteries, signal or coastguard stations, lighthouses or towns."

Furthermore, and remembering that practically everyone would wish to wear an ensign with pride, it is worth pointing out that most of our neighbours wear ensigns that are appreciably larger than those usually worn by small craft on our own coasts. Furthermore, they are invariably clean and untorn.

In the United Kingdom some yachtsmen show one, sometimes two, idiosyncrasies which are difficult to understand. The most unfortunate one is to wear a tatty little piece of bunting—once an ensign. The idiosyncrasy is also seen on some luggage, on which people will leave old and torn labels—supposedly to indicate how well travelled they are. With ensigns, the scruffier the better it seems—even on boats where thousands of pounds a year are lavished on maintenance.

The second British oddity is to have so-called privileged ensigns—blue or red; usually defaced with an emblem representing the owner's club, but often amazingly tatty. Overseas this practice is looked upon as very odd. Those that wear defaced ensigns are often mistaken for service yachts or other "official" representatives.

The custom of wearing defaced red or blue ensigns is one that is well engrained in the U.K. sport, and if it gives pleasure it would be difficult to make a case why it should not be continued at home. Nevertheless, when cruising to other countries the Red Ensign is the flag to wear—even if privileged ensigns are perfectly legal—because it causes no confusion.

After all, it is somewhat illogical for us to expect the visiting foreign yachts to wear a red courtesy ensign if we wear something different ourselves.

Finally, it must be stressed that the ensign represents the country with which the vessel is registered, not necessarily the country of origin of the skipper.

If a German were to charter a Swedish yacht and then take her to Danish waters, he must wear a Swedish ensign and a Danish courtesy ensign in his starboard crosstree or rigging when in Danish waters. If he wished to indicate his own nationality, it would be perfectly acceptable for him to wear a courtesy ensign representing his own country in the port rigging—with or without the courtesy ensign of the country being visited. In the example given, the German would thus wear a Swedish ensign with a German courtesy ensign in the port rigging all the cruise. When he was in Danish waters he would add a Danish courtesy ensign in the starboard rigging.

Complicated, but logical.

Customs and Excise

As has just been outlined, the requirements for ensigns are mandatory, but despite the extensive use of flags for yacht racing, for regattas and for decoration the only other mandatory requirement for the use of International Code flags is for the Code "Q" in some, but by no means all, countries.

Traditionally the Code "Q" flag has always been used for the request for health clearance. It signifies: "My vessel is healthy and I request free pratique." In practice, and for decades, the Port Health Authorities board at the same time as Customs and Excise officers and as far as small craft are concerned the two duties are often performed by the same man.

Now nearly all that has changed. Commercial vessels arrange for Customs and Excise clearance either by radio or via their agents. Health clearance, as far as north-western European countries are concerned, is virtually a thing of the past. Thus it is the Immigration Laws and the questions of the import of illegal goods that matter most, with the Customs Officers also being involved in Excise, the collection of taxes.

Thus the question of the "Q" flag is nowadays little or nothing to do with the health of those on board; it is used by the authorities in **some** countries and in **some** circumstances to announce the arrival of a vessel from another country and to indicate whether she has dutiable goods to declare or not.

France

The French now require all visiting craft to be registered, and for U.K.

yachts a new, simplified registration scheme was started in 1984, for those who were not previously registered under the Merchant Shipping Act (see later).

On arrival, the yacht is required to fly the Code "Q" if she has dutiable stores on board, and a member of the crew must report to the Customs Office, Douane. If, on the other hand, the visiting yacht is not carrying dutiable stores, there is no requirement to fly a "Q" flag; nor is there any need to report.

Since the new regulations were introduced, the French are much more strict than they were previously. For example, if a British yacht visits a French port with no dutiable stores on board; she then buys stores in France, for her return, but after leaving the French port bad weather forces her to re-enter France, to another port. She is then treated as a visiting foreign yacht *with* stores on board and *must* fly the "Q" flag, as well as report her arrival, despite the fact that the stores were bought in France.

The French are also very strict regarding the complications of crew changes. If one man brings the boat into the country and another intends to take her out, there are likely to be problems.

U.K. yachtsmen are advised to consult the Royal Yachting Association beforehand. Similarly, there can be very severe problems for any boats with paying passengers on board. Even school ships can have difficulties, and all charter boats and training ships tend to be treated as commercial vessels and taxed as such.

Belgium

The Belgian regulations require a Code "Q" flag to be flown by vessels entering Belgian ports from other countries, but in practice the authorities appear somewhat casual regarding whether it is used or not. Yachts are usually visited by Immigration officials (a blue uniform) when they first enter the country, but not often by Customs officials (a khaki uniform). In 1985 the authorities are introducing a computerized system to keep track of visiting small craft and their whereabouts. Thus the checks are likely to get more strict, rather than less so.

Holland

In Holland too the regulations have been tightened considerably since the beginning of 1985. In the past, yachts were expected to report to Customs only when they had dutiable stores on board. Now all yachts have to report at the first port-of-call and collect a certificate which will have to be carried on board—to show on demand—but which will serve for 12 months and can be produced on subsequent visits.

While cruising in Dutch inland waters, yachts are also visited by uniformed as well as plain clothes officials from time to time, but it seems to be tax, drug and immigration problems that concern the authorities, in so far as small craft are concerned, rather than the "traditional" ones of carrying tobacco or spirits.

Germany

Yet again the regulations are somewhat different. No "Q" flag is required if the yacht is coming from a Scandinavian or EEC country, but the first port of call **must** be a Customs port.

The exception is for boats passing straight through the Kiel Canal. They are required to fly the 3rd Substitute in the starboard rigging to signify that they have not cleared Customs, and they may pass straight through without clearance. Most yachts, however, would expect to go ashore in Germany and they would normally clear in Brunsbüttle or in Kiel itself. At Kiel there is also a special dock for clearing outward bound traffic, on the east side of the entrance to the Kieler Fiord.

Denmark

In Denmark we again see regulations that are much more strictly enforced than they used to be. Since 1983 the Danish authorities have enforced a regulation that has existed for years, but which was not enforced in the past. It says that all small craft shall clear customs, both in and out, "even if not calling at a Danish port".

Bearing in mind that it is not possible to enter the Baltic, via the Kattergat, without passing through Danish territorial waters, the regulation means that yachts bound say for the west coast of Sweden must visit two Danish ports on the way.

In practice, and after representation from the International Regulations Committee of the International Yacht Racing Union, the Danish authorities usually accept a "clearance" from a yacht making a suitable radiotelephone call on her approach. Officially the regulation remains, but in practice radio seems to be an answer to an otherwise onerous chore. It applies to all yachts, except those from EEC countries which have less than the "duty free" allowances on board. They are allowed to pass without calling in to clear.

Norway

Of all our near neighbours, Norway has the most relaxed attitude to visiting yachts. No "Q" flag is required, and apart from the need to report on first arrival there are no problems.

Sweden

Sweden, a country with a coastline almost as beautiful as that of Norway, and with amazingly good facilities for yachts, requires all visiting yachts to clear at a Customs port—not any port—on first arrival in the country. The Swedish authorities appear somewhat officious, by the standards of some other Scandinavian countries, but the regulations are clear.

Note too, when cruising in Swedish waters, that there are many prohibited areas—clearly shown on the excellent local charts—and that the Swedes seem particularly sensitive concerning the proximity of their Eastern European neighbours.

Republic of Ireland

On arrival in an Irish port yachts should fly the "Q" flag and a member of the crew must report to the local police—the Garda. U.K. citizens do not need either a passport or a visa.

United Kingdom

In some ways our own regulations are stricter than the others. For one thing, the use of the "Q" is mandatory for all, and must be exhibited when entering territorial waters. Also the regulations say that the flag should be "suitably illuminated" during the hours of darkness. In the International Code there is a reference to vessels requiring Customs clearance exhibiting "a red light over a white light where it can best be seen". However, as already explained, commercial vessels today arrange clearance by radio and the regulations for yachts no longer refer to the International signal. Precisely how a flag is supposed to be illuminated is not made clear.

What is clear, however, is the procedure that yachts must follow both outward bound and inward bound. Notice of Departure is given on a three-part Customs form—C1328. The top copy is to be deposited with the Customs before departure. The second sheet is for use, suitably amended, when the vessel returns. The third part is to be kept on board.

Arrival formalities are now very strictly enforced. Apart from the "Q" flag, a yacht is required to notify arrival, by telephone, within 2 hours of arrival. Then, assuming there is nothing to declare, no animals on board and no "non-patrials", the crew may leave the yacht and go their various ways after 2 hours. The second copy of the form, suitably signed, is then posted to the authority.

If, on the other hand, there are goods to declare or other reasons why the "quick report procedure" is not applicable, then the crew must await the arrival of a Customs Officer.

A part of the reason why our regulations are so strict is that H.M. Customs are also responsible for the prevention of the spread of rabies, and to bring in an animal or bird, including domestic pets, invites very heavy penalties.

From the Customs point of view, the Channel Islands count as a foreign country. A "Q" flag is required when visiting from a French port, but not when arriving from a U.K. one. However, the same arrival procedures must be followed, when returning to the United Kingdom from the Channel Islands as from any other foreign country.

The above summary may appear complicated. In practice, the system operates very smoothly. Full details are available in H.M. Customs and Excise booklet Notice No. 8 for boats based in the United Kingdom and Notice No. 8a for others.

The Notice No. 8 is straightforward, but nowhere is it made clear that the notification of arrival may be made by *radio*telephone. That notification has to be made within 2 hours, as already explained, and it has to be made when "...the vessel arrives at the place where the person responsible is required to clear customs...", but it might still be pouring with rain and the ship's own radio might well be the most convenient "tool" to use to make the notification of arrival.

Immigration

As has already been made clear in the summary of Customs procedures, Immigration arrangements differ from country to country. They also differ, in the United Kingdom, from port to port. By that I mean that some of the larger ports—London, for example—have separate Immigration Officers who may board visiting ships, but as far as yachtsmen are concerned the procedures are usually controlled by the Customs Officer. It is he who might call in an Immigration Officer if there were non-patrials (persons not having the right to live in the United Kingdom) on board; there is no requirement for the yachtsman to take any extra action other than the procedure for notification of arrival to the Customs authorities or Police.

Registration

As was briefly explained at the beginning of this chapter, there is more than one type of registration.

In law there has been a requirement since 1894 that all U.K. ships going more than a certain distance offshore must be registered British ships. Nevertheless, that is a law that has never been implemented.

Full Registration

A full registration as a British ship, now called a Part 1 Registration, is still available; not only does it prove that the vessel is British, it shows title and it shows who are the owners. It is still needed for many mortgage schemes, and the vessel has to have a professional measurement survey, the name has to be approved and there has to be a proof of ownership by means of a builder's certificate and suitable bills of sale. It is a complicated and expensive process.

Small Ships Register (SSR)

As was outlined earlier, the French authorities decided that as from January 1984 all vessels using their ports had to be registered to show their country of origin: their right to wear their ensign.

This decision was partly enforcing laws that already existed, but mainly to prevent tax-dodging within their own country. The effect was that the British Government had to introduce a simplified form of registration to satisfy the French requirements, and they arranged for the RYA to administer it.

The procedure is simple. It costs only £10—appreciably less than 10 per cent of the cost of the Part 1 Registration—and although the SSR does not prove title, it satisfies the French needs.

Those with a SSR carry an identification number, in letters 30 millimetres high, on a conspicuous position above deck. Over ten thousand British yachtsmen took advantage of the scheme in its first year.

International Certificate of Pleasure Navigation (ICPN)

An even simpler system of registration was introduced in the 1970s by the International Regulations Committee of the International Yacht Racing Union, to satisfy a demand for "ship's papers" for small craft passing from one country to another.

The document (which is not required in the United Kingdom, but which is still of use to many U.K. yachtsmen) merely lists the basic size, name and nationality facts, and it is issued to its members by fifteen national authorities throughout Europe.

The demand was primarily found on inland frontiers. A man might have adequate proof that the car he was driving was his, but he sometimes needed something to show that his national authority considered that his boat was his, even if the document had little standing in a court of law.

An official usually asks basic questions about name, length and the like. Considering that the cost—in time and in money—of obtaining an ICPN is minute, it is well worth carrying by all except those already having a Part 1 Registration or a Small Ships Register Certificate. However, even the holder of a SSR might find the ICPL of use when crossing inland frontiers with a boat on a trailer, because it is officially recognized by many and has been in use for years.

Among our near neighbours, the simple ICPN is recognized by Norway,

Denmark, Sweden, Poland, the German Democratic Republic, the Federal Republic of Germany, Holland, Belgium (NOT France) and Portugal, and it is recommended, although not officially recognized, for Spain.

In the United Kingdom we tend to smile a little at the procedures of frontier officials, but perhaps if we were not an island people we might be more understanding of how the various practices arose.

Crew List

One other "piece of paper" which is always worth carrying is a crew list. A commercial ship is usually required to carry both crew and passenger lists. For yachts there is no such requirement, but in my experience of extensive cruising in north-western European waters the value of having a well-presented list is enormous.

Almost always the visiting official, be he Customs, Immigration or Police or Harbour staff, will want some data about the boat or about those on board. The data of the boat is in the SSR papers or the INPN card. The crew list—with full names, addresses and passport numbers of all on board—seems to smooth the way in a remarkable manner.

Not only would I strongly recommend carrying the list, I would recommend carrying more than one copy. If the objective is to simplify the form-filling task of the harbour official, to be able to say "Please take it with you, if you wish" seems to act like magic.

Yachtsmen still benefit from the feeling that visiting yachtsmen are slightly eccentric men and women who are probably harmless, and who are usually welcome because of the money they are likely to spend in the town. That may not always be true, but a crew list on club notepaper seems to help the process of entering a foreign country out of all proportion to the little trouble it takes to prepare it.

Certificate of Competence

As with the question of "boat passports" just described, there is no *requirement* in the United Kingdom to carry any Certificates of Competence (other than for radio, to be described shortly), but there is such a requirement in certain other countries.

In the United Kingdom the RYA has a very full training programme, with "end-products" in the form of certificates ranging from Competent Crew to Master. These certificates are obtained through a number of different grades of RYA Approved Teaching Establishments, but the real beauty of the whole system, for us, is that it is all voluntary.

Increasingly, overseas there is a requirement from the government concerned to require qualifications, and for the congested waters of some of the Dutch and German rivers and canals it is not too surprising.

By 1985 there was no actual requirement for any **visiting** yachtsmen, with a small craft of low machinery power, to carry any certification, but in any case the RYA Yachtmaster is recognized by both The Netherlands and the German Maritime Authorities as adequate.

U.K. yachtsmen who have qualified themselves to that standard and are the holders of a Department of Trade and Industry/Royal Yachting Association "Yachtmaster (Offshore)" Certificate are well advised to have it on board while cruising. You may never be asked for it, but in the event of any problems it would establish a degree of status that could be invaluable.

Otherwise, the RYA can issue a very simple Certificate of Competence for "Sportsboats". In law it means little, but some countries recognize it, and if trailing a runabout across Europe while on holiday it might be well worth having.

Ship Licence

Despite the words used, a ship licence has nothing to do with a licence for a ship; it is the phrase used for a ship's radiotelephone licence.

As far as small craft are concerned, almost all will be equipped with VHF Only. The requirements for MF radio are much the same—but more so. Here it is VHF that matters, and the ship licence is the prime requirement for all who carry radio. The licence itself fills four pages of A4 with fine print. It specifies what is and what is not allowed, and it contains details of the frequencies which may be used.

When the ship licence is issued, it contains the ship's call sign and both licence and call sign stay with the ship unless she is sold out of U.K. ownership. At the same time, a selective call (Selcall) number will be issued, if asked for. As explained in Chapter 2, Selcall can be a most useful facility both for overall maritime safety and for the convenience of those on board.

The ship licence is issued in duplicate, and one copy has to be kept on board at all times; any suitably authorized officials at home, or overseas, can ask to see it.

Certificate of Competence

One of the more important regulations, outlined in the ship licence itself is that the set can be operated only by the holder of a "Certificate of Competence", "or in the presence of and under the supervision of a person so authorized".

Obviously it is desirable that everyone should take the "Certificate of Competence" because only by going through the hoop and studying for the test will the newcomer learn the reasons why the procedures are what they are.

Since 1983, when the RYA assumed responsibility for "VHF Only" examinations, thousands have taken the test, and there is reasonable evidence to suggest that the "bad old days", when many yachtsmen did not bother, have passed.

There is no age, or other, limit to those who can take the examination, except that they must have evidence to show they are British subjects, British protected persons or citizens of the Irish Republic. However, the "Authority to Operate" is issued only to those over 16.

The "Authority to Operate" is normally attached to the "Certificate of Competence"—and many do not realize that the "package" they receive contains two separate documents. However, there has to be two parts to the test. A moment's thought will show that a man might well be perfectly *competent* to operate, but still not have the *authority* to do so.

On the occasion when a man misbehaves, on radio, it is his "Authority to Operate" that can be revoked, not, necessarily, his "Certificate of Competence".

Light Dues

During 1985 there was considerable discussion concerning the question of light dues for small craft.

In many countries the costs of the lighthouse service are a part of the general taxation of the country, and ships, of whatever size, do not pay extra. In the United Kingdom, on the other hand, the costs of our lighthouse authorities—Trinity House, the Northern Lighthouse Board and Irish Lights—are levied from ships passing through our waters. About 85 per cent comes from foreign registered shipping. There are exceptions for ships such as ferries which make a large number of passages each year, but the principal exception as far as this book is concerned is that all vessels under 20 tonnes are not required to pay light dues.

Inevitably, with the numbers of pleasure craft rising by so much and the numbers of commercial ships falling, there have been many attempts to see a way through the maze of historical regulation and to find a cost-effective way to collect dues from small craft.

Morally there is no reason why all small craft should not pay in one way or another for the facility they enjoy. In practice, however, as there is no licensing or registration scheme in existence, there is no obvious way out of the dilemma.

For the immediate future, it seems likely that the exemption for vessels of under 20 tonnes will remain.

11

Distress and Urgency

Radio

The essence of any radiotelephone call anywhere, be it on land, sea or in the air, is that the call should be made on a frequency that will be monitored by the station to which the call is directed.

That should be self-evident, but a horrifying amount of rescue time is lost because ship-stations use incorrect frequencies. A man can call "Help, help, I am sinking" until his batteries run flat, but if he is calling on the wrong channel it is as if he was trying to semaphore to an astronaut: the message will not get through.

Much of what follows applies to distress and urgency working in general, rather than to any particular problems concerning working within a harbour. However, from the small craft point of view the procedures are usually the same, and it is possible to take full advantage of the system only if it is properly understood.

In the early days of ship's radio it was agreed internationally that the same frequency would be used both for calling and for distress. High-frequency radio (HF) uses 500 kHz, medium-frequency uses 2182 kHz and very-high-frequency (VHF), the type of short-range radiotelephony described throughout this book, uses Ch 16 (156.8 MHz).

Ch 16 is officially designated as the Distress, Safety and Calling frequency, and the principle of having the same frequency for all those functions was far easier to justify when the system was first introduced than it is today. To understand how the present system developed it is necessary to remind ourselves that the idea of every major port and every stretch of coastline having good VHF coverage had never been envisaged.

In contrast, airports have trained communicators on duty all the time, and aircraft distress traffic uses a dedicated distress frequency. At sea, without the back-up of "air traffic controllers" to monitor a dedicated distress frequency, the idea was that everyone listened on the same channel. Thus any call, for whatever purpose, was heard by everyone within range.

While the total volume of traffic was small, the system worked well; each

156

ship looked after her own. If anyone was in trouble the wireless operator on one ship knew that his fellow operator on the next ship would be using the same calling channel.

As far as VHF is concerned, the coastline of north-western Europe now has almost complete coverage on VHF via the Coast Radio Stations and, as far as the United Kingdom is concerned, we also enjoy virtually complete coverage via HM Coastguard stations as well. Furthermore, with most ports having VHF cover for their local area, we now have the situation where a vessel in distress—or even merely in difficulties and requiring assistance—has three different types of shore station that are likely to be within radio range, as well as numerous other ships that are likely to be in the vicinity.

In theory, that might sound as if there would be no problem in getting help. In practice, the problem that developed was that Ch 16 became so overloaded that, in certain areas and at certain times, it became almost useless for distress calls.

The answer, which has only recently become effective, is to keep Ch 16 clear by eliminating the calls that can, and should, be made on other frequencies. The point has been described in some detail in Chapter 2.

Almost all CRS now prefer, or require, calls on a Working Channel and all major ports prefer, or require, calls on a Working Channel. Thus Ch 16 has been relieved of most of the clutter, ship-to-ship calls being the only type of calling that is still normally made on the Distress, Safety and Calling channel.

An obvious problem is that, with Ch 16 now becoming less obstructed, the need for strict discipline in the way it is used is not so obvious. Nevertheless, education is better than legislation, and it is to be hoped that the considerable improvements in the arrangements for acquiring a Certificate of Competence, outlined in Chapter 10, will help in that direction; at least in the United Kingdom.

From that summary of the use of Ch 16 it should be obvious that more than one shore station is likely *to be able* to receive any distress call. In north-western European waters almost all CRS monitor Ch 16, but in the United Kingdom distress traffic, on Ch 16, is normally handled by HM Coastguard. A CRS would take action only if HMCG had not acknowledged. For MF distress calls, on 2182 kHz, the opposite is true. The CRS is the primary station to acknowledge. However, it is VHF frequencies that concern us here, and within a port itself there is the third alternative, a distress call might involve the harbour radio station as well as, or instead of, HMCG.

Despite what might appear a confusing pattern, the fact remains that there is remarkably good coverage of our inshore waters, and the actual agency that acknowledges the initial call is comparatively unimportant. What is important is that the call should be understood.

To achieve an acceptable standard for distress traffic the procedure for that traffic has been agreed internationally, and small craft need that discipline as much as, if not more than, their larger sisters.

The "Bible" for radiotelephony procedure is the *Handbook for Radio Operators*, for which the Department of Trade and Industry is now responsible. However, the problem for those unfamiliar with radio procedure is that it was written by those who were steeped in the theory of the subject. Thus, as a learning guide it is almost useless.

All procedures are easier to learn, and much easier to remember, if the reason for their format is explained. Thus mariners must appreciate both the agreed distress procedures as well as the occasions when different signals are appropriate.

The use of any distress signal is absolutely forbidden, except in the case of distress.

The distress signals are provided for use in cases of imminent danger, when immediate aid is necessary. Their use for less urgent purposes might result in insufficient attention being paid to calls made from ships which really require immediate assistance.

When the sending of the distress signal is not fully justified, the use should be made of the urgency signal which has priority over all other signals except distress.

Distress is defined to mean that a ship is threatened by grave and imminent danger, and that she requests immediate assistance.

Urgency is defined to mean that a ship has a very urgent message to transmit concerning the safety of a ship or the safety of a person.

Safety—the third order of priority—is defined as meaning that the station is about to transmit a message containing an important navigational or important meteorological warning.

Both HF and MF distress frequencies have auto-alarm systems associated with them, so that a particular signal triggers an alarm on the bridge, or in the wireless officer's cabin. With VHF, on the other hand, there is no auto-alarm, it is the procedure for the traffic which acts as the trigger.

It has been stressed repeatedly that there is likely to be a considerable amount of traffic on Ch 16. Thus, to break in to that traffic there has to be something to alert those listening, something to make them "switch on their ears".

Note carefully: distress traffic is divided into three parts:

(i)   a distress **signal**,
(ii) a distress **call**,
(iii) a distress **message**.

There is a good reason for that, and once the reason is understood the procedure will never be forgotten.

The distress *signal* (as there is no auto-alarm on VHF) is the word MAYDAY. It comes from the French *m'aider*, "Help me".

The distress *call* is the signal MAYDAY, spoken three times, followed by

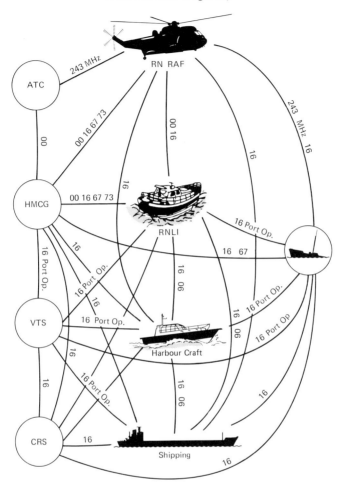

FIG. 11.1. *Distress frequencies: inshore and/or within harbour limits*

the procedural words THIS IS, followed by the name, or other identity, of the vessel in distress, also spoken three times.

The distress *message* is the signal (once) followed by the name or other identity of the vessel in distress (once), followed by the position, by the nature of the distress, and by any other information that might facilitate rescue, followed by OVER (the invitation to reply). Thus:

The Call

—distress signal (three times)	MAYDAY MAYDAY MAYDAY
—the words *This is*	THIS IS
—the name of the ship	FANFARE FANFARE FANFARE

The Distress Message

—distress signal	MAYDAY
—name of ship	FANFARE
—the position	ONE SIX ZERO DEGREES FROM SUNK HEAD TOWER DISTANCE ONE MILE
—nature of the distress	HIT SUBMERGED OBJECT AND AM MAKING WATER FAST—THREE PERSONS ON BOARD
—invitation to reply	OVER

The key point about that procedure—and it applies to everyone—is that the call and message will be acknowledged and the message may then be relayed, possibly several times. However, it is the *message* that is relayed, not the *call* and the *message*.

When relaying a distress message the word MAYDAY and the word FANFARE identify the message as distress traffic and identifies which ship is in distress.

In exceptional conditions, a single Marine Rescue Co-ordinating Centre (MRCC) might be handling several distress incidents at once. It might have to repeat relayed messages. Thus each message has to include the "trigger" words MAYDAY as well as the identity of the particular message being relayed.

Without that carefully planned procedure, a Mayday Relay or even an acknowledgement of a Mayday might be confused with a second Mayday message; it has happened.

An acknowledgement too has an agreed format.

—the distress signal (once)	MAYDAY
—the name of vessel in distress spoken three times	FANFARE FANFARE FANFARE
—the words *This is*	THIS IS
—name of vessel acknowledging, spoken three times	BARBICAN BARBICAN BARBICAN
—the word *received*	RECEIVED
—the signal *Mayday*	MAYDAY

Note that that is itself an acknowledgement, it does not include the invitation to reply.

In practice, a distress message would be received by a CRS or, in the United Kingdom, by HM Coastguard, and it is they who would acknowledge and otherwise conduct the subsequent traffic. Nevertheless, it is important to know the procedure. It is always possible that the vessel in distress was in a "black spot" and in those circumstances, and after a suitable interval, it is the duty of anyone who hears a distress message to acknowledge.

In that exceptional circumstance it is then the duty of the vessel that acknowledged the message to make every effort to relay the contents to the shore or to another vessel that could herself relay. The point is not purely hypothetical, because there are still "black spots" around the coast. Thus, in the rare event of having to relay a distress message, remember that it too has a recognized procedure.

A Mayday Relay is a formalized way of saying "Hey! Shut up a minute. There is a fellow in bad trouble out here." It opens with the phrase "Mayday Relay" which distinguishes it from a Mayday call itself.

—the signal, spoken three times	MAYDAY RELAY MAYDAY RELAY MAYDAY RELAY
—the words *This is*	THIS IS
—the name or call sign of the vessel making the transmission	BARBICAN BARBICAN BARBICAN

That is followed by the distress message being relayed:

—the signal	MAYDAY
—the name of the vessel in distress	FANFARE
—the position . . . and so on	POSITION ONE SIX ZERO . . .

Remember, all that is international procedure, and it applies when a vessel is in need of immediate assistance.

Urgency

Next in order of priority is what is called Urgency traffic. It has priority over everything except Distress traffic. For Urgency the signal is the expression "Pan Pan". It is derived from the French word *panne* meaning breakdown. An Urgency call can be addressed to All Stations or to a particular station. Thus:

—the urgency signal	PAN PAN PAN PAN PAN PAN
—the call (name of station called up to three times)	HARWICH HARBOUR CONTROL HARWICH HARBOUR CONTROL
—the words *This is*	THIS IS
—the name or call sign of vessel making the Urgency call	BARBICAN BARBICAN BARBICAN

—urgency message

POSITION—HALF CABLE SOUTH OF ROLLING GROUND BUOY—HAVE PICKED UP LARGE ROPE AROUND PROPELLER AND AM UNABLE TO RESTART ENGINE—I AM THUS DRIFTING EASTWARD ON THE EBB TIDE IN THE MIDDLE OF APPROACH CHANNEL—PLEASE ADVISE APPROACHING SHIPPING— OVER

The Harbour Authority might be able to arrange for a tow, it might advise the disabled vessel to anchor, or, if life was thought to be at risk, they might involve the local Coastguard and the local RNLI lifeboat. However, the point of the example is that a small craft with a rope around her propeller is almost certainly not in distress, but in many circumstances she could be in very urgent need of assistance. Thus it might be appropriate to use the priority given by an Urgency call.

At sea an Urgency call would usually be addressed to "All Ships", but the "Pan Pan" signal is enough to alert ships in the area as well as to give priority to a call to Harwich port.

When there is a port operation service, it is they that control what happens, not the ship in need of assistance. It would be far more satisfactory to inform the port station (the VTS) of your predicament rather than for you, yourself, to broadcast vague warnings to approaching shipping.

In all other circumstances, however, except the somewhat specialized problem given as an example of an Urgency call, HM Coastguard is the authority to whom small craft should turn for assistance. It has already been pointed out that it is HMCG who would normally acknowledge distress calls in U.K. waters. We also enjoy a first rate advice service.

Safety

As far as small craft are concerned, there are two types of Safety traffic. First there is the *Sécurité* call, the third order of priority in so far as radio silence is concerned. The word *Sécurité*, sent three times, precedes a message concerning an important navigational or meteorological warning. A CRS, for example, might use it before giving details of a gale warning. The call will be on Ch 16, but the message would be sent on a working frequency.

Yachts will frequently hear the *Sécurité* call, but would be unlikely to need to use it themselves.

HM Coastguard

The other type of traffic that comes under the general heading of "Safety" is the use, by small craft, of Ch 67. That is the only way in which a vessel can speak directly to a shore station on maritime channels, other than by using a port operation channel (for matters affecting the business of the port) or via a CRS to make a link call. Ch 67 has been allocated, in the United Kingdom, for direct communication between small craft and HM Coastguard on any matters affecting the safety of the vessel.

In practice, that last expression—matters affecting the safety of the vessel—is loosely interpreted. It can be used to pass details of a passage, under the Coastguard Safety Scheme; it can be used to make enquiries regarding sea state or weather and visibility; and it can be used to pass the details of any subject of concern to the mariner.

Any calls are made on Ch 16, and they should be as brief as possible.

THAMES COASTGUARD—THIS IS BARBICAN
BARBICAN—OVER

is sufficient. The Coastguard will acknowledge with:

BARBICAN [and it does not matter at that stage if the name is
precisely correct or not]—THIS IS THAMES
COASTGUARD—Ch 67—ACKNOWLEDGE—OVER.

In practice, HMCG might not bother to use "Over", but they usually include the instruction to acknowledge, because so much of the traffic is with comparative beginners, it lessens the chance that the yacht switches to Ch 67 (on receipt of the instruction to do so) without first acknowledging that instruction.

After the change to Ch 67, yachtsmen will find the Coastguard officers most helpful, even if the "help" is mainly reassurance. If "things" seem to be going wrong, it can make all the difference to know that somebody else knows where you are and what is happening. Furthermore, the ability to express a concern can often avoid the temptation to use distress signals when that would not otherwise be justified.

Distress Other Than Radio

Only a few years ago it would have been unthinkable to devote several pages to the use of Distress and Urgency radio, because the facility hardly existed. Today it has transformed a man's ability to seek help, but by no means has it totally superseded the more traditional signals.

The Collision Regulations list no less than fourteen recognized distress signals, some of which, like flames from a burning tar barrel, must go back centuries. However, several are fundamental to an understanding of the responsibilities of going to sea, and the use of distress pyrotechnics is the most obvious.

Even within a harbour the red hand-held flare could easily prove to be the best possible distress signal, because not only does it indicate the state of being in distress, it indicates the position of the boat.

All too often a small boat gets into trouble because of an error in navigation. Thus, a radio call for help cannot always given an accurate position, whereas a flare can.

The way in which flares should be used will obviously depend on the circumstances, but the best advice is always to think of the use of flares in pairs. Experience suggests that one flare is not enough, because it is so difficult to get an accurate bearing; the flare is so totally unexpected. A second, fired half a minute after the first has expired, is the best practice.

Coupled with that advice is the thought that there is little point in firing all the available flares in the first few minutes of any incident. Parachute rockets go up 300 metres and therefore they are obviously the right choice if well offshore, but low cloud, as well as strong winds, can cause problems. First, because the rocket disappears and second, because—contrary to what most would imagine—the rocket climbs *into* the wind as it is fired. Thus a parachute flare needs to be fired pointing downwind—10 to 20 degrees from the vertical—not pointing against the wind, as everyone seems to assume.

The hand-held precise location flare is the right "tool" for indicating position, and having made an initial distress call on the radio, HMCG might well ask the casualty, once a lifeboat is thought to be in the vicinity, to fire flares so that she can be located.

There is much that could be written about distress in general and the use of flares in particular, but remember two points above all else. When a flare is needed it will be needed in a hurry, possibly in a state of near panic. That is not the time to have to start looking for them. I stow mine in pairs of plastic clips between the deck beams in my coach roof. They are dry and they are accessible. To me, the more usual plastic bag or screw top plastic box is a crazy way to stow something that may be needed in the dark.

The second overriding point concerns the number to be carried. The RYA recommended minimum for coastal cruising is two rockets, two hand flares and two orange smoke signals. I believe that at least three times that number would not be excessive for both parachute rockets and hand-held flares.

Other Visual Distress and Urgency Signals

From the long list of distress signals in the Collision Regulations, the two most likely to be of use to yachtsmen are:

"Slowly and repeatedly raising and lowering arms outstretched to each side" and

> "a signal consisting of a square flag having above or below it a ball or anything resembling a ball".

The former might be the only way to signal distress sitting in, or even sitting astride, a sunken dinghy. It could be made when on shore, and it could be made ground-to-air, to signal to a helicopter.

The latter (of the two distress signals mentioned) is the best distance signal "in the book". Any large flag, such as an ensign, could be used above or below an anchor ball, and the signal is one that would be recognized at a mile or more by any seaman. Also, like most other day signals and all other signals composed of flags and shapes, it goes on sending its message while the crew are otherwise occupied.

Distress is the unqualified state when a man seeks immediate assistance, but, as with radio, where there are degrees of urgency in Mayday, Pan Pan or Sécurité, so there are degrees of urgency with other visual signals.

It is distress that catches the attention, and all seamen soon learn the essential rules that govern it. However, the international urgency signal—V—which is a visual Pan Pan, is something that deserves to be better understood than it is.

The introduction of radio has largely superseded the use of flags for conversation, but single-letter flags, in the International Code, are still as important, internationally, as they ever were.

They have the advantage over radio that language problems do not arise and most of the single letter signals can be made by several different methods of signalling.

Several are of of obvious importance to small craft, but unfortunately yachtsmen rarely carry flags as a signal; they tend to think of them as decorations.

By all means let us keep the rather pleasant custom of "dressing overall" on special occasions; it is a nice tradition and one that goes back a long time. However, let us also preserve the common sense of the tradition. Flags for dressing overall must never be flown when under way.

Flags, when under way, are signals, and signals are there to be read. Tatty little bits of bunting saying "Volvo Penta" or "Shell" ought not to have any place on board any vessel *when under way*. The same applies to flags of the RNLI, the RYA or any other organization.

If a man wants to indicate his allegiance to an organization let the "signal" be confined to use when made fast alongside: it would be madness to let "advertising" flags overwhelm the use of single-letter flags from the International Code.

Flag "V"—"I require assistance"—is the one that is easily recognized, and, especially in a harbour environment, the most obvious to have stowed so that it is available.

To be worth carrying as a visual Pan Pan, a flag "V" ought to be, say, 1 metre in the hoist at a minimum. Statistically it is highly unlikely to be needed, but when needed it might save your life.

A man with a severely sprained wrist and a flat battery—who is unable either to start his engine or get his anchor up—is most certainly in need of assistance. However, he is probably not in distress and the use of distress signals when they are not really necessary soon devalues the whole "currency" of the sea.

"V" is one of the signals that can be made by other methods, and the German manufacturer of small craft navigation lights, Ahlemann & Schlatter, has recently produced a clever device—little bigger than a matchbox—that can be wired into the existing circuit of any all-round white light to cause it to flash "V" when needed. An all-round white light at the masthead would be the obvious choice.

A man might have a rope round his propeller or he might be in one of many other predicaments. He might even have operational radio and have already been in touch with the rescue authorities. In all those circumstances the ability to signal "I am the chap who needs help" would, at the very least, save someone a certain amount of time. Inshore lifeboats often waste hours trying to identify which boat, out of dozens in an area, was the one that called for help.

The problem ought not to arise, but it does. Even if the situation was one of genuine distress, the casualty might well have exhausted all the available pyrotechnics. Thus a simple way to indicate an urgent need for assistance might still be a blessing.

Club Rescue Boats and the Use of Ch "M"

One other, more specialized, type of "rescue" is found in the use of yacht club "rescue" boats. In practice, although called "Rescue Boats" by most clubs, they are really safety and patrol boats to accompany racing for small craft and to assist those in need. In no way does that denigrate their purpose, but the word "rescue" is better reserved for the actual operation when somebody needs rescuing.

In the United Kingdom yacht clubs and yacht marinas can both be licensed for the use of what is usually named Ch "M"—157.85 MHz. To have such diverse organizations as clubs (using the frequency for yacht race management) and marinas (using the frequency for the booking of overnight berths) is not a particularly happy mix, and the problems regarding the marina use of the frequency have already been discussed in Chapter 10. Here it is the rescue side of the problem that matters.

The licence that a club can obtain allows the use of the channel for yacht race management and other business of the club. It is not a general ship-to-shore channel, and it is not licensed for messages to be passed to third parties.

The club licence includes permission for the channel to be used in the club safety boats, but problems arise because a Certificate of Competence is not a prerequisite. Thus although, when the Regulations were formed, the intentions were sound, the huge number of people now using the frequency, at certain times, means that without the discipline imposed by a familiarity with maritime channels Ch "M" can be seriously abused to the detriment of all.

However, as with other forms of radiotelephone abuse, much of the problem is ignorance rather than arrogance. A club that mounts an aerial on a flagstaff outside the club for example—giving a range of say 25 miles—when it wishes to transmit to its own safety boats 0.5 mile away, is causing problems that can easily be minimized, if not overcome. On the other hand, a club that looks on the use of Ch "M" as if it were a private channel for the club's exclusive use is an even more obvious abuse of the system.

By no means is the system itself perfect. The regulations were introduced many years ago to satisfy a need. Now, to a large extent, technology has overtaken the system we use. From the safety side of "safety boat" work—as opposed to the organizational side of "safety boat" work—Ch "M" is fine if there are not others using the channel at the same time. It allows a group of safety boats to keep in touch with each other and to speak to the Race Officer whether he is afloat or ashore.

What safety boat use of Ch "M" cannot do—without a good deal of goodwill from neighbouring clubs and marinas—is to have any priority on the use of the channel when casualty working.

Perhaps the best answer of all is to have a club licence for the use of Ch "M" but also to license the club boats with a ship licence as well. That has the slight disadvantage, from the club's point of view, that the radio operator in the safety boat must be the holder of a Certificate of Competence, but it means that the club boats can change to maritime ship-to-ship or distress frequencies when necessary.

By no means am I suggesting that the maritime ship-to-ship VHF channels are generally available for yacht race management. They are not. Maritime ship-to-ship channels must not be used in port except on matters affecting the safety of the ship, but the ability to change to ship-to-ship channels on occasion, to transmit directly to HM Coastguard, or to speak directly to other vessels that might be involved or become involved in assisting a yacht in trouble could be invaluable.

Without a ship licence in the club safety boat the boat would have to communicate with any other authority via the club and then a land-line telephone. With a ship licence, on the other hand, a safety boat could communicate directly to HM Coastguard or to the Harbour Authority if necessary: something that might well be of great advantage to all concerned.

Citizen's Band (CB)

Concerning club safety boats, there is yet another means of communication that is not as clearly understood as it deserves to be. Citizen's Band radio has acquired a very bad reputation because of the extraordinary behaviour of some of our fellow men and the silly abuse of the commoner channels. However, when the use of CB was made legal in the United Kingdom, in 1981, yachtsmen did not adapt their thinking to adopt CB in the way that they might have—and still could—do.

To make a point about CB, and the abuse of CB, is that it is in the popular 27 MHz band—where there are forty channels—that all the abuse occurs. When the regulations were devised there was also provision for twenty more channels in a 934 MHz band, and it is there where the answers to inshore yacht race management might lie.

Part of the problem is basic supply and demand. All the demand went into the 27 MHz equipment, so that there is very little of the 934 MHz available. Nevertheless, in the longer term, the slightly shorter range of the 934 MHz band might be an actual advantage. The range over water will be more than adequate, and safety boats, club launchmen, club secretaries and even a car park attendant could all be in touch with each other at regatta times. And with twenty channels from which to choose, and ranges of only a few miles, the 934 MHz group seems to offer advantages that neither Ch "M" nor the maritime channels can offer.

There would still be a need for a mother ship to monitor the race traffic and to be capable of getting in touch with other authorities on VHF maritime channels, but that applies in any case. Most clubs include members with cruising boats that can be used for that type of rôle, and the idea of having a mother ship at any regatta is a sound one, regardless of the communications advantages. The younger members can dash about in safety boats for hours on end, but even they can appreciate a hot coffee, or a chance to get out of the wind for a while. The custom of having regatta mother ships as communications bases as well as "kitchen boats" has never been developed as much as it deserves to be.

Safety Boats

Bearing in mind that the theme throughout this book is that small craft navigators should be encouraged to behave in a sensible and intelligent manner—especially within the environs of a commercial harbour—I shall end by highlighting a weakness in some yacht club organization itself.

In many aspects of sailing—especially cruising offshore and racing offshore—there are long periods when those taking part are well beyond the immediate help of others. They have to be self-sufficient and a part of the challenge and the attraction of the sport is that it should be so.

On the other hand, those organizing events inshore—often with children involved—may be in a different category. They are training the children to be like themselves—independent and self-sufficient. When so-called club Rescue Boats are provided for an event, then the preparation of those boats, and the training of the crews to man them, should be treated at least as carefully as the boats that club members themselves take offshore.

There are many instances when the quality of the crews of safety boats and the degree of maintenance of the boats is not as it should be. The result is that if the weather does turn nasty other rescue authorities have to be called in.

Both official bodies like HM Coastguard and voluntary bodies such as the Royal National Lifeboat Institution are there to serve the public. It is not they that complain. My concern is that yachtsmen themselves are becoming too ready to rely on "official" back-up.

The more the younger generation can be encouraged to treat the problems with a responsible seriousness—without inhibiting their enjoyment of a challenge—the better for them and for the future of the sport.

A part of that responsible approach is that if a club does organize an event with "safety cover", then that cover needs to be suitably trained and equipped. A "safety boat" is not just any old boat, and the crewing of safety boats is not a job for anyone who happens to be available.

Sailing is a very safe sport—so long as we never forget how dangerous it can be.

APPENDIX A

VHF Procedural Words and Their Meanings

Acknowledge: Used to ask for an acknowledgement of a request.

All After: Used after the pro-words "Say Again" to request a repetition of the rest of a message after a certain phrase.

All Before: Used after the pro-words "Say Again" to request a repetition of all that preceded a certain phrase.

Confirm: Asking for confirmation that a message, just transmitted, was the correct version.

Copy: Used by a third station that has monitored an exchange between two other stations. During a search, "A" and "B" might have been exchanging messages and then "A" might ask "C" "Did you copy?" An acknowledgement, "This is 'C'—copied", would mean that "C" had monitored the exchange and that therefore it need not be repeated.

Correct: The message you have just transmitted was correct.

Correction: Spoken during a transmission means an error has just been made in what was said. The transmitting station then goes back to a correct phrase and carries on with the sentence. For example: "I shall be with you in about five—correction—in about one five minutes."

Date–Time Group: As a time group, but with the date of the month added to make the group a six-figure expression. Messages are often identified by time or date–time group. HM Coastguard might refer to "My zero three one one two five", meaning the message I transmitted at 1125 on the third of the month.

In Figures: The following numeral or group of numerals is to be written in figures.

In Letters: The following numeral or group of numerals is to be written in letters.

I Say Again: I shall repeat what I have just said. *See also* Repeat in Appendix B.

I Spell: I shall spell out the next word or group of words phonetically. For example: "Barbican—I spell—Bravo Alpha Romeo Bravo India Charlie Alpha November—Barbican."

Out: The end of working to you, the station addressed. It does not necessarily mean the end of my transmission. (See also the Ten Golden Rules in Appendix C.)

Over: The invitation to reply. Ideally every message ends with "Over", during an exchange, up to the point when the traffic is complete and the final sentence ends with "Out". (See also the Ten Golden Rules.)

Received: When a message is received and acknowledgement only is needed, say: "Received". Do not use the jargon "Roger": it means different things to different people, and it cannot be used at all internationally.

Radio Check: The best way to obtain reassurance that the radio is working correctly. For example: "Thames Coastguard—This is Barbican—Radio check—Over". The reply might be: "This is Thames Coastguard—Loud and clear—Out".

Say Again: Used to ask for a message to be repeated or as "I say again" to repeat what has just been said.

Station: All ships and shore establishments are referred to as "stations". The station initiating the call is the "calling station" and the station that was called is referred to as "station called".

This Is: The expression immediately preceding the name or other identity of a station.

Time Group: A four-figure identification of the time or the time of a message followed, if necessary, by a time zone letter. Time is normally expressed as UTC unless otherwise stated.

Wait: If a station is unable to accept traffic it might reply: "Wait—Out" or "Wait one—Out". The station called would then call back when able to do so, and if the delay was likely to be more than a short period, the number of minutes would be indicated in the acknowledgement.

APPENDIX B

Standard Marine Navigational Vocabulary

As outlined in Chapter 3, the world has changed to the use of English for all VHF radiotelephone traffic, and the teaching discipline "Seaspeak" is likely to be used more and more by those instructing others, particularly non-English-speaking students. In the meantime, the principle of Message Markers—which is the essence of the discipline—has recently been introduced into the *Standard Marine Navigational Vocabulary*.

The vocabulary itself is not a booklet that yachtsmen will normally use, but it is a valuable guide to how English should be used to avoid confusion, particularly in port operational traffic. The recommended procedures will increasingly be used by port operators in VTS traffic and by ships themselves. Thus, the more yachtsmen accustom themselves to the style recommended, the easier it will be for them to understand what they hear and for them to be understood.

The vocabulary itself is a Merchant Shipping M. Notice. Here the procedural advice that precedes the glossary is summarized.

Procedure/Message Markers (see also Chapter 3, "Seaspeak")

If necessary, external communication messages may be preceded by the following message markers:

Question: Indicates that the message is of an interrogative character.

Answer: Indicates that the following message is the reply to a previous question.

Request: Indicates that the contents of the following message is asking for action from others with respect to the ship.

Information: Indicates that the following message is restricted to observed facts.

Warning: Indicates that the following message informs other traffic participants about dangers.

Advice: Indicates that the following message implies the intention of the sender to influence the recipient(s) by a recommendation.

Responses

Where the answer to a question is in the affirmative, say "YES" followed by the appropriate phrase in full.

Where the answer to a question is in the negative, say "NO" followed by the appropriate phrase in full.

Where the information is not immediately available, say "STAND BY".

Where a message is not properly heard, say "SAY AGAIN".

Where a message is not understood, say "MESSAGE NOT UNDERSTOOD".

(See also Appendix A for additional procedural words.)

Repetition

If any parts of a message are considered sufficiently important to need safeguarding, use the word "repeat". For example: "I have picked up six repeat six survivors." Otherwise, repetition of words or phrases should be avoided unless specifically requested by the receiving station.

Position

When the position is related to a mark, the mark shall be a well-defined charted object. The bearing shall be in the 360 degree notation from True North and shall be the position **from** the mark. "Position is 137 degrees from Barr Head lighthouse. Distance 2 miles."

Course

Always expressed in 360 degree notation.

Bearings

The bearing of a mark or a vessel is the bearing in the 360 degree notation, but the bearing may be from the mark or from the vessel.

Note: as stated above, the bearing, when quoting position, is always from the mark.

Relative Bearings

Relative bearing can be expressed in degrees relative to the ship's head.

Distances

Preferably expressed in nautical miles or cables (tenths of a mile). When precision is necessary, metres can be used, but the unit must always be stated.

Speed

In knots. Without further notation, speed means speed through the water, otherwise state "ground speed".

Numbers

Numbers spoken as "One-five-zero" or "Two decimal five".

Geographical Names

Place names should be those on the chart. Göteborg *not* Gothenburg, Oostende *not* Ostend *or* Vlissingen *not* Flushing.

Time

Time should be in the 24-hour notation, with a zone time letter as a suffix unless UTC is being used. However, within a VTS area boundary times are usually given in local time with the phrase "local time" as the suffix. If there is any doubt as to the time used locally, time can be expressed as relative to now: " . . . in three hours time".

APPENDIX C

Ten Golden Rules for the Use of VHF Radiotelephones

1. Listen and think before starting to transmit.
2. Although Ch 16 is the calling channel, in addition to being the distress and safety channel, always call on a working channel if one is known to be watched.
3. When calling a station likely to be listening to more than one channel, name the channel being used for the call in that initial call.
4. When calling on Ch 16 for a ship-to-ship exchange, it helps if, before making the call, the station about to call listens to the available working channels, to find one that appears to be free, before making her initial call. Then she can suggest the use of a working channel, in her initial call on Ch 16.
5. Always acknowledge acceptance of a request to change channel before changing. Similarly, when making a request for a change, await acceptance before changing.
6. Use low power whenever it will give a satisfactory result.
7. When a call is complete, and subsequently during an exchange of messages, a station invites a reply by saying "OVER".
8. The end of work is indicated by each station adding "OUT" to the end of her last transmission.
9. When conditions are good, abbreviated procedures should be used:
   (a) Repetition of words or phrases should be avoided.
   (b) The words "This is" may be omitted and, after the opening exchange, the name of the station called may also be omitted but the identity of the calling station must always be included in every exchange.
   (c) At the end of work only one station need use "OUT"; the other need not reply.
10. When traffic is complete, make sure that the Press-to-speak switch is properly released and that a carrier wave is not being transmitted by the microphone in its cradle.

APPENDIX D

Metric Units and Their Symbols and Other Useful Measurements

Quantity	Name	Symbol and/or explanation
length	metre	m
	nautical mile	n mile or M, as in abbreviation for light: Iso 4 s 43 m 18 M.
	cable	One-tenth of a nautical mile.
mass	kilogram	kg
	tonne	Written "tonne" to avoid confusion with short or long tons of American Imperial measure. Do not abbreviate "t" to avoid confusion with "l" or "1".
time	year	Abbreviated to last two digits: '82.
	month	Abbreviated to first three letters.
	day(s)	d
	hour(s)	h
	minute(s)	min In a tabulation minutes can be shown as 3 h 45 as in tidal information or as H+20. Otherwise time is given as four-figure notation: 1435. Assume UTC unless marked otherwise.
	second(s)	s
plane angle	degree	Bearings in three-figure notation. True unless stated otherwise.
electric current	ampere	A
power	watt	W
electrical potential	volt	V The derivation is W/A.
electrical resistance	ohm	Ω The derivation is V/A.

frequency	Hertz	Hz The derivation is 1 cycle per second.
temperature	degree Celsius	°C
luminous/ intensity	candela	cd
area	square metre	m²
	hectare	ha Equals 10 000 m².
volume	cubic metre	m³
	litre	Always write litre, not l, because a small letter "l" will be confused with the figure 1.
speed	knot	kn Nautical mile per hour.
	metres per second	m/s The quantity normally used by meteorologists.
	kilometres per hour	km/h The quantity normally used in aviation.
pressure	millibar	mb Shortly the bar is likely to be replaced by the Pascal in weather forecasts. However as one hectopascal equals one millibar the figures will be the same even if it is kilopascals that are used as the unit; hecto is not a preferred SI prefix.

Prefixes

mega	one million times	M
kilo	one thousand times	k
milli	one thousandth	m
micro	one millionth	μ (The Greek letter, not a small u).

APPENDIX E

Useful Abbreviations

ALRS	Admiralty List of Radio Signals
AM	Amplitude modulation
ATC	Air Traffic Control
CG	Coastguard
Ch	Channel(s)
CROSSMA	Centre Régional Opérationnel de Surveillance et de Sauvetage pour la Manche
CROSSA	Centre Régional Opérationnel de Surveillance et de Sauvetage pour l'Atlantique
CRS	Coast radio station (operated by British Telecom in U.K.)
D/F	Direction finding
DSB	Double sideband
DST	Daylight Saving Time. Note: it can be confusing to use the expression British Summer Time (BST) because most neighbouring countries now change to a summer time that may differ from that used in the U.K.
EPIRB	Emergency Position Indicating Radio Beacon (also called a PLB Personal Locator Beacon)
ETA	Estimated time of arrival
ETD	Estimated time of departure
FM	Frequency modulated
GRT	Gross Registered Tonnes
h	hour(s)
HF	High frequency
Hz	Hertz
H+...	Commencing at ... minutes past the hour
H24	Continuous
ICAO	International Civil Aviation Organization
Inop	Inoperative
IMO	International Maritime Organization (until 1982 Inter-governmental Maritime Consultative Organization)
ITU	International Telecommunication Union
KHz	Kilohertz
MF	Medium frequency
MHz	Megahertz
min	Minute(s)
MRCC	Maritime Rescue Co-ordination Centre
MRSC	Maritime Rescue Sub-Centre
RNLI	Royal National Lifeboat Institution
R/T	Radiotelephony
Rx	Receiver
RYA	Royal Yachting Association
s	second(s)
SAR	Search and rescue

SITREP	Situation report
SSB	Single Sideband
temp inop	Temporarily inoperative
Tx	Transmitter
ufn	Until further notice
UHF	Ultra high frequency
UTC	Co-ordinated Universal Time. For general use UTC is the same as what has been known, for decades, as GMT, but the use of GMT is being phased out in favour of the more accurate method
VHF	Very high frequency
VTM	Vessel Traffic Management
VTS	Vessel Traffic Services
W/T	Wireless telegraphy
Wx	Weather

Index

Abbreviations 177
  Supplement, inside cover
Alongside others 131
Anchoring 116
  scope 117–118
Anchors 119
  pawl 123
  weights 121
Authorities 138
  moorings 141
Authority to Operate 153

Bad visibility (aide memoire) 95
Belgian Customs 147
Buoys, picking up 102

Capture effect 13
Certificate of Competence 153
Channel "M" 166
Charts 65
  correction 66
  scales 68–69
Citizen's band (CB) 168
Close quarters 48
Coastguard Supplement 5
Coast Radio Procedure
  UK Supplement 4
  France Supplement 4
  Belgium Supplement 4
  Holland Supplement 4
  Germany Supplement 4
  Channels Supplement 6–17
Coming alongside 108
Collision Regulations
  Rule 9 44, 47
  Rule 10 45
Compass 81
Correction service Supplement 2
Courtesy flags 145

Crew list 153
Crossing a channel 50
Customs and Excise 147
  "Q" flag 147–150

Danish Customs 149
Depth indicators 76
Distress
  radio 22, 156–161
  other than radio 163
  signals 164
Drogues 104–107
Dual installation 18
Dual watch 17
Duplex 14

Electronic aids 74
  integration 77
Ensigns 145

Fairleads 129
Fenders 125–127
Fog 88
Fog signals 90
French Customs 147

German Customs 149
Guidelines Supplement 3–5

Hampered vessels 53
  at anchor 53
  not-under-command 54
  restricted 55
Harbour radio 18
  data Supplement 6–17
Heaving-to 100

Human eye 84
Hyperbolic aids 78

Immigration 151
Insurance 141
Irish Customs 150

Leaving a berth 135
Light dues 155
Lights
  anchor 63
  obscured 60
  positions for small craft 59
  scatter 62
  shielding 61–62
  small craft 57
Locks, making fast 133

Making fast 124
Marinas, manoeuvring 111
Metric units 175
Moorings 141
Motor-sailing 51

Narrow channels 45, 96
Navigational warnings 79
Netherlands Customs 148
Night sailing 83
Night vision 84–88
Norwegian Customs 149

Out, procedural word 30
Over, procedural word 30

Port Radio Supplement 6–17
  correction service Supplement 2

"Q" flag 147–151

Radar 93
  reflectors 94
Registration 151
  small ships 152
  ICPN 152
Rescue boats 166
Ropes, slip 112

Safety boats 168
Salvage 142
Sea anchors 104
Seaspeak 36
Selective calling 31

Ship licence 154
Ship-to-ship traffic, dangers of 25
Signals
  international port entry 2
  national port entry 5
  special signals 139
  tidal 8
  way-point reporting 9
Simplex 14
Slip ropes 112
Slowing and stopping 97
Speech, rhythm, speed, volume and pitch
  Supplement 3
Speed indicators 77
Stopping distances (ship's) 56
Swedish Customs 150

Tide
  tidal height 70–74
  tidal stream 69–74

United Kingdom Customs 150
Urgency 161

VHF
  calling on working channels 24
  calling port operations 26
  capture effect 13
  installation 20
  loudspeakers 21
  model calls 23
  payment for calls 29–32
  procedural words 170
  procedures 22
  safety 162
  ten golden rules 174
  urgency 161
Visibility from the bridge 59
Vocabulary, standard marine 172
VTS
  development 19
  principles 33

Warps
  alongside others 131
  anchor 116
  chafe 129
  in locks 133
  mooring 125
  tidal height 130
Weather messages 81

Yacht clubs, custom and behaviour 144
Yacht signalling (Macmillan) 14

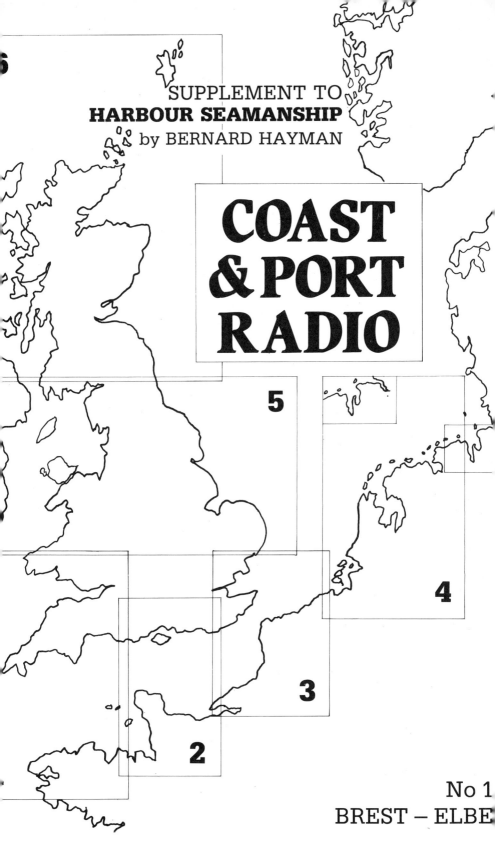

SUPPLEMENT TO
HARBOUR SEAMANSHIP
by BERNARD HAYMAN

COAST & PORT RADIO

5

4

3

2

No 1
BREST — ELBE

COAST AND PORT RADIO

INTRODUCTION

WITHIN a comparatively few years the ability to communicate by radio has changed—as far as small craft are concerned—from being something almost unthinkable, to something that is taken for granted.

■ There are two main areas of development: this supplement to *Harbour Seamanship* deals with both. First, and most obvious, is the need to communicate with the Coast Radio Stations (CRS): to make a "Link Call". Secondly, there is an increasing need to be able (on occasion) to communicate with, and frequently to listen to, the Harbour Radio.

■ *Harbour Seamanship* deals, in some detail, with all aspects of the movements of small craft both in, and in the approaches to, ports and harbours. But what a book cannot do so easily is to give details of the facets of a subject that are continually changing. That is the objective of this supplement.

■ The lesser of the two problem areas is the question of Coast Radio Frequencies and the differing procedures that apply in the U.K. and to stations run by our near neighbours. Details are shown on p. 5. Also in each of the six "double-openings" throughout this booklet, the channels to be used for calling CRS, and for passing messages to them, are shown geographically. If in doubt, call the nearest station.

■ The second, and the principal, purpose of the supplement is to summarize the procedures that apply to port operation traffic.

■ The subject is so new that many may not have appreciated how many of our ports are now controlled by radio. The days when men in black oilskin coats walked to the end of the pier to hoist black balls or to signal with flags on signal masts have almost gone. Today all commercial ports, as well as many small harbours used primarily for pleasure, have their own radio bases. It is there that there has been a revolution.

■ There is an old saying: *"The man who makes the rules controls the game."* In this context it can be paraphrased as: *"The man who understands the rules can enjoy playing the game."* In other words, the man who knows what is going on is far less likely to make an error of judgement and thus far more likely to enjoy what he is doing.

■ As far as most commercial ports are concerned, the objective ought to be *"listen, don't talk"*. The man who monitors the Port Operational radio traffic is not only infinitely better informed than were his forefathers but better informed than they would ever have dreamed possible.

2

■ If the port radio—the Vessel Traffic Service (VTS), as it is called today—is doing its job, he will learn about weather forecasts, about the general movements of shipping and about any *special* movements. He will hear about visibility, about any vessel with special problems, about dredgers or other hazards. In other words, he will be informed.

Apart from this introduction, and the advice on p. 4, this booklet is about facts. What frequency, what time, what facilities and, above all, what procedures apply?

■ The whole subject is alive. Something changes almost every week and for that reason a correction service is available.

Inserted between pages 8 and 9 is a postcard designed to be cut out and then posted to the publisher, Pergamon Press.

About six months after publication the first list of corrections will be sent out—without charge—in the form of sentences or paragraphs on self-adhesive paper. That will allow this radio guide to be corrected with the minimum of trouble.

■ As with a chart, data which is out of date is, at the very least, confusing and it may be highly dangerous. The correction service is designed to keep the booklet up to date. Periodically it will have to be re-printed but, by the issue of a series of correction sheets, it is hoped to keep the Supplement up-to-date until at least the 1987 sailing season.

Burnham-on-Crouch 1985   BERNARD HAYMAN

ABBREVIATIONS AND LEGEND

Ch 11 16; 11	Call Ch 11 or 16. Ch 11 will be used for working
Ch 16; 12 14	Call Ch 16 and you will work Ch 12 or 14
Ch 12 14	Ch 12 and 14 are the channels used for working
Ch **12** 14	Call Ch 12 and you will work Ch 12 or 14 as directed
Ch 23 **25** 27	Choice of CRS working channel with Ch 25 the primary frequency
Fcst	Forecast
GRT	Gross registered tonnage
NRT	Nett registered tonnage
Times	All UTC (Co-ordinated Universal Time) unless shown otherwise. [Note: the expression GMT is being phased out for navigation because, for scientific purposes, UTC is marginally more accurate]
2h before to 1h 30	The operation begins two hours before and lasts until one hour thirty minutes after . . .
H+20 H+50	Commencing at twenty minutes past and fifty minutes past each hour
HJ	Daylight service only
HX	No specific hours
H24	Continuous
Hr Mr	Harbour Master
LT	Local Time
Lt Ho	Lighthouse
miles	Nautical miles
VTM	Vessel Traffic Management
VTS	Vessel Traffic Service

VHF Guidelines

FOR the cruising yachtsman, as well as the offshore racing yachtsman, it is important to remember that when using Coast Radio, as well as Port Radio, one person will frequently be speaking to another whose mother tongue is not English. That is the main reason why it is so important to speak clearly and to use procedures that will easily be understood.

There is no one magical answer. *Harbour Seamanship* has a good deal to say about radio procedures in general, and it introduces the principles of the language discipline "Seaspeak", a discipline designed to organize the use of the English language and to eliminate ambiguities and uncertainties.

What follows here, on the other hand, applies to the use of any language when communicating via a radiotelephone.

Rhythm. Any phrase spoken in ordinary conversation has a natural rhythm which helps to make it intelligible. That same rhythm should be maintained on a radiotelephone. Where possible, a message should be given in complete sentences—or in phrases that make sense—not word by word.

Avoid hesitation and never add "er" or "um" after a word.

Speed. Speak steadily at a medium speed, and try to ensure that the speed of speech is kept constant throughout.

Volume. Speak slightly louder than in normal conversation, but do not shout. In ordinary conversation certain words are stressed and others may be slurred. On a radiotelephone that must be avoided; each word should be spoken with equal clarity.

Pitch. High-pitched voices are transmitted more successfully than those of lower pitch. Thus any tendency to lower the pitch on the last syllable of a word, or the last word of a phrase, should be avoided.

Calling Coast Radio Stations

United Kingdom

The United Kingdom has now changed to the system when all calls to CRS should be made on the appropriate working channel. Look up the available channels in the following six maps and then listen to each channel in turn, until one is found to be free. An engaged channel is indicated by speech, or by pips; a free channel is silent.

The initial call should be the name of the station that is being called (usually once) followed by "This is" and the call sign of the station calling, twice. Then listen.

"NORTH FORELAND RADIO—THIS IS MIKE ALPHA BRAVO ALPHA—MIKE ALPHA BRAVO ALPHA—OVER."

That is the complete call. The acceptance of the call is indicated by the engaged pips, and the operator will then speak as soon as he is free to do so.

Jersey and Crockalough are the only two CRS around our shores that still need to be called on Ch 16. The procedure is the same, except that there are no "pips" to indicate that the channel is engaged.

Call, as outlined, but on Ch 16. When the operator answers, you will be transferred to one of his working channels, and if he is busy you may be given a turn number and told to wait.

France

The French CRS do not operate on Ch 16 for ship-to-shore traffic at all. To call a French CRS look up the appropriate frequency on pages 6 to 9 and, if it is free, call as for the United Kingdom: the operator will then call the ship and ask for further details of the station calling.

Belgium

The Belgian CRS at Oostende and Antwerpen accept calls on Ch 16 or on the appropriate working channels as shown on page 11. For all the Belgian coast the call is Oostende Radio regardless of which channel is being used.

Holland

Scheveningen Radio accepts calls on Ch 16 (as do Belgian and U.K. stations), but it prefers calls direct on the appropriate working channel. Look up the channel, on pages 12 and 13. The call is Scheveningen Radio for all of them. The acceptance of a call is indicated by a jingle, and if the operator has not called back within about 90 seconds the jingle switches off and you may call again.

Germany

Norddeich Radio also accepts calls on Ch 16. There are three channels used on this comparatively short coastline by Norddeich and three more by Helgoland Radio. There is no engaged signal.

Port Radio

As a generalization, the larger the port the more likely it is to use working channels for all calling.

Throughout the following pages there is a summary of the facilities offered by all the ports that have a port operations radio—a Vessel Traffic Service (VTS).

The expression VTS covers everything from the highly sophisticated port control operation off an entrance like the Hoek van Holland to the use of radio by the harbour master's launch at Chichester. Both are important, and both offer a service to small craft. However, as another generalization, remember that most port operational radio is precisely that: it is a commercial operation.

"Listen, don't talk" should be the aim. Increasingly, port radio is being used to include traffic, weather and other important information of use to everyone, including those participating in the VTS only by listening.

When it is necessary to call a VTS look up the primary working channel (usually shown in **bold type**) and then listen. If the channel is free, give the name of the station called—usually once—followed by "This is" and the name of the calling station—twice. Then wait.

There are numerous reasons why a man may not be able to reply straight away, and repeated calls merely clutter the channel as well as annoy others monitoring it.

Coastguard

Around much of the U.K. coast, HM Coastguard has installed VHF D/F equipment that allows bearings of any vessel in trouble to be taken within a transmission time of only a few seconds. The service is for emergency use only. Whenever it is necessary to call HM Coastguard to use the VHF D/F position fixing facility, or for any normal traffic to HMCG, call on Ch 16.

Since 1985 many Coastguard stations have adopted the useful practice of broadcasting the inshore weather forecasts at regular intervals—after a preliminary announcement on Ch 16—on Ch 67.

When it necessary to speak to HMCG, call, as for a call to a port radio, but on Ch 16. When free to reply, the Coastguard will, except in an emergency, ask you to change to Ch 67.

CORRECTION SERVICE

This Supplement is supported by a correction service—for which there is no charge.

An application form for the first list of corrections is enclosed.

The number of correction sheets to be issued will depend upon the volume of correction thought necessary. However, it is hoped to keep the Supplement up-to-date until at least the 1987 season before it has to be reprinted.

The first distribution will be made about six months after publication of the "parent" book *Harbour Seamanship,* but it will help all concerned if the application forms can be posted as soon as possible.

A separate copy of the Supplement will be sent immediately on receipt of the application form.

Detail reproduced from *Admiralty List of Radio Signals,* volumes 6 and 6a, with the sanction of the Controller, HM Stationery Office, and the Hydrographer of the Navy.

FRENCH COAST

All foreign vessels 25m or more in length navigating or at anchor in French internal waters from the Cherbourg Peninsular westwards to the Spanish border, are required to maintain a continuous listening watch on Ch 16 or other frequency specified by the local authority.

BREST
CALL: Brest Port. Ch 16; 08
Any vessel entering the charted approach should listen Ch 16 and, if over 25m or 150 NRT, request permission from Goulet de Brest Control Post before entering Goulet de Brest or Baie de Douarnez.

César Tour Signal Station
CALL: Tour César. Ch 08 16
Broadcasts information of dredgers in Rade de Brest.

Le Guilvinec Ch 12

Moulin Blanc (yacht harbour) Ch 09

La Forêt-Fouesnant (yacht harbour) Ch 09

ROSCOFF
Ch 16; 12. 0700–1100, 1300–2200
Any vessel intending to enter should listen Ch 16

LE LÉGUÉ (St Brieuc)
CALL: Légué Port. Ch 12 16. 2h–1h before to 1h–1h 30 after HW.
Any vessel intending to enter should listen Ch 16

OUESSANT (Ushant)
Mandatory Vessel Traffic Management System that applies to all vessels including pleasure craft.

AREA: Inshore traffic zone of Ouessant, Chenal du Four, Chenal de la Helle, Passage du Fromveur and Raz du Sein.

Ushant Control Centre
CALL: VTM: Ouessant Traffic. Ch 11 (English), 13 (French), 16

AREA: Inshore traffic zone and Passage du Fromveur.

Saint Mathieu Signal Station
CALL: Saint Mathieu. Ch 16
AREA: Chenal de la Helle and Chenal du Four.

Pointe du Raz Signal Station
CALL: Le Raz. Ch 16
AREA: Raz de Sein

Le Stiff Signal and Radar Staion
CALL: Le Stiff Ch 16
Vessels report to Ouessant Traffic (or Saint Mathieu or Le Raz) and maintain listening watch on Ch 16. H24

INFORMATION: Ouessant Traffic (in English) Ch 11, following announcement on Ch 16.
General bulletins H + 20 and H + 50. Weather 0150 0450 0750 1050 1350 1650 1950 2250

Urgent information from CROSSCO (Centre Regional Operationnel de Surveillance et de Sauvetage Corsen-Ouessant) Ch 13 (in French) following announcement Ch 16

WESTERN APPROACHES

MILFORD HAVEN

Signal Station
CALL: Milford Haven Radio. Ch 09 10 11 **12** 14 16 67 H24

Patrol Launches
CALL: Milford Haven Patrol. Ch 06 08 11 12 14 16 67
Inward-bound (or outward-bound) contact Signal Station on Ch 16 and then maintain listening watch on Ch 12 or 14 as directed.

INFORMATION: local weather Ch 12 14 0300 0900 1500 2100; gale warnings on receipt; shipping movements Ch 12 0800–0830, 2000–2030 LT.

Milford Docks
Ch 09 12 14 16 2h before HW to HW.

SWANSEA
CALL: Swansea Docks Radio. Ch 16; 14

Swansea Yacht Haven Ch M

PORT TALBOT
Ch 16; 11 12 H24

BARRY DOCKS
Ch 16; 10 11 22 4h before to 4h after HW

CARDIFF
Ch 16; 11 14 4h before to 3h after HW

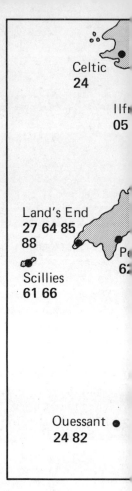

Celtic
24

Ilf
05

Land's End
27 64 85
88

P

Scillies
61 66

6

Ouessant
24 82

NEWPORT
Ch 16; 09 11 4h before to 4h HW

SHARPNESS
CALL: Sharpness Control. Ch 1
AREA: River Severn from sea end of The Shoots to site of f Severn Bridge; Gloucester Sharpness Canal. Vessels repc entering the area.

PORT OF BRISTOL
Avonmouth Signal Station
CALL: Avonmouth Radio. Ch 1 11 **12** 14 H24
AREA: Upper Bristol Channe Severn Estuary; River Avon to Rock.

Royal Portbury Dock
CALL: Royal Portbury Radio. C 12 **14** 4h 30 before to 3h 30 afte
AREA: Portishead Pt to Royal bury lock.

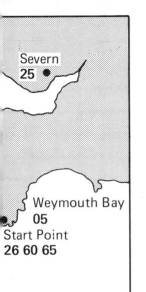

Severn
25

Weymouth Bay
05
Start Point
26 60 65

u
Paimpol
27

28

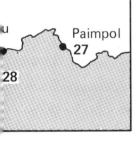

ST MARY'S HARBOUR, Isles of Scilly
Ch 16; 14 0800–1700 LT

NEWLYN
CALL: Newlyn Harbour Ch 16; 12 0800–1700 (Mon–Fri) 0800–1200 (Sat) LT

FALMOUTH
CALL: Falmouth Harbour Radio. Ch 16; 11 12 13 14 0900–1700 (Mon–Fri) 0900–1200 (Sat) LT. Watch kept outside these hours if required
Vessels keep watch on Ch 16

Mylor Yacht Marina, (Falmouth) Ch M

Falmouth Yacht Marina Ch M

CHARLESTOWN, St Austell Bay
Ch 16; 14 1h before to 1h after HW and when vessels expected.

PAR
CALL: Par Port Radio. Ch 16; 12 Office hours and 2h before to 1h after HW.

FOWEY
Ch 16; 11 12 HX

tishead Dock
16; 12 **14** 2h 30 before to 1h 30 r HW.
A: Portishead Pt to Portishead

y Docks
16; 12 **14** 3h before to 1h after

A: River Avon from Black Rock ntrance lock.

stol Floating Harbour
16; 73 Office hours.

rmation Service: From Avon-ith Radio on request Ch 12.

TCHET
16; 12 14 HX

NEHEAD
16; 12 14 HX

DE
16; 12 When vessel is expected.

DSTOW
14 HJ

PLYMOUTH

Ship Movement Control
CALL: Long Room Port Control. Ch 16; 08 12 14. All vessels listen Ch 16. Vessels over 70 GRT request permission to proceed.

Millbay Docks Ch; 16 12 14 H24

Sutton Harbour
CALL: Sutton Harbour Radio. Ch 16; 12. 0830–2000 (April–Oct 15); 0900–1800 (Oct 16–March) LT

Cattwater Harbour
CALL: Cattwater Harbour Office. Ch 16; 12 0900–1700 (Mon–Fri) LT

Mayflower Marina (Plymouth) Ch M H24

SALCOMBE
Ch 16; 14 0830–1600 (May-Sept 14); 0830–1630 (Sept 15–April) LT
Local weather, tidal information and berthing instructions on request

DARTMOUTH
Dart Marina Ch M 0730–dusk LT

Kingswear Marina Ch M 0730–dusk LT

Darthaven Marina (Kingswear) Ch M 0830–1800 LT

BRIXHAM (Torbay)
Ch 14 16 0900–1300, 1400–1700 (May–Sept); 0900–1300, 1400–1700 (Oct–April, Mon–Fri) LT

TORQUAY
Ch 14 16 0900–1300 (Oct–Feb, Mon–Fri); 0900–1300, 1400–1700 (March–April, Mon–Fri); 0900–1300, 1400–1700, 1800–2200 (May–Sept) LT

Torquay Yacht Harbour Ch M 0900–1800 LT

TEIGNMOUTH
Ch 16; 12 0900–1230, 1400–1700 (Mon–Fri); 0930–1200 (Sat) LT
Vessels should not call unless within 3h of harbour.

EXETER
Ch 16; 06 12 0730–1630 (Mon–Fri) LT and when vessel is expected.

LYME REGIS
Ch 16; 14 0900–1200, 1600–1800 (May–Sept) LT.

WEYMOUTH
Ch 16; 12. When vessel is expected. Station may be contacted Ch 13 via Portland Naval Base.

Portland Naval Base
Ch 13 14

FRENCH COAST

All foreign vessels 25m or more in length navigating or at anchor in French internal waters from the Cherbourg Peninsular westwards, are required to maintain a continuous listening watch on Ch 16 or other frequency specified by the local authority.

SAINT MALO
Ch 12 16 0800–1200, 1300–1800 LT (except Sun and holidays) and 2h before to 2h after HW.
Any vessel intending to enter should establish listening watch Ch 16

Yacht harbour Ch 09

Grand Jardin Lighthouse
CALL: Grand Jardin. Ch 12 16 0800–1100, 1300–1700 (except Sun) and 1h 30 before to 1h 30 after HW

GRANVILLE
CALL: Granville Port. Ch 12 16 1h 30 before to 1h after HW. Pilotage compulsory over 45m

JOBURG
Radar Surveillance Station
CALL: Jobourg Traffic.
INFORMATION: Ch 05 11
SAFETY: Ch 13 16 H24

CHERBOURG
Naval Port. Ch 11

Yacht harbour Ch 09

CARENTAN
Ch 09

PORT-EN-BESSIN
Lock. Ch 18 2h before to 2h after HW

CAEN-OUISTREHAM
Any vessel intending to enter should maintain listening watch Ch 16

Ouistreham
CALL: Ouistreham-Port. Ch 12 16 68 2h 30 before to 3h after HW. Vessels anchored, awaiting tide, listen Ch 16

Canal de Caen
Ch 12. Maintain listening watch Ch 12

Caen
CALL: Caen Port. Ch 08 68

PORT DEAUVILLE
Ch 09

LA SEINE
Rouen Port
CALL: Rouen Port. Ch 11 13 73 74
AREA: Rade de la Carosse to Jeanne d'Arc Bridge

Honfleur Radar Ch 16; 11 71 74 H24
AREA: Rade de la Carosse to Courval Lt

Radicatel Radar
Ch 11 13 73 74. 2h before to 2h after HW Le Havre
AREA: Risle Rivière entrance to Courval.

Vessels over 20m not equipped with VHF Ch 06 11 13 16 to request for portable radio.
Vessels in the Seine between Rade de la Carosse and Rouen listen Ch 11.
Water level and fog warnings Ch 11

Honfleur
Ch 12 16. 2h before to 4h after HW Le Havre

Tancarville
Ch 11 16 H24. Lock Ch 18

Rouen
CALL: Rouen Port Capitainerie. Ch 16; 06 11 13 73 H24

LE HAVRE
CALL: Havre-Port. Ch 12 16 20 22
Vessels bound for Le Havre maintain watch Ch 16. Radar assistance on request in fog (in French).

SHIP MOVEMENT REPORT SYSTEM (MAREP)

A voluntary system which applies mainly to large commercial ships but also to any vessel not-under-command, restricted in her ability to manoeuvre or with defective navigational aids.

Ouessant
CALL: Ouessant Traffic
Ch 11 16

Casquets
CALL: Portland Coastguard or Jobourg Traffic. Ch 10 16 (English), Ch 11 16 (French)

Dover Strait
CALL: Dover Coastguard or Gris Nez Traffic
Ch 10 16 (English) Ch 11 16 (French)

Weymouth
Bay 05

C
2

St Peter
Port
62

Jersey
16; 25 82

Saint Ma
01 02

Vessels should maintain liste watch on Ch 16 and, if possibl Ch 10 or 11 as appropriate. Information broadcasts, follo announcement Ch 16, Ch 1 H + 10 H + 40 and H + 23 H when visibility less than 2 miles 11 H + 20 H + 50 and H H + 55 Radar Assistance on re from Dover Coastguard.

CHANNEL ISLE:

BRAYE (Alderney)
CALL: Alderney Radio Ch 16; 1 0800–1200, 1400–1700 (N Fri); 0900–1200, 1400–1600 Sun). Outside those hours ca Peter Port. Pilotage compulsory 40 GRT

Mainbrayce Marine Ch M 08 2000 (April–mid Sept) LT

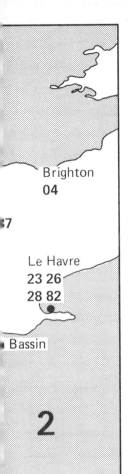

Brighton
04

7

Le Havre
23 26
28 82

Bassin

2

ETER PORT
Port Control Ch 12 H24
s over 18m contact Port Con-
fore entering

Sampson Ch 16; 12 H24

ELIER, Jersey
H24 Vessels over 25m con-
ort Control before entering

EY HARBOUR, Jersey
3h before to 3h after HW,
ner)

NGLISH COAST

MOUTH
12. When vessel is expected.
n may be contacted Ch 13 via
nd Naval Base

POOLE
CALL: Poole Harbour Control.
Ch 16; 14. 0900–1700 (Mon–Fri)
LT

Cobbs Quay Ch M 0800–1700 LT

Poole Harbour Y C Marina Ch M
0800–1800

LYMINGTON

Lymington Marina Ch M Office
hours

Lymington Yacht Haven Ch M
Office hours

COWES
Ch 16; 06 11. 0900–1700 LT

West Cowes Marina Ch M
0845–1730 LT

Medina Yacht Harbour Ch M

**THE SOLENT, SOUTHAMP-
TON AND PORTSMOUTH**

Southampton Port Signal Station
CALL: Southampton Port Radio or
SPR
Ch 16 Calling and Safety
Ch 12 14 Port Op.—calling, work-
ing
Ch 18 20 22 Radar information
Ch 10 Pollution

**Queen's Harbour Master,
Portsmouth**
CALL: Queen's Harbour Master or
QHM
Ch 11 Working
Ch 13 Naval Port Operations
Ch 73 Dockyard craft
All craft north of Outer Spit buoy use
Ch 11

Fort Gilkicker
CALL: Gilkicker. Continuous watch
Ch 16

Portsmouth Commercial Port
CALL: Portsmouth Harbour Radio Ch
11

Southampton Patrol
CALL: Southampton Patrol or SP. Ch
12 16;
All vessels over 20 m contact SPR
when approaching Nab or Needles
and report as instructed.
Within the area all vessels should
maintain listening watch Ch 12 or
14: Ch 11 13 north of line Gilkicker
to Outer Spit.

Information of shipping movements
and tide on request. All H24
ACCIDENT PROCEDURES: SPR or
QHM become "Emergency Control": broadcasts as appropriate.

Hamble Point Marina Ch M
0800–2000 LT

Port Hamble Marina Ch M H24

Mercury Yacht Harbour Ch M
H24

Swanwick Marina Ch M
0700–2400 LT

Camper & Nicholsons Marina Ch
M Office hours

LANGSTONE HARBOUR
Ch 16; 12 0830–1700 (Summer).
0830–1700 (Winter Mon–Fri),
0830–1300 (Winter Sat–Sun). LT

Northney Marina Ch M Daylight
hours

CHICHESTER
Ch 14 16; 14 0900–1730 (April–
Sept). 0900–1300 (Mon–Sat),
1400–1730 (Mon–Fri) (Oct–Mar).
AREA: within 5 miles of entrance.
PROCEDURE: Visitors advised to
make prior arrangements.
Requests for overnight swinging
moorings should be made when in
vicinity of Chichester Bar buoy

LITTLEHAMPTON
Littlehampton Marine
Ch M 0900–1700 LT

SHOREHAM
Ch 16; 14 Vessels over 50 GRT
contact Hr Mr. Maintain listening
watch Ch 14 when entering.

BRIGHTON MARINA
CALL: Brighton Control. Ch 16; 11
68

Brighton Marina Ch M H24

NEWHAVEN
Ch 16; 12 H24

FRENCH COAST

FÉCAMP
Ch 12 16 From 2h 30 before to 0h 30 after HW.

Yacht harbour Ch 09 0800–2000 LT

DIEPPE
CALL: Dieppe Port Ch 06 **12** 16
All vessels should report arrival in the roads and then maintain listening watch Ch 12

LE TRÉPORT
Ch 16

BOULOGNE
Port Captain Ch 12 16 H24 All vessels should contact Port Captain on Ch 12 on arrival in outer anchorage.

Control Tower Ch 12 16

CROSSMA (Central Régional Opérationnel de Surveillance et de Sauvetage pour la Manche) co-ordinates SAR operations.
SAR: Ch 16; 13.

INFORMATION: Ch 11 21 68 79 H24

CALAIS
Ch 12 16 H24

Calais Ecluse Carnot
Lock Ch 12 16 HX

DUNKERQUE
Ch 12 16 **73** H24 Dredgers work Ch 12

BELGIAN AND NETHERLANDS COASTS

NIEWPOORT
Ch 09 16

OOSTENDE
Ch 09 16 H24

Mercator Marina Ch 14

ZEEBRUGGE
Ch 09 13 H24

WESTERSCHELDE
Schelde Information Service

Vlissingen
CALL: Vlissingen Radio
Ch 14 H24

AREA: Near Wandelaar, Scheur 2 and Akkaert NE buoy to Pas van Terneuzen

ENGLISH COAST

NEWHAVEN
Ch 16; 12 H24

RYE
Ch 16; 14 1h before to 1h after HW
Vessels communicate only when less than 10 miles from harbour

DOVER
CALL: Dover Port Control Ch 16 **74;** 12 H24
Vessels passing or inward-bound for Dover Harbour should contact Dover Port Control on Ch 74 to advise ETA and then maintain listening watch Ch 74

DOVER STRAIT
Channel Navigation Information Service Ship Movement Report System (MAREP)
A voluntary system which applies mainly to large commercial ships but also to any vessel not under command, restricted in her ability to manoeuvre or with defective navigation aids.

Ouessant
CALL: Ouessant Traffic Ch **11** 16

Casquets
CALL: Portland Coastguard or Jobourg Traffic. Ch **10** 16 (English), Ch **11** 16 (French)

Dover Strait
CALL: Dover Coastguard or Gris Nez Traffic Ch **10** 16 (English) Ch **11** 16 (French)
Vessels should maintain listening watch on Ch 16 and, if possible, on Ch 10 or 11, as appropriate, as well.

INFORMATION BROADCASTS, following announcement on Ch 16, Ch 11 at H + 20 H + 50. Also at H + 05 and H + 35 when visibility less than 2 miles. (English and French).
Ch 10 at H + 10 and H + 40, and H + 25 and H + 55 when visibility less than 2 miles, (English).

Radar assistance from St Mar Bay or Dungeness Radar Stati request to Dover Coastguard.

RAMSGATE
Ch 16; 14 H24

WHITSTABLE
Ch 16; 09 12 0800–1700 (M LT and 3h before to 1h after H

MEDWAY
CALL: Medway Radio Ch 09 **74**

PATROL: Medway Patrol Ch 1 Vessels over 50 GRT to report All vessels should keep lis watch Ch 74

Gillingham Marina Ch 0830–1700 LT

Kingsferry Bridge Ch 10

Ne
05

Thames
02 83

Hastings
07 63

Dieppe 02 24

Le Havre
23 26 28 82

Rouen
25 27 64

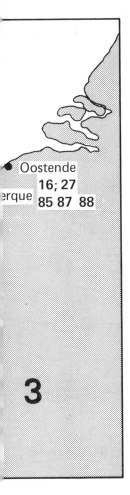

Oostende
16; 27
erque 85 87 88

3

THAMES BARRIER
CALL: Woolwich Radio Ch **14** 16 22
AREA: Crayfordness to Tower Bridge.
Control zone from Margaret Ness to Blackwall Point. All vessels intending to navigate Thames Barrier Control Zone report Woolwich Radio on Ch 14 stating ETA at barrier. H24
INWARD-BOUND when passing Crayford Ness and when passing Margaret Ness.
OUTWARD-BOUND when clearing Tower Bridge and when passing Blackwell Point.
All vessels obtain clearance to proceed before entering the Zone.
Spans to be used for navigation, or barrier closures, are included in the routine messages

RIVER THAMES
St Katherine Yacht Haven
Ch 14; 06 12 2h before to 1h 30 after HW between 0600–2030 LT in summer. 2h before to 1h 30 after HW between 0800–1800 LT in winter.

Brentford Dock Marina Ch 14 16; 14 M

RIVER CROUCH
Essex Marina Ch M 0900–1700 LT

West Wick Moorings Ch M 0900–1730 LT

RIVER BLACKWATER
Bradwell Marina Ch M Office hours

Tollesbury Marina Ch M Office hours

COLCHESTER
Ch 16; 11 **14** 0900–1230, 1400–1630 (Mon–Fri) LT and 2h before to 1h after HW

IPSWICH River Orwell
CALL: Ipswich Port Radio Ch 16; 12 14
Local weather, visibility and tidal information on request. H24

Suffolk Yacht Harbour Ch M

HARWICH
CALL: Harwich Harbour Control
Ch 16 Calling and safety
Ch 14 **71** Harbour operations
Ch 11 Harbour services
Ch 10 Pollution H24

Vessels of 50 GRT and over report ETA when inward-bound at South Bawdsey buoy or Medusa Buoy.
Vessels within the area maintain watch Ch 71

INFORMATION SERVICE: local weather, tidal information and vessel movements on request.

ACCIDENT PROCEDURE—Harwich-cap—(Harwich Combined Accident Procedure) vessels maintain watch keeping requests for information to a minimum.

SOUTHWOLD
Ch 16; 12 0800–1800 LT

OF LONDON
es Navigation Service
ich Radio Ch **14** 16 22

Thames above Crayford Ness

send Radio Ch **12** 14 16 18

Thames below Crayford Ness
of 50 GRT and over to

MATION MESSAGES from Radio Stations; Thames Ch stings Ch 07 Orfordness Ch

rnings on receipt; end of first period after receipt.

ENT PROCEDURES: Polecap; f London Authority Combined nt Procedure) All vessels mini-radio traffic. Polasea; major t to seaward of Sea Reach

BELGIAN AND NETHERLANDS COASTS

NIEWPOORT
Ch 09 16

OOSTENDE
Ch 09 16 H24

Mercator Marina Ch 14

ZEEBRUGGE
Ch 09 13 H24

WESTERSCHELDE
Schelde Information Service

Vlissingen
CALL: Vlissingen Radio
Ch 14 H24
AREA: Near Wandelaar, Scheur 2 and Akkaert NE buoy to Pas van Terneuzen

Terneuzen
CALL: Radar Terneuzen
Ch **03** 14
AREA: Vlissingen east limit to Hoek van Baarland Lt and Pv83 buoy

Hansweert
CALL: Hansweert Radio
Ch 71
AREA: Terneuzen east limit to Kruiningen harbour and Perkpolder harbour

Zandvliet
CALL: Zandvliet Radio
Ch 12 14
AREA: Hansweert east limit to River Rupel
INFORMATION BROADCASTS: visibility reports, tidal data and vessel movements H + 35 by Zandvliet on Ch 12 and 14, H + 50 by Vlissingen on Ch 14 and H + 55 by Radar Terneuzen on Ch 03
Traffic lists and navigational reports by Antwerpen Ch 16

Vlissingen (Flushing)
Ch 09

Locks Ch 22

Terneuzen
CALL: Havendienst Terneuzen Ch 11 H24
Information H + 00 for vessels in the Terneuzen-Ghent Canal

Terneuzen-Ghent Canal Ch 11
Vessels intending to enter report Ch 11

Ghent
CALL: Havendienst Ghent Ch 05 11 H24

Antwerpen
CALL: Antwerpen Havendienst Ch 18 H24

NETHERLANDS

OOSTERSCHELDE
CALL: Roompotsluis Ch 18
Pleasure craft less than 20m are not required to report

Zeelandbrug
Ch 18

Kreekraksluizen, Schelde-Rijn-kanaal
Ch 20

HOEK VAN HOLLAND
CALL: Maasmond Radar Ch 02

Recommended procedure for coastal-recreational traffic crossing roadstead.
Follow track west of line joining MV, MVN and Indusbank N buoys.
Before crossing report name, position and course and subsequently maintain a listening watch.

NIEUWE (ROTTERDAMSCHE) WATERWEG
Traffic Management and Information Service
All vessels report to Maas Approach on Ch 20 before arrival at the Maas Center buoy and subsequently maintain listening watch on Ch 20.

INFORMATION BROADCASTS: In Maasmond, from Maas Approach Ch 20, including visibility on request for vessels inward-bound. Vessels outward bound from HCC Centrale Post (the pilotage centre) on Ch 01.
Reports also from Rijkshavendienst (RHD) (the State Harbour Service) on Ch 14 for the area from the estuary to Oude Maas when visibility below 4000m
Weather reports H + 00 from Traffic Centre Hook on Ch 14

Oude Maas
CALL: RHD Post Hartel Ch 10 13.

Oude Maas bridges; Botekbrug and Spijkenissergrug Ch 13

Botlekhaven
CALL: Botlekhaven Traffic Control Ch 09

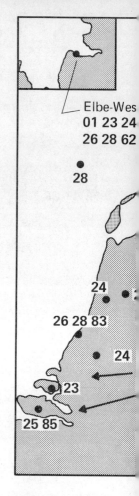

Elbe-Wes
01 23 24
26 28 62

28

24

26 28 83

24

23

25 85

Dordrecht
CALL: Post Dordrecht Ch 08 1 14 71

SCHEVENINGEN
CALL: Scheveningen Haven C H24

IJMUIDEN
CALL: Traffic Centre IJmuiden nounced 'eye mouden') Ch 12
Vessels report when within range of IJmuiden Lt buoy

Radar assistance
CALL: IJmuiden Radar
Ch 12 (west of IJmuiden buoy)
Ch 19 (IJmuiden Lt Buoy to pierhead)
Ch 09 (pierhead to North Sea l

NOORDZEEKANAAL
IJmuiden
CALL: IJmuiden Port Contr IJmuiden Port Control Locks f rect contact with locks Ch 09

Helgoland ●
03 27 88

deich
86

8
jen

4

ug
Jmuiden Locks Ch 11
Locks to Hembrug

dam

in Noordzeekanal maintain
g watch as appropriate

ation broadcasts
Ch 12 by Coastguard IJmui-

Ch 05 11 by IJmuiden
Ch 14 by Amsterdam

IELDER
14 H24

DEVER
1 20

WERDERZAND
1 18

MEER
emmer Ch 20

Sluis Enkhuizen Ch 22

Sluis Houtrib (Lelystad) Ch 20

Sluis Schellingwoude "Orange" Ch 18

HARLINGEN
Ch 11 0000 (Mon)–2200 (Sat) Vessels report 30 min before arrival

LAUWERSOOG
Ch 22 H24

EMSHAVEN
Ch 14 H24

Emshaven Radar
CALL: Emshaven Radar Ch 04 0900–1700 (Mon–Fri) LT
Radar assistance when visibility falls below 2000m

DELFZIJL
FOG. CALL: Loodskantoor Delfzijl Ch 14
Report when visibility below 500m on entering harbour

CALL: Havendienst Delfzijl Ch 14 0800–1200; 1300–1700 and last 15 min of each additional hour

Locks Ch 11 Mon–Sat H24

Bridge Ch 22 0000 (Mon)–1200 (Sat) LT

FEDERAL REPUBLIC OF GERMANY

DIE EMS
Inform WSA (Wasser und Schiffahrtsamt) Emden through Ems Revier Ch 18 inward-bound or Ch 21 outward-bound H24 Radar advice on request in German

Information broadcasts H + 50 in English and German by Ems Revier

Emden Lock Ch 13 16

DIE JADE
CALL: Jade Revier or Jade Radar Ch 16 **20** Mandatory reporting system for vessels over 50m
Information broadcasts H + 10 in German on Ch 20 and 63

Wilhelmshaven
Ch 11 16 H24

DIE WESER
Mandatory reporting system for vessels over 50m controlled by WSA (Wasser und Schiffahrtsamt) Bremerhaven-Weser-Revier Ch 22 inward-bound or Ch 21 outward-bound

Bremerhaven Ch 12; 12 16 H24

Bremerhaven Weser Ch 14; **14** 16 H24

DIE ELBE
Mandatory reporting system for vessels over 50m controlled by WSA (Wasser und Schiffahrtsamt) Cuxhaven.
Inward-bound report Elbe 1 Lt V Ch 11.
Outward-bound to Brunsbüttel Elbe Port Ch 14

INFORMATION BROADCASTS in English and German, every odd H + 00 by Cuxhaven Radar Centre Ch 21; odd H + 05 by Brunsbüttel Radar Centre; H + 55 Revierzentrale Cuxhaven Ch 19

Cuxhaven Elbe Ch 12 16; 12 14 16 H24

Brunsbüttel Elbe Ch 14 16; **11** 14 16 H24

NORD-OSTSEE KANAL (KIEL KANAL)
Brunsbüttel Entrance and locks Ch 13

WEST COAST

FISHGUARD
Ch 16; 14 H24

ABERDOVEY
Ch 16; 12

PORTHMADOG
Ch 16 HX

CAERNARVON
Ch 16; 12 14 HJ

Port Dinorwic Yacht Harbour Ch
M 0800–1800 LT

HOLYHEAD
Ch 16; 14 H24

CONWY
Ch 16; 06 08 **12** 14 72
0900–1700   (Apr–Sept);
0900–1700 (Oct–Mar, Mon–Fri) LT

LLANDUDNO PIER
Ch 16; 06 **12** 0700–1500 (end
May–mid Sept)

LLANDDULAS
Ch 16; 14 0900–1200,
1400–1700 LT and from 4h before
HW when vessel expected

MOSTYN DOCK
Ch 16; **14** When vessel expected

LIVERPOOL
CALL: Mersey Radio
Ch **12** 16; 04 09 12 18 19 22 H24
General situation and movement
statement on Ch 09 at 3h and 2h
before HW.
On request on Ch 04.
Local warnings on receipt on Ch 12
and on Ch 09 every 4h from 0000
LT
All vessels over 50 GRT are required
to carry VHF R/T and to report.

Garston Dock Ch 20 H24

Bromborough Dock Ch 21 H24

Tranmere Stages Ch 19 H24

Alfred Dock Ch 05 H24

Waterloo Dock Ch 20 H24

Langton Dock Ch 21 H24

Gladstone Dock Ch 05 H24

PORT OF MANCHESTER
Ch 14 Vessels approaching from
River Mersey contact Assistant Har-
bour Master.
When in canal listen Ch 14

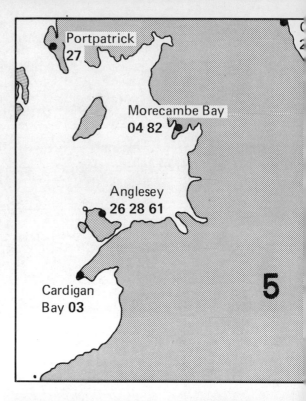

Portpatrick **27**

Morecambe Bay **04 82**

Anglesey **26 28 61**

Cardigan Bay **03**

5

Eastham Locks
CALL: Eastham Control Ch 14

Weaver Navigation Ch 14; 71 **73**
H24 except 1800–1900 LT
Vessels intending to enter establish
contact when approaching locks.

Latchford Locks Ch 14 20 H24

Barton Locks Ch 14 18 H24

Mode Wheel Locks Ch 14 18 H24

FLEETWOOD
CALL: Fleetwood Harbour Control Ch
16; 11 12 H24
CALL: Fleetwood Docks Ch 16; 12
2h before to 2h after HW
All vessels entering contact Harbour
Control

GLASSON DOCK
Ch 16; 19 2h before to 1h after HW
and on request.

Heysham Ch 16; 14 H24

Barrow Docks Ch 16; 12 H24

DOUGLAS, Isle of Man
CALL: Douglas Harbour Control Ch
16; 12 H24
Inward-bound send ETA 2h–1h in
advance and then listen Ch 16.
Within the harbour listen Ch 12

CASTLETOWN, Isle of Ma
CALL: Castletown Harbour C
12 when vessel expected

PORT ST MARY, Isle of M
CALL: Port St Mary Harbour C
12 when vessel expected

PEEL, Isle of Man
CALL: Peel Harbour Ch 16; 12
vessel expected

RAMSEY, Isle of Man
CALL: Ramsey Harbour Ch 1
when vessel expected

WHITEHAVEN
Ch 16; 12 2h before to 2h afte

WORKINGTON
Ch 16; 11 14 2h 30 before
after HW

IRELAND

COLERAINE
Ch 16; 12 0900–1700 LT
when vessel expected

Coleraine Marina Ch M

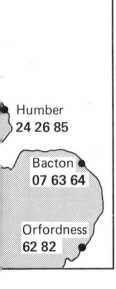

Humber
24 26 85

Bacton
07 63 64

Orfordness
62 82

4 HX

CKFERGUS
2 14 3h before to 1h after
ssel expected

ST
lfast Harbour Radio
8 10 (emergency) 11 **12** 14

requested to establish con-
ntering Belfast Lough

OR
08 When vessel expected

VOGIE
4 0900–2000 (Mon-Fri)

EAGH
2 HX

EEL
2 14 0900–2000 (Mon-Fri)

NPOINT
2 H24

ORE
erry Greenore Ch 16; 13

ALK
06 12

HEDA
1 HX

DUBLIN
CALL: Dublin Harbour Office Ch **12**
16; 09 **12** 13 14 H24
Lifting bridge
CALL: Eastlink Ch 12 13

DUN LAOGHAIRE
CALL: Carlisle Pier Ch 16; 14 H24

ARKLOW
CALL: Roadstone Jetty Ch 16 HJ

ROSSLARE
Ch 16; 06 14 H24
VHF contact before entering the har-
bour

NEW ROSS
Ch 16; 12 14 H24

EAST COAST

LOWESTOFT
Ch **14** 16; 14 H24
Vessels inward-bound should request instructions before approaching harbour entrance.

GREAT YARMOUTH
CALL: Yarmouth Ch 16; 12 H24
All vessels inward-bound send ETA
at least 1h in advance of arrival.

Haven Bridge Ch 12

WELLS HARBOUR
CALL: Wells Harbour Base Ch 16; 12
when vessel expected

KING'S LYNN
Ch 14 16; 11 12 14 0900–1700
(Mon–Fri) 1000–1200 (Sat) LT.
Also from 4h before HW to HW

WISBECH
Ch 16; 09 **14** 4h before HW to HW
when vessel expected.

BOSTON
CALL: Boston Dock
Ch 16; 12 0700–1700 (Mon–Fri)
and 2h 30 before to 1h 30 after HW

HUMBER
Vessel Traffic Service
CALL: VTS Humber Ch 12 16; 10 **12**
13 H24 All times to be given in LT
Mandatory reporting for vessels over
50 GRT.
Vessels approaching Humber estab-
lish listening watch Ch 16

Grimsby Docks
Ch 16 Calling and safety H24
Ch 18 Docking instructions
Ch 09 Short range berthing instruc-
tions

Grimsby Marina Ch 16; 09 18

River Hull Port Operations Service
CALL: Drypool Radio Ch 16; 06 **14**
0800–1800 (Mon-Fri); 0830–1300
(Sat) LT and 2h before to 0h 30 after
HW Hull

Hull Marina Ch M H24

Goole Docks Ch 16; 14

Boothferry Bridge Ch 16; 12 H24

Selby Railway Bridge Ch 16; **09**
12 Inward-bound vessels contact 10
min in advance

Selby Toll Bridge Ch 16; **09** 12
Outward-bound vessels contact 10
min in advance

BRIDLINGTON
Ch 16; **12** 14 HX

SCARBOROUGH
CALL: Scarborough Lighthouse Ch
16; 12 14 H24

WHITBY
Ch 16; 06 **11** 0900–1700 LT

Whitby Bridge Ch 16; 06 **11** 2h
before to 2h after HW

TEES
CALL: Tees Harbour Radio
Ch 16; 08 11 12 **14 22** H24
Vessels over 20m in length to advise
Hr Mr at least 6h in advance and 1h
in advance before navigating in the
Tees. Listening watch Ch 14

Hartlepool Docks
CALL: Hartlepool Radio Ch 16; 11
12 H24

SEAHAM
CALL: Seaham Harbour Ch 16; 06
12 2h 30 before to 1h 30 after HW

SUNDERLAND
Ch 16; 14 H24

PORT OF TYNE
CALL: Tyne Harbour Ch 16; 11 **12**
14
Vessels over 50 GRT to report. Ves-
sels maintain listening watch Ch 12.
Information on request

BLYTH
CALL: Blyth Harbour Control
Ch 16; 12 H24 Restricted to within
1h sailing time from port.

SCOTTISH COAST

BERWICK
Ch 16; 12 3h before to 1h after HW

FORTH NAVIGATION SERVICE
Ch 09 10 11 12 13 14 16 **20 71**
Ch 16 71 H24
AREA: River and Firth of Forth west of North Carr to Great Carr.
When visibility less than 0.5 miles vessels to obtain clearance before passing No 19 buoy.
Vessels of 50 GRT and over maintain continuous listening watch.

Methil Docks Ch 16; 14 3h before to 1h after HW.

Leith Docks
CALL: Leith Harbour Radio Ch 16; 12 H24 Contact Leith Harbour Radio before arrival in Leith Roads.

North Queensferry Naval Signal Station
CALL: Queensferry Ch 16; 12 13 H24

DUNDEE
CALL: Dundee Harbour Radio
Ch 16; 10 11 **12** 13 14 H24
Information service on request

MONTROSE
Ch 16; 12 H24 Contact Harbour Office 1h prior to arrival

ABERDEEN
Ch 16; 10 11 12 13 H24 All movements in harbour strictly controlled from Port Control

PETERHEAD
Ch 16; 09 11 14 H24
Vessels make contact 1h from breakwaters

FRASERBURGH
Ch 16; 12 H24 Inward-bound call 2h before arrival

MACDUFF
Ch 16; 12 0900–1700 LT and 1h before vessel expected

BUCKIE
Ch 16; 09 11 12 0900–1700 (Mon–Fri) LT and every H + 05 to H + 15 when vessel expected

LOSSIEMOUTH
Ch 16; 12 0800–1700 LT and 1h before vessel expected

INVERNESS
Ch 16; 12 14 0900–1700 (Mon–Fri) LT

INVERGORDON
CALL: Cromarty Firth Port Control Ch 16; 06 08 **11** 12 13 14 H24

BALTASOUND HARBOU
Ch 16 20 Office hours or as re

**SULLOM VOE HARF
Shetland**
CALL: Sullom Voe Harbour C
Ch 16 Safety
Ch 19 Initial contact
Ch 10 Emergency
Ch 20 Information broadcast:
Small craft send ETA 24h in a
and confirm 6h in advance
LOCAL WEATHER: 0830
Gale warnings on receipt ar
broadcast information every 4
0000, Ch 20

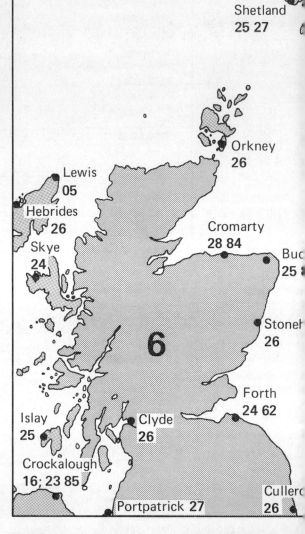

Collafirth
24

Shetland
25 27

Orkney
26

Lewis
05

Hebrides
26

Skye
24

Cromarty
28 84

Buc
25

Stoneh
26

6

Forth
24 62

Islay
25

Clyde
26

Crockalough
16; 23 85

Culler
26

Portpatrick 27

.LOWAY, Shetland
5; 12 0800–1700 (Mon-Fri),
–1200 (Sat) LT

WICK
5; 10 11 **12** H24 All vessels
: to Port Control before arrival
efore leaving. Maintain listen-
atch Ch 16

NEY HARBOUR NAVIGA-
I SERVICE
Orkney Harbour Radio
6 20; 09 11 H24 Service
ble to all vessels navigating
Flow.
ier Messages Ch 11
–1715.

vall Harbour Office
5; 12 0900–1700 (Mon-Fri)

iness Harbour Office
5; 12 0900–1700 Mon-Fri

ray Pier
5: 14 When vessel expected

ABSTER, Thurso
5; 12 H24

RNAWAY
5; 12 H24

LOCHBERVIE
5 HX

APOOL
6; 12 June 26–Nov or Dec
Nov or Dec–June 25 office

elford Yacht Haven, (Argyll)
M 0830–1730 (May-Sept);
–1730 (Oct-April)

LAIG
5; 12 Office hours

N
5; 12 0900–1700

BELTOWN
5; 12 14 0845–1700 LT

CLYDEPORT
CALL: Clydeport Estuary Radio Ch
16; 12 H24

Conservancy vessels Ch 16; 11.
Information service on request.

Ardrossan Ch 16; 12 14 H24

Rothsay, Bute Ch 16; 12
0600–2100 (May–Sept),
0600–1900 (Oct–April) LT

Stroul Bay Yacht Haven, (Clynder)
Ch M 0800–2200

Rhu Marina Ch M Office hours

Kip Marina Ch M H24

Largs Yacht Haven Ch 12
0830–1730

Troon Marina Ch M H24

GIRVAN
Ch 16; 12 0900–1700 (Mon–Fri)
LT

STRANRAER
Ch 16; 14 H24 Station owned by
Sealink (Scotland) but accepts mes-
sages from any vessel bound for
Stranraer.

Continued from:

Time (Min)	Speed (knots)										
	2.5	3.0	3.5	4.0	4.5	5.0	5.5	6.0	6.5	7.0	7.5
1	- -	- -	- -	0.1	0.1	0.1	0.1	0.1	0.1	0.1	0.1
2	0.1	0.1	0.1	0.1	0.1	0.2	0.2	0.2	0.2	0.2	0.2
3	0.1	0.1	0.2	0.2	0.2	0.2	0.3	0.3	0.3	0.3	0.4
4	0.1	0.2	0.2	0.3	0.3	0.3	0.4	0.4	0.4	0.5	0.5
5	0.2	0.2	0.3	0.3	0.4	0.4	0.5	0.5	0.5	0.6	0.6
6	0.2	0.3	0.3	0.4	0.4	0.5	0.5	0.6	0.6	0.7	0.7
7	0.3	0.4	0.4	0.5	0.5	0.6	0.6	0.7	0.8	0.8	0.9
8	0.3	0.4	0.5	0.5	0.6	0.7	0.7	0.8	0.9	0.9	1.0
9	0.4	0.4	0.5	0.6	0.7	0.7	0.8	0.9	1.0	1.0	1.1
10	0.4	0.5	0.6	0.7	0.8	0.8	0.9	1.0	1.1	1.2	1.3
11	0.5	0.5	0.6	0.7	0.8	0.9	1.0	1.1	1.2	1.3	1.4
12	0.5	0.6	0.7	0.8	0.9	1.0	1.1	1.2	1.3	1.4	1.5
13	0.5	0.6	0.8	0.9	1.0	1.1	1.2	1.3	1.4	1.5	1.6
14	0.6	0.7	0.8	0.9	1.0	1.2	1.3	1.4	1.5	1.6	1.7
15	0.6	0.7	0.9	1.0	1.1	1.2	1.4	1.5	1.6	1.8	1.9
16	0.7	0.8	0.9	1.1	1.2	1.3	1.5	1.6	1.7	1.9	2.0
17	0.7	0.8	1.0	1.1	1.3	1.4	1.6	1.7	1.8	2.0	2.1
18	0.7	0.9	1.0	1.2	1.3	1.5	1.6	1.8	1.9	2.1	2.2
19	0.8	1.0	1.1	1.3	1.4	1.6	1.7	1.9	2.1	2.2	2.4
20	0.8	1.0	1.2	1.3	1.5	1.7	1.8	2.0	2.2	2.3	2.5
21	0.9	1.0	1.2	1.4	1.6	1.7	1.9	2.1	2.3	2.4	2.6
22	0.9	1.1	1.3	1.5	1.7	1.8	2.1	2.2	2.4	2.6	2.8
23	1.0	1.1	1.3	1.5	1.7	1.9	2.1	2.3	2.5	2.7	2.9
24	1.0	1.2	1.4	1.6	1.8	2.0	2.2	2.4	2.6	2.8	3.0
25	1.0	1.3	1.5	1.7	1.9	2.1	2.3	2.5	2.7	2.9	3.1
26	1.1	1.3	1.5	1.7	1.9	2.2	2.4	2.6	2.8	3.0	3.2
27	1.1	1.3	1.6	1.8	2.0	2.2	2.5	2.7	2.9	3.1	3.4
28	1.2	1.4	1.6	1.9	2.1	2.3	2.6	2.8	3.0	3.3	3.5
29	1.2	1.5	1.7	1.9	2.2	2.4	2.7	2.9	3.1	3.4	3.6
30	1.2	1.5	1.7	2.0	2.2	2.5	2.7	3.0	3.2	3.5	3.7
31	1.3	1.6	1.8	2.1	2.3	2.6	2.8	3.1	3.4	3.6	3.9
32	1.3	1.6	1.9	2.1	2.4	2.7	2.9	3.2	3.5	3.7	4.0
33	1.4	1.6	1.9	2.2	2.5	2.7	3.0	3.3	3.6	3.8	4.1
34	1.4	1.7	2.0	2.3	2.6	2.8	3.1	3.4	3.7	4.0	4.3
35	1.5	1.7	2.0	2.3	2.6	2.9	3.2	3.5	3.8	4.1	4.4
36	1.5	1.8	2.1	2.4	2.7	3.0	3.3	3.6	3.9	4.2	4.5
37	1.6	1.8	2.1	2.4	2.8	3.1	3.4	3.7	4.0	4.3	4.6
38	1.6	1.9	2.2	2.5	2.8	3.2	3.5	3.8	4.1	4.4	4.7
39	1.6	1.9	2.3	2.6	2.9	3.2	3.6	3.9	4.2	4.5	4.9
40	1.7	2.0	2.3	2.7	3.0	3.3	3.7	4.0	4.3	4.7	5.0
41	1.7	2.0	2.4	2.7	3.1	3.4	3.8	4.1	4.4	4.8	5.1
42	1.7	2.1	2.4	2.8	3.1	3.5	3.8	4.2	4.5	4.9	5.2
43	1.8	2.2	2.5	2.9	3.2	3.6	3.9	4.3	4.7	5.0	5.4
44	1.8	2.2	2.6	2.9	3.3	3.7	4.0	4.4	4.8	5.1	5.5
45	1.9	2.2	2.6	3.0	3.4	3.7	4.1	4.5	4.9	5.2	5.6
46	1.9	2.3	2.7	3.1	3.5	3.8	4.2	4.6	5.0	5.4	5.8
47	2.0	2.3	2.7	3.1	3.5	3.9	4.3	4.7	5.1	5.5	5.9
48	2.0	2.4	2.8	3.2	3.6	4.0	4.4	4.8	5.2	5.6	6.0
49	2.0	2.5	2.9	3.3	3.7	4.1	4.5	4.9	5.3	5.7	6.1
50	2.1	2.5	2.9	3.3	3.7	4.2	4.6	5.0	5.4	5.8	6.2
51	2.1	2.5	3.0	3.4	3.8	4.2	4.7	5.1	5.5	5.9	6.4
52	2.2	2.6	3.0	3.5	3.9	4.3	4.8	5.2	5.6	6.1	6.5
53	2.2	2.6	3.1	3.5	4.0	4.4	4.9	5.3	5.7	6.2	6.6
54	2.2	2.7	3.1	3.6	4.0	4.5	4.9	5.4	5.8	6.3	6.7
55	2.3	2.8	3.2	3.7	4.1	4.6	5.0	5.5	6.0	6.4	6.9
56	2.3	2.8	3.3	3.7	4.2	4.7	5.1	5.6	6.1	6.5	7.0
57	2.4	2.8	3.3	3.8	4.3	4.7	5.2	5.7	6.2	6.6	7.1
58	2.4	2.9	3.4	3.9	4.4	4.8	5.3	5.8	6.3	6.8	7.3
59	2.5	2.9	3.4	3.9	4.4	4.9	5.4	5.9	6.4	6.9	7.4
60	2.5	3.0	3.5	4.0	4.5	5.0	5.5	6.0	6.5	7.0	7.5